NAVY

COAST GUARD

W9-BXB-845

MARINES

ADMIRAL

VICE ADMIRAL

REAR ADMIRAL

CAPTAIN

COMMANDER

LIEUT. COMMANDER

LIEUTENANT

LIEUTENANT JUNIOR GRADE

ENSIGN

CHIEF WARRANT OFFICER

WARRANT OFFICER

CHIEF PETTY OFFICER

PETTY OFFICER 1ST CLASS

PETTY OFFICER 2ND CLASS

PETTY OFFICER 3RD CLASS

DECONTAM—
INATION CORPS

DEMOLITION
CREWS

AUXILIARY
POLICEMEN

RESCUE SQUADS

NURSES' AIDS

DRIVERS CORPS

ROAD
REPAIR CREWS

EMERGENCY
FOOD & HOUSING

PICTOGRAPH CORPORATION

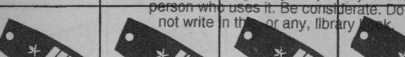

America organizes to win the war

America organizes to win the war

A Handbook on the American War Effort

PRESIDENT ROOSEVELT	PRIME MINISTER CHURCHILL
VICE-PRESIDENT WALLACE	SECRETARY WICKARD
JOHN CHAMBERLAIN	WALDEMAR KAEMPFFERT
HENRY STEELE COMMAGER	MAX LERNER
DAVID CUSHMAN COYLE	LAUREN D. LYMAN
ALVIN E. DODD	S. L. A. MARSHALL
PAUL DE KRUIF	ARTHUR UPHAM POPE
LADISLAS FARAGO	BYRON PRICE
DOROTHY CANFIELD FISHER	PAUL SCHUBERT
CHARLES H. JUDD	FREDERICK L. SCHUMAN
	HAROLD M. VINACKE

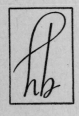 *Harcourt, Brace and Company, New York*

CONTENTS

LIST OF GRAPHS

PUBLISHERS' FOREWORD

Americans took up arms in 1917 in order to "make the world safe for democracy" and to win "the war to end war." These were the purposes to which Woodrow Wilson then pledged the United States and all the Allies. These were the purposes which the Americans of Wilson's day regarded as worth living for and therefore worth fighting for. In the name of these purposes America and its associates in the war against Imperial Germany won the victory of 1918.

Americans were again plunged into war in 1941 through a treacherous attack launched against them by the new tyrants of Tokyo, Berlin, and Rome. The aggressors had spent most of a tragic decade destroying democracy in Europe and Asia and waging brutal wars of conquest against weaker peoples on three continents. Because war had not been ended and because the world had not been made safe for democracy, the people of the United States were summoned to new sacrifices of blood and treasure on a scale vastly greater than that of 1917. They were called upon to fight anew not only to ensure the survival of the democratic way of life and to reconquer the peace that had been thrown away during the wasted years but to preserve their very existence as a free people from the fanatical onslaught of the world-conquering hosts of greed and hatred.

"Twice in a single generation," said Winston Churchill to the Congress of the United States on the day after Christmas, 1941, "the catastrophe of world war has fallen upon us. Twice in our lifetime has the long arm of fate reached out across the oceans to bring the United States into the forefront of the battle. Do we not owe it to ourselves, to our children, to tormented mankind, to make sure that these catastrophes do not engulf us for a third time?"

Only one answer is possible to the British Prime Minister's question. But that answer, if it is to have any meaning, must be translated into action to win the war, to rebuild the peace on firm foundations, and to safeguard the future against new disasters. Action, if it is to be effective, must be based on knowledge of why and how the victorious democracies of the First World War lost the peace of 1919 and brought upon themselves twenty years later a Second World War. Action, if it is to be democratic, must be based not on the wisdom of a few leaders but on earnest thought and talk by all Americans and by all the free peoples of the earth. This book is published to encourage such talk and to make it as informed as possible. Only by understanding the task is it possible to meet the challenge of the present and to win mastery of the future.

Each of the distinguished contributors, of course, is responsible only for the views in his own chapter.

America organizes to win the war

I. What are the fundamental issues of the war?

HENRY STEELE COMMAGER

Henry Steele Commager is professor of American history at Columbia University. He is the author (with Samuel Eliot Morison) of 'The Growth of the American Republic,' editor of 'Documents in American History,' and (with Allan Nevins) of 'The Heritage of America,' is coauthor of textbooks in American history for the schools, and author of many articles on American history and contemporary events.

"The true goal we seek is far above and beyond the ugly field of battle. When we resort to force, as now we must, we are determined that this force shall be directed toward ultimate good as well as against immediate evil. . . . We are now in the midst of a war, not for conquest, not for vengeance, but for a world in which this nation, and all that this nation represents, will be safe for our children."

Thus President Roosevelt proclaimed, in his war speech of December 9, 1941, the nature of the conflict, the stakes of war, and of the peace to follow. Thus he made clear that while we are fighting for the defense of our territory, we are fighting, too, for something bigger than this — for something that concerns more than America, something that concerns all the peoples of the earth. We are fighting for ourselves and our generation, but we are fighting, too, for the past and for the future, for all that we have been and all that we might be — the kind of world, in short, in which " this nation, and all that this nation represents, will be safe for our children."

AMERICA MEANS LIBERTY AND DEMOCRACY

Let no one be deceived by a narrow or superficial interpretation of the nature of this conflict. This war is not merely a struggle between rival imperialisms — a struggle into which the United States happened to get caught up. It is not merely a struggle for control of far-flung territories, or of raw materials, or of trade. It is not merely a struggle against the ambitions and pretensions of one " wicked " man. It involves far more than this. For ours is truly a nation " conceived in liberty and dedicated to the proposition that all men are created equal," and this war is to test once more whether a nation " so conceived and so dedicated " can endure. It is to test whether liberty and democracy and the reign of law are to flourish in a peaceful world or whether they are to go down before a " New Order " based on different principles and proclaiming different values.

The United States, to be sure, has no monopoly on freedom or on democracy, no copyright on the reign of law. Devotion to these principles is shared by liberty-loving and peace-loving peoples everywhere, and above all by the peoples of England and of the British Commonwealth of Nations. For it was in England that the principles of government under law were first stated, and it is the English-speaking peoples in the far corners of the globe — in the United States, in Canada, in Australia and New Zealand, in South Africa — who have built, upon the firm bases of freedom and law, liberal governments and democratic societies.

Yet in a peculiar and heart-lifting sense the defense of liberty and of democracy and of law is our responsibility. It is en-

tirely fitting that the men and women who love liberty, everywhere in the world, should turn in this hour of peril to the United States — entirely fitting that Winston Churchill should speak with confidence of the time when " the New World, with all its power and might, steps forth to the rescue and liberation of the Old."

For America has always been, in the words of the French statesman Turgot, " the hope of the human race " and Americans have themselves recognized this and have done much to justify that hope. Jefferson spoke of this nation as " the world's best hope." Longfellow reminded us that

> Humanity with all its fears,
> With all the hopes of future years,
> Is hanging breathless on thy fate

and Whitman that

> Thou holdest not the venture of thyself, not of the Western Continent alone.
> Earth's résumé entire floats on thy keel, O ship, is steadied by thy spars,
> With thee Time voyages in trust, the antecedent nations sink or swim with thee,
> With all their ancient struggles, martyrs, heroes, epics, wars, thou bear'st the other continents,
> Theirs, theirs as much as thine, the destination-port triumphant.

And this was not the expression merely of patriotic ardor, of the pride of a new nation growing so mightily. For it is historically true that here in this New World it was to be determined whether men could live the good life and build the good society. Here, under the most favorable conditions ever enjoyed by man — with abundance of free land, with fabulous richness of natural resources, with temperate climate and gen-

erous Nature, with freedom from the wars of the Old World and from the institutions that had so long tyrannized over the bodies and the minds of men — here men were to have a chance to establish a democratic government, to be secure in their liberties and to be worthy of them, and to live in peace with one another. Here men and women were to have a chance to live their own lives in comfort and security, to worship as they would, to marry whom they would, to follow such careers as their talents and abilities permitted, to make and unmake their own governments, to be subject to equal laws.

And if Americans sometimes took all this for granted, or forgot it, other peoples never did. Throughout the nineteenth century and into the twentieth it was to the New World that the underprivileged and the oppressed of the Old World turned — to the Promised Land. To this world of hope, to this land of the second chance, they came by the hundred thousand, by the million — from famine-ravaged Ireland, from overcrowded Scandinavia, from poverty-stricken Germany, from war-ravaged Poland, from the persecutions of Russia, from the teeming cities of Italy and the sterile uplands of Spain and the lovely valleys of the Danube and the Moldau, darkened by racial strife. They came to America because they knew they could find freedom here, and tolerance, and a chance for themselves and for their children.

OUR LONG STRUGGLE FOR FREEDOM

Their hopes were in large part fulfilled. It is well for us to remember that they were not fulfilled without effort and struggle. For the United States has faced, from the beginning, many dangers, has met many challenges, has survived many and serious threats. It won independence against overwhelming odds, and against odds defended it — against the British, against threats from the French and the Spanish. It overcame

the dangers of vast distances, vast expanses of territory, of sec-
tionalism and States Rights, and maintained national union at
the cost of the greatest war of the nineteenth century. For
two centuries and more, Americans faced the test of the frontier
— of a wilderness that might have barbarized men if men had
not first tamed it, of continuous uprooting and transplanting,
continuous adjustment of men to environment and adaptation
of environment to men. They faced, for an equally long period, the test of the melting pot — of making Americans of millions of newcomers with different and often clashing back-
grounds, cultures, and faiths, and they fused out of these varied
elements a united people. They faced the test of continuous
economic readjustments — the changes in ways of working
and living that resulted from the Industrial Revolution, the
shift from a domestic to a world-wide agricultural economy,
the swift rise of cities, successive business panics and depressions. All of these dangers the nation survived, all of these
crises it weathered, preserving intact the essentials of liberty
and democracy. Within three generations after the establishment of the republic, the United States had grown from an
uncertain confederation of thirteen small states to be the first
Power in the world.

Then, in 1914, the United States faced a new threat and was
called upon in a new way to justify the experiment in democracy and liberty it had so long conducted. This was the threat
against world order and world peace from Imperial Germany
and its allies. When the war came, the United States took refuge in " splendid isolation " while President Wilson sought
anxiously some way whereby the differences between the warring powers of Europe could be arbitrated. But splendid isolation proved a delusion, and soon the United States was forced
to protect itself against aggression. And as American ships
were sunk and American lives lost on the high seas it became

clear that we would have to fight to protect our rights, to take our part in the First World War.

But at no time did Wilson fail to see that more was involved than the property or the lives of individuals, more even than the " rights " of Americans. What was at stake here was the whole system of international law that had been painfully built up over the years. What was at stake here was the rights and liberty of nations everywhere, of peoples everywhere in the world. And when Wilson came to set forth the American " war aims " it was this aspect of the war and of the peace to which he gave chief emphasis:

We entered this war because violations of right had occurred which touched us to the quick and made the life of our own people impossible unless they were corrected and the world secured once for all against their recurrence. What we demand in this war is therefore nothing peculiar to ourselves. It is that the world be made fit and safe to live in; and particularly that it be made safe for every peace-loving nation which, like our own, wishes to live its own life, determine its own institutions, be assured of justice and fair dealing by other peoples of the world as against force and selfish aggression. All the peoples of the world are in effect part-ners in this interest, and for our own part we see very clearly that unless justice be done to others it will not be done to us. The pro-gram of the world's peace is, therefore, our program.

And when the war was over, and the aggressors had been defeated, Wilson proposed a world organization — the League of Nations — which should maintain peace, enforce law, and help nations work together for a better world. But his own people would not follow him.

WE CANNOT LIVE ALONE

Disillusioned by the war and lulled into false security by victory, Americans thought that they could keep their own liberties and preserve their own safety regardless of what went on elsewhere in the world. They refused to take any responsibility for the political and economic reorganization of the postwar world, refused to co-operate in winning a lasting peace as they had co-operated in winning a war.

We know now how shortsighted was that policy of isolation which the United States adopted after 1920. Yet it is worth while reminding ourselves again of its causes, its character, and its consequences, for all this entered into the making of the present war and may enter into the making of the peace that is to follow. The causes of that isolationism were in part weariness with the war and with war efforts, in part ignorance about the nature of world organization and economy, in part a selfishness which other nations shared, and in part the accidents of our party politics.

Isolationism did not stop with refusal to enter the League of Nations and the World Court. It assumed that the United States was superior to other nations in its ways of living and thinking, and that it could better preserve that superiority if it avoided contamination with the Old World — with its wars, its secret diplomacy, its racial and national hatreds, its selfish struggle for raw material and trade, its decaying culture. And the consequence of that isolationism was that the United States abandoned the field to the antidemocratic and warmongering nations, permitting them to organize as they pleased for war and conquest.

What was wrong with the isolationism of these years is now clear. In the first place, it was based on a mistaken idea of the nature of the modern world. Actually we were not, nor could we be, isolated from the rest of the world. Our economic life was and has to be part of world economic life; our trade was international, our investments were world-wide. The prosperity of farmers in Texas depended upon their ability to sell cotton in England; the prosperity of farmers in Minnesota depended upon their ability to sell wheat in Germany. The prosperity of the worker in a Detroit automobile factory, of the miner in a Montana copper mine, of the small investor or the large banker — and of all the middlemen and white-collar workers who depended on these — was intimately bound up with conditions abroad. Nor was this all. Actually — as we were to learn to our cost — we had to do business with the rest of the world. We needed raw materials from abroad — normal things like sugar, coffee, tea; and military necessities like rubber, tin, manganese, chromium. And we had to sell abroad.

The depression of the 1930's and this war were to bring home to us the failure of isolationism as an economic formula. Meanwhile it was equally clear that isolationism had not worked in the political and diplomatic field. Our refusal to join the League of Nations, the World Court, or any other really effective organization for the maintenance of international law and order resulted in the growth of international anarchy. Our neutrality legislation of 1935, 1936, and 1937 erected an American Maginot Line behind which we lulled ourselves into insensibility with the opium of isolation. Our refusal to rearm or to make arms for the other democracies exposed us and them alike to the ruthless force of those nations which were ready to rearm and which cared nothing for law or for peace.

It was during these fateful years, while the United States was turning away from its responsibilities, ignoring its duties, rejecting the teachings of the past, forgetting the whole moral of its own history, flouting its destiny, that the totalitarian nations and the dictators became powerful. It was during these years, while we were living in a dream world of isolation, that we were confronted with the gravest challenge that has ever come to us — a challenge which was to test not only whether we could survive, but whether the things for which we had always stood, the values which we had always cherished, would survive or would disappear.

THE THREAT TO DEMOCRACY

For the totalitarian states of Germany, Italy, and Japan presented to the democratic states a challenge not only military and economic, but moral as well. It was not merely a contest for territory, for raw material, for control of the routes of trade, that they entered upon. It was a contest that reached much farther than this — a contest for the very hearts and souls of men. It would be disastrous if we failed to realize what was involved in this totalitarian threat. It would be calamitous if we failed to appreciate what were the fundamental issues of that war which began a decade ago and has now, with our entry, reached its climax.

Now once again, as in the past, we are called upon to defend that hope which we thought we had fulfilled — the maintenance for ourselves and for the peoples of the world of liberty, democracy, security, law, and peace. The totalitarian states have not only challenged these concepts, they have denied them. Our ideal of democracy is condemned by totalitarian beliefs or philosophies, which announce that democracy is the weakest of all systems of government and oppose to it systems that they think more efficient. Our economic individualism and freedom and our system of free enterprise are threatened by systems of economic collectivism and governmental control, or by the complete subordination of business and economy to political ends. Our traditional beliefs and ethics are confronted by a new system which denies in large part the democratic values which we have always taken for granted and always cherished. Our faith in man is challenged by a new faith — a faith in the state or in the party or in some New Order

which is to benefit the " master races " of Germany or Japan
at the expense of the rest of mankind.

It is difficult for the average American — who lives in the
intellectual atmosphere of freedom and of Christian principles
and ethics — to grasp the real nature of this challenge. It is a
new thing to us — new, and for the most part incomprehensible, and it is not remarkable that it has taken us a decade to
appreciate it. For none of the numerous challenges which we
have encountered in the past has been of this nature, none of
them has struck so fearfully at the very foundations of
our government, our economy, our society, our whole way
of life.

WE BELIEVE IN THE COMMON MAN

The very basis of the American system is the concern for
the welfare and the happiness of individual men and women.
Government exists to advance this welfare, to enhance this
happiness. Men make government, and men can unmake government. Men have rights and liberties — rights and liberties
in society, to be sure, but nevertheless individual: the right to
worship, to speak, to write, and to go about their own affairs
undisturbed by the state, to give the fullest freedom to their
talents and capacities. No matter how socialized our thinking,
our administration, our business, have become, it is still true that
the final objective of our government and of our social system
is the creation and protection of the free man.

To this democratic philosophy totalitarianism opposes a directly opposite one. The Nazi and Fascist governments
agree in subordinating the individual to something which they
think larger — the State. In these governments the individual
is unimportant; his liberties, his property, his ambitions and
hopes, his social and family relationships, even his religious
faith, are negligible. And this profound difference between

the democratic and the totalitarian ideas has affected the whole system of values which they cherish.

It is because we have failed to appreciate this that we have been so startled and so shocked by what has occurred in Europe and in Asia during the last decade. The record is familiar to all of us: the violation of treaties and of international law, ruthless conquest and invasion, fifth-column activities, religious and racial persecution, barbarous punishments and barbarous conduct of war, the regimentation and control of life and the subordination of all normal activities to the needs of the warring State — the whole strategy of terror and the strategy of totalitarianism. By our standards of values these things are wicked, and we wonder how they could come to pass. We have even been inclined to doubt their reality, to put them down as exaggerations, to argue them away as propaganda. But they have not been exaggerations, nor can they be explained away as mere propaganda. They are realities, and they are harsh realities. To the Nazis and the Fascists, who deny our standards of values and subscribe to very different standards, these things are not wicked at all, but normal and right. For in the totalitarian view the end inevitably justifies the means.

It is well to dwell for a moment on this matter of means and of ends, for both are important. The means are different from those to which we have long been accustomed — that much is clear — and the democracies have not yet learned to imitate them. Democracy appeals to reason, Nazism to authority. Democracy depends upon voluntary co-operation, Nazism exacts unquestioning obedience. Democracy has faith in education and knows that the truth will make men free, Nazism perverts understanding and emotions through propaganda. Democracy exalts tolerance, Nazism exploits intolerance.

The means are different, and the ends are different. The ends of the totalitarian systems are not, as with us, the liberty and happiness of the individual. Their ends are the power and the wealth of the State, or of the party or, perhaps, of the " race." The means reject the age-long habits of society, the ends deny human values and even life itself. For totalitarian doctrines, in Germany, in Italy, in Japan, embrace the mistaken concept of the superman and the slave, and rest on the brutalizing notion of the survival of the fittest. These doctrines are doctrines of negation, of rejection of all that we stand for. They are antiliberal, antidemocratic, anticapitalist, anti-Semitic, antirational, anti-Christian, antihuman.

WE FIGHT TO REMAIN AMERICAN

This is the challenge, then, that now confronts us — the challenge which denies and attacks everything that our philosophy holds dear. This is the fundamental issue of the war — the issue whether our way of life is to survive or is to go down before this new thing coming out of Hitler's Germany and advancing menacingly over two hemispheres.

For however wrong the totalitarian philosophy may be, it cannot be denied that it has proved itself immensely powerful and terrifyingly dangerous. Ideas are weapons, and if truth can make men free, falsehood can make them slaves. And these ideas confront us backed by every instrument, every weapon, every technique, which the energy and the cunning of men can devise.

The record of the last decade is sufficient evidence of this. For that record is one of almost unbroken successes for the totalitarian states. While the democracies were paralyzed by false security, or by passion for peace at any price, or by internal dissensions, the three leading totalitarian nations marched from triumph to triumph. Japan, long nursing an ambition to dominate the whole Eastern Hemisphere and the Pacific, struck into Manchuria in 1931 and six years later began that " China incident " which has developed into a full-scale war for the East. Its war was not only an utterly unprovoked attack upon China, but an outright violation of long-standing treaty agreements with the United States and other Powers, and it has been waged with a barbarism probably unmatched in the annals of modern warfare. Germany, under the leadership of Hitler, tore up the Versailles Treaty, denounced the Locarno Pact, remilitarized the Rhineland, marched into Austria, seized the Sudetenland, dismembered Czechoslovakia, and — arrogantly confident now of its strength — assaulted Poland and brought on a world war. Italy, the first state to devise a totalitarian government, aped its more powerful neighbor to the north by conquering an unoffending Ethiopia, supporting a Fascist revolution in Spain, seizing Albania, and finally assaulting Greece.

These violent acts undermined all the international law that had been built up over centuries, and constituted, therefore, a direct threat to the peace and safety of the United States. Yet most Americans thought them far-distant and senseless, and refused to concern themselves with them. Soon the war moved nearer, and the threats became more immediate. For the conflagration which Germany set in Poland in September, 1939, spread swiftly to the whole of Europe, and beyond. In a few weeks Germany overran Poland, and then settled down to organize for bigger game. In the spring of 1940 the German military machine moved into helpless Denmark and Norway, struck savagely into the Lowland countries, battered France into submission, and pushed the British Army off the sands of Dunkirk and across to its island stronghold. That fall German planes rained death and destruction upon England itself, and it seemed that the last outpost of democracy in Europe might fall. It did not fall, and Germany turned southward. With lightning strokes the Nazis pushed into the Balkans, rescued the Italians stranded in Albania, shoved the British out of Greece, took Crete from the air, and from the sandy shores of northern Africa threatened Egypt, the Suez Canal, and the fabulous East.

The pattern of conquest was now clear, and it was a world pattern. It involved more than " living-room " for Germans; it involved the domination of the entire globe. Soon Americans were reading with new understanding passages in *Mein Kampf* (*My Battle*) or authentic reports of Hitler's conversations: " Can a dynamic revolution stop at a sharing of the world? Must not the struggle continue until the final world dominion of a single nation? At the back of Germany's Continental empire stands the will of absolute dominion of the world, the technical means of which are no longer lacking." And again: " We, as the true chosen people, shall become the masters of the earth." And still again: " Our true object is to set up a rule for all time, and to anchor it so firmly that it will stand firm for a thousand years. Today we are faced with the iron necessity of creating a new social order. Only if we succeed in this shall we solve the great historical task which has been set for our people."

It was clear that here was something more than one of a long series of European wars. And soon it was equally clear that here was something that involved America. For Hitler himself recognized in the United States the last great threat to his plans. He recognized that democracy must be destroyed here, and that its destruction here would remove the last threat to his New Order. And he moved with customary efficiency to achieve that destruction. He concluded a pact with Japan designed to help Japan clear the Pacific area of American as well as of British and Netherlander control. He built up throughout the South American states racial and economic and political groups which were to be used to turn those states against the United States. In the United States itself he organized fifth-column activities, financed skillful propaganda, and agitated among the German-born for support of his new doctrines. " I guarantee," he said arrogantly, " that at the right moment a new America will exist as our strongest supporter when we are ready to take the stride into overseas space."

So we were faced not only with the distant and perhaps imaginary threat of a new and dangerous philosophy; we were faced with the immediate and concrete threat of economic encirclement, demoralization of our people, and military attack. Now every American could see — if he would — what a German and Japanese victory would mean for the United States. It would mean the end of the Monroe Doctrine. It would mean the end of the Open Door in the Far East. It would mean the end of the great principle of freedom of the seas. It would mean that we would lose our all-important sources of raw material in Latin America and the Pacific, that we would lose our markets everywhere in the world — or hold them only at the pleasure of the totalitarian states. It would mean that we would have to live to ourselves, as best we could, the while we armed frantically to ward off final defeat.

Faced with these consequences of a totalitarian victory, the United States aroused itself to arming the democracies and rearming itself. It announced that the cause of the democracies everywhere was its cause, and that it would not fail them. Swiftly it prepared to support this announcement by deeds. Most of the neutrality legislation was repealed. The Lend-Lease Act started an immense flow of war material to Britain and to its allies. Billions, and more billions, were appropriated for Army, Navy, and Air Force. Air and naval bases were obtained from Iceland and Greenland south to the Caribbean and British and Dutch Guiana. The American Navy joined the British in the Battle of the Atlantic. And Roosevelt and

Churchill, meeting in mid-ocean, drew up the Atlantic Charter which opposed to Hitler's New Order a democratic formula for peace and justice among nations.

Faced with this implacable determination that the democracies should be victorious, the Axis Powers struck — swiftly and treacherously. Their initial strokes were successful, yet it is clear that they had already lost the opening rounds, lost the one advantage which might have given them victory. For the totalitarian Powers had so conducted themselves that they had, at last, united the American people. They had made perfectly clear to Americans the real nature of the struggle, the real stakes of battle, the real issues of the war.

Those issues must have emerged from this brief survey of the opposing forces in the war. They stand out, illumined by history, unobscured by propaganda. We realize now that while the things we are fighting may be new, the things we are defending are old and familiar. Freedom and democracy and peace, the right of men to govern themselves and to find happiness in their own way, the right of peoples, great and small, to live their own lives — all these things wait upon the outcome of this war. We have come to understand more fully what President Roosevelt said two years ago:

There comes a time in the affairs of men when they must prepare to defend not their homes alone, but the tenets of faith and humanity on which their churches, their governments and their very civilization are founded. The defense of religion, of democracy and good faith among nations, is all the same fight. To save one we must now make up our minds to save all.

II. How did the war begin and spread over the world?

FREDERICK L. SCHUMAN

Frederick L. Schuman taught for fifteen years at the University of Chicago. He is now Woodrow Wilson Professor of Government at Williams College. He has traveled and studied extensively, and on the eve of the Second World War, was in England, France, Germany, Italy, and Russia. Among his more recently published books are 'International Politics' (a standard textbook in the colleges), 'The Nazi Dictatorship,' 'Europe on the Eve,' 'Night over Europe,' and 'Design for Power.'

THE RIDDLE OF ARMAGEDDON

How did the Second World War come about? The easiest answer would be that Nazi Germany invaded Poland on the first day of September, 1939, in a criminally insane attempt to conquer the world, that Britain and France declared war on Hitler two days later, and that Italy, Russia, Japan, the United States, and a dozen smaller nations were all dragged into the conflict by 1942. Another easy answer would be that the triumphant Allies of 1918 dealt too harshly with Germany and too ungenerously with Italy and Japan, and thereby created rankling resentments which later exploded in aggression. Still a third easy answer, the opposite of the second one, would be that the Allies of the First World War dealt too leniently with Germany and too indulgently with Italy and Japan and thereby enabled the militarists of these countries to prepare their peoples for new wars of conquest.

Easy answers to hard questions, however, seldom lead to wisdom. All these answers are in some sense " true." But they furnish few clues to comprehension of the past and little guidance for the future. In reality the Second World War did not begin in September of 1939 but in September of 1931. The tragedies of the last few years have been products of many years of ignorance and weakness, and of cruelty and malice, in a period before 1939. To deal generously and justly with the vanquished in the making of the next peace, moreover, will not by itself prevent future war. Nor will peace be ensured in the years ahead by bitter punishment for monstrous crimes, however much such punishment may be deserved.

Some broader view than this, some fuller understanding of modern man's tragic road to war, are needed if we are to avoid new failures and despairs and keep ourselves from saying once again, some five or ten years hence, that " all our yesterdays have lighted fools the way to dusty death."

GOVERNMENT AND ANARCHY

The Second World War, like the First and like all outbreaks of disorder and crime in human affairs, is a result of something harder to grasp than the evil motives of wicked people or the weaknesses of virtuous ones. Order and justice are products not alone of good motives but of good government based on goodwill. When government breaks down, gangsters flourish and sinners prosper by robbing and murdering their neighbors. Where government does not exist or is inadequate to its tasks, people live in anarchy and become victims of a savage warfare of each against all.

Modern mankind, by a slow and painful process, has through

the centuries replaced anarchy by government, violence by order, brutality by justice, and lawlessness by law *inside* of the nation-states into which the human race has somehow gotten itself divided. But modern mankind has not yet succeeded in doing anything resembling this in the relations *between* the nation-states in that larger community of which the nation-states are members. All of us as citizens of our own nations have long lived under government and have taken it for granted that our governments will at the very least maintain order and enforce the law. But all of us as members of the world community have lived and continue to live under conditions of international anarchy which leave national governments free to play " power politics " against one another by trickery and violence and to indulge in periodical outbreaks of arson and murder on a world scale.

The evil of war is not a thing to be blamed upon " human nature." Nothing is more " human " than Tom, Dick, and Harry who live around the corner or in the next block. Yet we do not expect them to draw guns on one another (or on us), nor to plunder and burn down their neighbors' houses. On the contrary, we know that they are law-abiding and peaceable citizens and that if, perchance, they are tempted to misconduct themselves, they will be forced to behave by the police, organized and paid for our own protection and for theirs by all of us. By the same logic, if the national tribes of men engage in wholesale killing, robbing, and burning at one another's expense, to the common ruination of all, this is not at all due to " human nature " but to the peculiar conditions in the family of nations in which human nature has hitherto been obliged to express itself.

Such misconduct is due, in short, to the fact that the community of nation-states is not yet organized to prevent and punish the commission of evil acts or to put a stop to the pursuit

WORLD-WIDE EXCHANGE OF GOODS
IN PEACE TIME

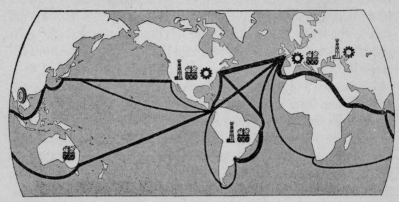

SYMBOLS REPRESENT INDUSTRY, FOOD, OIL, AND RUBBER

PICTOGRAPH CORPORATION

The goods of the world are unequally distributed. One country may have an abundance of one thing but lack another one. Thus the United States abounds in food and oil and industrial products, but lacks rubber. In times of peace the regions of the world exchange some of the goods in which they abound for some which they need more. Most of these goods are carried over the highways of the sea, which link the great ports of the world. For thousands of miles the ships travel over routes which are wide and safe. But wherever coast lines press the traffic into narrow lanes, those who control the coasts control the life-lines of trade which pass between them.

of national purposes by violence or threat of violence. It is therefore possible to " get away with murder " in the society of nations, though this is no longer possible within any well-governed nation or neighborhood. In both cases human nature is the same. The difference lies in the presence of " government " within nations and in the absence of " government " among nations.

For many long centuries it mattered little to the common run of men and women that the nation-states lived with one another in anarchy. In the old and simple world of our fore-fathers, who earned their livelihood by farming and local trade, wars were hatched by professional diplomats and fought by small armies of professional soldiers. Other people went about their business and were little affected. But the coming of science, of modern technology and of the factory system, has in the past century and a half bound all the world together into one market and one small neighborhood — growing smaller year by year — in which most people live by machine industry on a world scale. In such a brave new world as this, war becomes " total," war anywhere affects the lives and fortunes of everybody everywhere, war threatens the destruction of the whole world-wide network of commerce and finance upon which all of us depend for the very necessities of life. Mankind in the Machine Age must abolish war or war will abolish the Machine Age and bring to humanity a new epoch of darkness in which the miserable survivors of man-made catastrophes return to poverty, brutishness, and ignorance.

THE PRICE OF PEACE

If war is a result of anarchy in the family of nations, then peace can be assured only by the organization of government in the family of nations. This proposition is fundamental to any clear thinking about war aims and peace aims and world reconstruction. It means that international violence springs from the lack of any higher authority above the nations which can compel the keeping of the peace. It means that the peace can be kept only by the creation of some world-wide concert of power which will abolish " power politics " and the " balance of power " through some paramount organization of authority reflecting the highest purposes of all mankind and commanding a paramount respect and allegiance. That allegiance must be broader than our present national loyalties, just as those loyalties are already much broader than the earlier loyalties of men to their local creeds and classes and provinces.

Another proposition which is equally fundamental is that the world government of the future, if it is to guarantee world peace, must have effective power at its disposal to enforce the law. In the last analysis that power must be military power. It must be so organized that leaders and peoples will be able and willing to use it, promptly and completely, against any men or groups of men anywhere in the world who seek to defy the community and endanger the safety of all by taking the sword against their neighbors. A further central truth, made clear as day by the tragic lessons of our generation, is that the United States of America, as the richest and most powerful of the Great Powers, has the largest stake in world peace and the largest opportunity to help in the creation of world government. No nation in the modern world can live alone and like it, least of all America. No people can find safety by " avoiding foreign entanglements " and " keeping out of other peoples' wars," least of all Americans. The world is one and all men are brothers.

If America is to have a future, Americans must recognize and act upon these facts. If America is to play the role of world leadership imposed upon it by destiny, Americans must assume the responsibilities and run the risks involved in the establishment of the world government of tomorrow. By refusing to face these facts, the democracies of the world brought upon themselves the Second World War. By refusing to face these facts, Americans have inflicted upon themselves a new ordeal by blood and fire. If the future is to be better than the past, these facts must be made our guides to action. If the past is to be understood, these facts must be made the basis of our understanding.

HOW THE LAST PEACE WAS LOST

The pity of it all lies in the circumstance that these things were clearly seen a quarter of a century ago. In 1915–16 a nation-wide organization called the League to Enforce Peace won the support of most Americans to a program of world order involving American membership in an association of nations with adequate power to put force behind peace. In 1918 the leaders of Britain, France, Italy, and the United States, with the full approval of their peoples, pledged themselves to the creation of a League of Nations to enforce peace. In 1919 the Covenant of the League, which was largely written by Woodrow Wilson, was made a part of the peace treaties. Early in the following year the League came into being as the fulfillment of the hopes of all free peoples, who were then convinced by the ordeal of war that all must join forces to keep the peace for the future.

The weakness of the League lay in the fact that it was not a " superstate " nor even a federation of nations, but only a loose confederation of fully sovereign members, like the unsuccessful government of the United States under the Articles of Confederation (1781–89). The League had no authority over individuals, no power to regulate commerce or levy taxes, no police force at its disposal, no ability to act at all save through its member states. There were provisions in the Covenant, to be sure, for " peaceful change," for mutual guarantees of the independence and integrity of the members, and for economic and military sanctions against states violating the Covenant. But the members of the League could take no action against lawbreakers or peace-breakers except insofar as each member, acting as a sovereign and independent government, might choose to take action. And national governments necessarily act not in the interest of the whole community of nations but only to protect and promote " national interests " in the name of " My country, right or wrong! " No " government " in any community of states has ever proved effective for the maintenance of order and the preservation of peace on the basis of such arrangements as these. The League would perhaps have been found wanting under the most hopeful of circumstances.

The circumstances, however, were not the most hopeful. Woodrow Wilson became a prophet without honor in his own land. A little group of willful men in the United States Senate vetoed American membership in the League, as they later vetoed American membership in the World Court. They alleged that the League and the Court were a " superstate " with power to " drag America into foreign quarrels." They contended that American peace could be made secure by " avoiding foreign entanglements " and " minding our own business." The League of Nations, although " made in America " and founded by a President of the United States, thus began its work under the handicap of nonmembership by the greatest of the Great Powers.

HOW POVERTY LED TO TYRANNY AND WAR

The Geneva adventure in international government might yet have succeeded had it not been for the consequences of the Great Depression which began in 1929. All national governments, and that of the United States above all, sought the economic well-being of their citizens in the 1920's not by organizing and planning world prosperity in a world market, but by subsidizing exports to other countries, taxing or prohibiting imports, encouraging risky investments of private capital abroad, seeking to collect war debts and reparation payments without being willing to accept imports of goods as payment, and indulging in a variety of other policies designed to increase private profits at public expense or to foster national prosperity at the expense of other nations. The crazy structure of world trade and finance which was erected by the economic nationalists of all countries toppled into ruin at the end of a decade and plunged scores of millions of people all over the globe into bankruptcy, unemployment, hunger, and despair.

This disaster was fatal to democracy and to peace alike. Democracy is government by talk and by free co-operation and compromise. It can work only when people are reasonable and tolerant. They can be reasonable and tolerant only when they have food, clothing, shelter, and some measure of dignity, security, and confidence. People who are jobless and desperate cannot value freedom highly, nor can they easily be patient and sweetly reasonable. As early as 1917 the mass misery produced by the First World War had led to revolution in Russia and to the establishment of a " dictatorship of the proletariat " whose leaders were pledged to giving people bread and hope through the violent establishment of a new social order. As early as 1922 mass misery in Italy led to the Fascist revolution and to the tyranny of Mussolini, who, in the name of " saving Italy from Communism," promised bread and hope to the masses through the boasted efficiency of a totalitarian despotism. The Great Depression produced similar miseries elsewhere, enabling the gangster elements in the Japanese Army and Navy to secure more and more influence in Tokyo and bringing to power in Germany, early in 1933, Hitler's Nazi fanatics, sworn to hatred, persecution, and revenge.

The despairs which led in Japan, Italy, and Germany to tyranny and to plans for conquest led in France, Britain, and America to desperate efforts to escape war by running away from danger and bribing the aggressors to be good. These efforts led to the betrayal of the League of Nations, to the constant weakening of the democratic Powers, and to a steady increase in the ambitions and the armaments of the war-mad adventurers who had hypnotized and enslaved the Japanese, Italian, and German peoples.

The attempt to escape war by running away expressed itself from 1935 to 1939 in the neutrality legislation of the United States, which by denying American arms and money to all foreign states at war, with no distinction between aggressors and their victims, helped to make the world safe for aggression. It also expressed itself in the fatal " appeasement " policies of the British and French governments. Many democratic leaders were completely " taken in " by Nazi and Japanese pretensions of " saving the world from Communism." If the new war lords were, as they said, preparing only to attack Red Russia, then, reasoned many of the timid and the blind, no harm would be done by permitting them to build up their war machines and to launch their crusade against Moscow. Still less harm would come, thought many people, from permitting them to attack and enslave the weaker peoples of Asia, Africa, and Europe. The great democracies said, in effect, that they were not their brothers' keepers, and they sought peace for themselves by encouraging the warmakers to attack others.

AGGRESSORS AND APPEASERS

The Second World War began in fact, though few realized it then, with the Japanese seizure of Manchuria in the fall of

1931. China appealed to the League. But Britain, France, and America, all alike in the throes of business paralysis, would not " risk war " to compel Japan to keep its promises in the League Covenant, the Nine Power Pact of 1922, and the Pact of Paris of 1928. It seemed easier and " safer " to do nothing beyond passing pious resolutions and making futile recommendations which the aggressor ignored. America's Secretary of State Stimson sought a common Anglo-American front against Japan's aggression, but Britain's Foreign Minister, Sir John Simon, refused to co-operate in any joint action out of fear that any action to preserve peace might lead to war. The conquest of Manchuria was thus completed. Tokyo left the League and created the puppet state of Manchukuo. All the elements of lawlessness and violence in a sick world were plainly told that Americans, Britishers, and Frenchmen would do nothing to prevent or punish lawlessness and violence if doing something seemed to involve risks and responsibilities.

The little Caesar of Rome, Benito Mussolini, and the Caesar-to-be of Germany, Adolf Hitler, drew conclusions from the Manchurian crisis. After seven months in the Chancellorship of the Reich, which he secured by trickery and lies, Hitler announced Germany's withdrawal (October, 1933) from the League of Nations and the World Disarmament Conference. His destruction of German democracy, his persecution of the Jews, and his preparations for the conquest of Europe went on quite openly with no interference from the democratic Powers. When in March of 1935 he publicly repudiated the disarmament clauses of the Treaty of Versailles, the Allies did nothing beyond writing notes of protest — and selling arms to Germany. Three months later the British Cabinet headed by Stanley Baldwin signed a treaty with Hitler granting him a Navy 35 per cent as large as the British with 100 per cent equality in submarines.

The Italian tyrant had already laid his plans. In January, 1935, he persuaded the French Foreign Minister, Pierre Laval, to acquiesce in his designs against Ethiopia in return for a vague promise of an alliance against Germany. All that spring and summer Fascist troops, tanks, and planes poured through the Suez Canal while Paris and London, both inside the League and outside the League, sought to give Ethiopia to Mussolini without war. In October, 1935, he ordered the invasion of Ethiopia. Emperor Haile Selassie appealed anew to the League of Nations. The United States banned arms and loans to both the aggressor and his victim. The Anglo-French appeasers were obliged by public opinion to go through the motions of imposing " economic sanctions " against Italy in November, all the while secretly assuring Mussolini that nothing would be done to impede the conquest. In December, Laval and Sir Samuel Hoare, then British Foreign Minister, cooked up a " peace plan " to give two-thirds of Ethiopia to Italy if Mussolini would call off his war. He refused. By May of 1936 the conquest was complete. Ethiopia was enslaved. Haile Selassie, with dark predictions of doom for the Western Powers, went into lonely exile. In July League sanctions were lifted. The League Powers surrendered to the aggressors.

REHEARSALS FOR CONQUEST

The Nazi despot, perceiving clearly how the wind was blowing, lost no time. In March, 1936, he repudiated the Locarno Treaty and ordered his troops into the demilitarized Rhineland. The Allies wrote notes of protest. In July of 1936 Hitler and Mussolini laid the basis for the " Axis " by supporting the Franco Rebellion against the Spanish Republic. France, Britain, and America forbade their citizens to sell arms to either side in Spain, while the Fascist rebels were given guns, planes, and whole army corps by the Fascist Powers, all in the name of "saving Spain from Communism." In November, 1936, Germany and Japan signed the "Anti-Comintern" pact, the better to befuddle the democracies. Italy joined a year later, and then Manchukuo, Hungary, and Franco's Spain.

The Tokyo militarists meanwhile launched their new assault on China in July of 1937. China appealed to the League — in vain. China appealed to America, Britain, and France — in vain. In the name of "peace" and "friendly relations," Americans, Britishers, and Frenchmen were permitted by their governments to sell oil and metal, planes and guns, ships and tanks, to the Japanese war lords for the conquest of China. Only the heroism of the Chinese people, with a little aid from Russia, enabled them to hold out, just as the Spanish Republic was enabled to survive for almost three years by Russian arms and by the courage of its loyal soldiers and civilians. Tokyo said that the Chinese Republic was "Communist," as Rome and Berlin said that the Spanish Republic was "Communist." Democratic irresponsibility led to the complete breakdown of the League system. It also led to the spread of international anarchy, lawlessness, and violence and to the growth of Fascist plans for the conquest of a world which the democratic peoples were unwilling to govern.

THE YEAR OF DISHONOR

In March, 1938, Hitler seized Austria. Lord Halifax, busily engaged as British Foreign Minister in appeasing Tokyo, Rome, and Berlin, cried "Horrible! I never thought they would do it!" Otherwise there was no action. In the late spring and summer Hitler cleverly organized a campaign of threats against the Czechoslovak democracy, which was the ally of France, the heart of the Little Entente (Czechoslovakia, Yugoslavia, and Rumania, all allied with France), and the bastion of the Danube basin and the Balkans. Hitler's slogan this time was

" self-determination " for the Sudeten Germans, who had lived contentedly in the Czech borderlands for seven centuries. Premier Daladier and Prime Minister Chamberlain were sympathetic — not toward President Beneš and the Czech Republic but toward Hitler.

In September, amid terrifying rumors of war, Chamberlain flew three times to Germany, and finally made the " peace " of Munich. By its terms Germany secured the Sudetenland, including all the Czech border fortifications, while Hungary and Poland grabbed off smaller pieces. The whole French alliance system therewith collapsed. Chamberlain signed a separate peace pact with Hitler, as did French Foreign Minister Georges Bonnet two months later. Said Chamberlain to cheering crowds: " I bring you peace with honor. I think it is peace for our time." Said Winston Churchill: " Britain and France had to choose between war and dishonor. They chose dishonor. They will have war."

The Munich men of France and Britain took it for granted that Hitler's machine, once dominant in eastern Europe and the Balkans, would attack the Soviet Union. The assumption was tragically mistaken. Gangsters invariably attack those who show themselves to be weak. The U.S.S.R. had aided China and Spain and had sought, always without success, to persuade London and Paris to make the League an effective weapon of collective security against Fascist aggression. The U.S.S.R. had concluded alliances with France and Czechoslovakia and had offered to defend Czechoslovakia against Germany even after the Anglo-French betrayal. The Western Powers had shown themselves incapable of defending or even understanding their own interests. In March of 1939 Hitler occupied Prague, destroyed the pathetic remnant of Czechoslovakia, and made clear (as indeed he had done long ago in *Mein Kampf*) that he was bent upon crushing the Western

Powers before launching his armies of conquest against Russia. In May of 1939 he concluded a formal military alliance with Italy against France and Britain.

EUROPE ON THE BRINK

At long last frightened into a sense of realities, Chamberlain and Daladier now sought to rebuild the alliance system they had thrown away. The British Government, which had refused to defend China, Ethiopia, Spain, Austria, and Czechoslovakia, guaranteed Poland against German aggression at the end of March and concluded an Anglo-Polish alliance in August, 1939. After Mussolini's seizure of Albania in early April, London and Paris together concluded an alliance with Turkey and gave " guarantees," for which they got nothing in return, to Greece and Rumania. But this combination, as Churchill, Eden, and others pointed out, was useless against the Axis without Russian support.

Russia was willing to give its support on condition that France and Britain enter into a binding alliance with the U.S.S.R., give Soviet troops access to Poland (which they would be called upon to defend), and authorize the Soviet Union to " protect " the Baltic States against possible Nazi conquest. These terms Chamberlain could never bring himself to grant. His refusal convinced Stalin that the Western appeasers were still hoping for a German-Soviet war in which Britain and France might be neutral. He concluded that any agreement with such leaders would be highly dangerous. He therefore prepared to come to terms with Hitler and to abandon the Western democracies to their fate.

Hitler had meanwhile brought heavy pressure on Poland for cession to Germany of the Polish Corridor and acquiescence in German annexation of the Free City of Danzig. When Warsaw refused, fearing the fate of Vienna and Prague, the Führer

manufactured another summer war crisis, hoping either to
drive Paris and London into another Munich at Warsaw's expense or to crush Poland by force before the Western Powers could act. By mid-August Chamberlain and Daladier were
warning him that any attack on Poland would mean war with
Britain and France.

Hitler was doubtful. London still seemed willing to bribe
him to keep the peace. The French appeasers were shouting:
"Danzig is not worth a war!" But he told the British Ambassador, Sir Nevile Henderson, that although he had the soul
of an artist, he would prefer war when he was fifty to war when
he should be fifty-five or sixty. On August 21 Berlin announced that Foreign Minister Ribbentrop would fly to Moscow two days later to sign a neutrality and nonaggression pact
with Russia. With Poland now left defenseless by Moscow's
adoption of a policy of appeasement, the Nazi leaders expected
Chamberlain and Daladier to surrender. The Nazi-Soviet pact
was signed on August 23, 1939. But the British and French
leaders warned Berlin that they would nevertheless come to
the defense of Poland if Germany attacked.

The final crisis centered on the meaning of "negotiations."
Hitler and Ribbentrop told Henderson that they would "negotiate" a settlement providing that a special Polish envoy arrived in Berlin by midnight of August 30. They denied that
this was an "ultimatum." London and Paris sought to encourage German-Polish negotiations but indicated that they could
not deliver a Polish envoy or compel Poland to accept a dictated
settlement. When Ribbentrop saw Henderson at midnight of
August 30, the Nazi Foreign Minister gabbled through some
"sixteen points" of a proposed agreement, threw the document contemptuously on the table, and said it was "too late,"
since no Polish envoy had appeared. The proposals were
never officially transmitted to Warsaw, Paris, or London, and

AXIS POWERS TRY TO CUT
LINES OF EXCHANGE

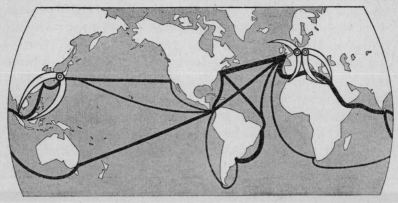

There were four major spots on the map where shipping could easily be controlled. Two are man-made: The Panama and Suez canals. And two are natural: Singapore and Gibraltar. Although all four were controlled by English-speaking nations, traffic through them was open to the ships of all nations who followed peaceful trades. The Axis Powers, intent upon conquest of the world, planned their effort against all four of these spots.

Japan drove against British control over Singapore.

Germany, lacking a navy comparable to Britain's, prepared air and land drives against Britain's control over the Suez Canal and Gibraltar.

The conquest of the Balkans and the drives in Libya point toward Suez.

Look at a map of occupied France; it will show you that the Germans hold a long strip of France along the Atlantic reaching clear down to the Pyrenees. Continue this strip through Spain and you will find that this strip points right to Gibraltar.

Only the Panama Canal is not yet under a direct threat.

were therefore never accepted or rejected. They were in fact a sham to conceal carefully laid plans of aggression. To negotiate with madmen whose appetite for power can never be satisfied and whose morals are those of professional criminals is always impossible save at the cost of liberty or life. To appease such power-drunk fanatics is equally impossible, as even Stalin was to discover.

WAR IN THE EAST

At dawn of September 1, 1939, formidable Nazi armies poured across the Polish frontiers, slaughtering, burning, and plundering wherever they went, as they were destined to do in a dozen other unhappy lands. The Second World War therewith became a war of blood as well as a " war of nerves."

After two days of delay, caused by Bonnet's last-minute efforts to arrange another Munich with the aid of Mussolini, Britain and France delivered ultimatums to Berlin on Sunday morning, September 3, demanding an end of the invasion of Poland. The demands were scornfully rejected. Britain was at war with Germany from 11 A.M. France followed suit six hours later. All appeals for peace from America, the Vatican, and other sources were ignored by the Nazi adventurers. Mussolini, by prearrangement with Berlin, remained " nonbelligerent," confident that the Allies would continue to appease him until he should be ready to strike.

Fascist strategy, as always, was to confuse and befuddle enemies and intended victims by the propaganda of anti-Semitism and anti-Communism, and to strike down one foe at a time while others were drugged into inactivity by reassurances and empty promises. This strategy, coupled with the terrible striking power of armed forces skillfully prepared for world conquest, worked wonders so long as the Western Munich men remained at the helm, for these architects of disaster were no more capable of waging war than of preserving peace.

Poland was destroyed in two weeks and partitioned between Germany and the U.S.S.R. Moscow not only shared in the spoils but imposed " protectorates " on the Baltic states in the fall of 1939 and waged war against Finland (December 1, 1939–March 12, 1940) to compel the Finns to cede islands, border areas, and naval bases deemed essential for Soviet defense. The last gasp of the League of Nations was the expulsion of the U.S.S.R. from membership. Chamberlain and Daladier laid plans to fight Russia. But they had none for fighting Germany, except blockade and passive defense. In the West the Reichswehr stood on its " West Wall " and did nothing for eight long months of " phony war," while appeasers, defeatists, Fascist sympathizers, and Nazi agents busily sowed the seeds of demoralization among Frenchmen and Britishers.

WAR IN THE WEST

On the ninth day of the eighth month of the war the Nazi hosts, aided by " Trojan horses " and " fifth-columnists " galore, struck down Denmark and Norway. Air power immobilized sea power along the northern coasts. All of Britain's might was helpless to save the Norwegians from conquest. On the tenth day of the ninth month of the war the Nazi hosts, once more aided by secret agents and sympathizers, invaded Luxemburg, the Netherlands, and Belgium. Luxemburg was occupied in a day. The Netherlands was crushed in five days and Belgium in seventeen. Chamberlain at last resigned in favor of Winston Churchill. In Paris Daladier had given way to Reynaud in March. On May 14 the Nazi tank divisions and dive-bombers smashed through the French border positions near Sedan and drove down the valleys of the Meuse, the Aisne, and the Somme. They split the British Expeditionary Force and the French divisions in the north from the main French armies to the south. The invaders reached the sea on May 21, turned northward, and encircled the entire B.E.F. Most of its members managed, by a miracle of heroism on the part of British seamen and airmen, to cross the Channel to England before the Nazis ended the Battle of Flanders by taking Dunkirk on June 3.

On the eleventh day of the tenth month of hostilities Mussolini ordered Italy into war against Britain and France. This "stab in the back" was due to his belief that the war was practically over. On June 2 the German armies had struck south from the Somme at the heart of France. Premier Reynaud had named defeatist General Weygand as Generalissimo and defeatist Marshal Pétain as Vice-Premier. They and their Fascist-minded colleagues were neither willing nor able to save the French Republic. Paris fell on June 14. Two days later Churchill, in a desperate attempt to keep France in the war, offered to the French Government at Bordeaux a "Union Now" proposal by which France and Britain would fight on together as a single federated democracy. But on June 17 Reynaud was ousted by Pétain, Weygand, and Laval, who hastened to surrender rather than continue the war from the French colonies.

A few heroic Frenchmen were able to follow General de Gaulle to London and to continue the fight in the name of "Free France" in exile. But the defeatists signed an armistice with Germany on June 22 and with Italy on the next day. Hostilities in France ceased on June 25. The defeatists set up an anti-Semitic, semi-Fascist regime in Vichy and agreed to "collaborate" with Hitler. Like Mussolini, they were sure that Britain would be conquered within a few weeks.

WAR FOR THE WORLD

The fall of France was not the end but the beginning of a gigantic contest for mastery of the globe. Churchill's Britain stood firm as a rock under the rain of bombs which Nazi airmen poured upon its cities in the summer and fall of 1940. Russia annexed the Baltic states and took Bessarabia and northern Bucovina from Rumania for better protection against the Nazi menace. The United States transferred fifty destroyers to Britain (September 2) in return for naval bases and embarked on a program of all-out aid " short of war " under the terms of the Lease-Lend Act signed by President Roosevelt on March 11, 1941. Germany, Italy, and Japan meanwhile signed the Triple Alliance Pact (September 27, 1940) in an effort to frighten America. Mussolini attacked Greece in October, 1940, only to have his armies beaten back into Albania. British troops overran Italian East Africa, restored Haile Selassie to his throne, and invaded Libya while British warships blasted the Italian Navy in the Mediterranean.

The spread of the war over all the earth during 1941 was the result of the desperation of Adolf Hitler and of his allies in Europe and Asia. His conquests of all of central, western, and northern Europe brought him no victory over Britain, even though Britishers stood almost alone against him. He therefore decided to conquer the Balkans and strike at Suez. In April, 1941, Nazi troops invaded Egypt from Libya. With Hungary, Rumania, and Bulgaria forced into the Triple Alliance and occupied by German soldiery, the Nazi war machine struck down Yugoslavia and Greece in a few swift blows and then sought, with the help of the Vichy men in Syria, to strike at Britain in the Near East.

But British troops beat back the invasion of Egypt. British and Free French forces occupied Iraq in May and Syria in

June, thus thwarting the furious Führer. He dared not attempt an invasion of Britain so long as British sea power was unbroken and so long as the Red Army stood at his back. He therefore decided in late spring to attack Russia, despite his five-year nonaggression pact with Moscow and despite Stalin's benevolent neutrality toward Germany. The Nazi Napoleon expected that the Soviets would be speedily defeated and that his new " crusade against Communism " might lead to a " negotiated peace " with Britain and to confusion and paralysis in America.

Hitler's hopes were doomed. His machines of murder invaded the Soviet Union on June 22, 1941, and won great victories in western Russia. Finland, Slovakia, Italy, Hungary, and Rumania joined in the assault. But the invaders this time met an army and a people ready to die rather than yield. For the first time the Nazi divisions were stopped and then defeated. By late fall the Nazi armies were forced for the first time to retreat — from the gates of Moscow, from the mouth of the Don, from the sources of the Volga, and from the plains before Leningrad. The invasion of Russia had failed. The " war of nerves " against Britain and America had also failed, for London made an alliance with Moscow while Washington extended aid to the Soviet Union.

THE ATTACK ON AMERICA

The perfidious assault of the Triple Alliance on the United States, launched at Pearl Harbor on December 7, 1941, was the result of Hitler's failure to conquer Britain and Russia and of the failure of the Japanese war lords to conquer China. The Nazi debacle in the land of the Soviets meant that with the passage of time the Axis would face certain defeat unless the flow of American supplies to Britain and Russia could be stopped. The Japanese debacle in China meant that the Tokyo militarists would ultimately face disaster unless the flow of American supplies to China could be stopped. In September, 1940, Vichy had surrendered northern Indo-China to Japanese troops, thus helping Hitler to bribe Tokyo into signing the Triple Alliance. In July, 1941, Vichy surrendered southern Indo-China to Japanese troops, thus helping Hitler and Hirohito to prepare an eventual attack on American, British, and Dutch territories in southeastern Asia. America's reply was to shut off the shipment of oil, metal, and other war materials which for four years had gone from the United States to Japanese ports. Tokyo demanded that the embargoes be lifted and that America accept Japanese mastery of East Asia, hypocritically disguised as a " New Order " or a " Co-Prosperity Sphere " for defense against " Communism." Washington refused to betray China but offered Tokyo fair and generous terms toward settlement if only the war lords would withdraw their troops from China and Indo-China.

In the midst of pretended negotiations the Japanese military fanatics struck their blow at the United States Pacific Fleet and at the same time occupied Thailand and attacked Hong Kong, the Philippines, Singapore, and the Netherlands East Indies. On December 11 Hitler declared war on America. His lackey Mussolini followed suit, as did the shadow rulers of Slovakia, Croatia, Hungary, Rumania, and Bulgaria. Against this coalition of gangsters and puppets there was ranged a counteralliance of twenty-six " United Nations," headed by America, Britain, Russia, and China. Their representatives pledged themselves in Washington on January 2, 1942, to wage war together and to make no separate peace or armistice until final victory should be won.

THE PRICE OF VICTORY

That victory is inevitable, whatever new defeats may be met with during 1942, if all Americans do their duty with the courage and determination already shown by the peoples of Britain, China, Russia, and many smaller countries. That victory will be only half won, however, if the United States does not lead the United Nations on a course of common action which will win the peace as well as the war. This purpose will not be realized merely by firm resolve to make a " just peace " after the fighting ends. Neither will it be achieved merely by destroying the German and Japanese military machines and by teaching the deluded peoples of the enemy countries in the hard school of tears and blood that militarism and aggression do not pay.

In the future, as in the past, punishment will lead to cries for revenge, " justice " will become a catchword to hide irresponsibility or lust for power, " peace " will be but a time of preparation for the next war — unless international anarchy in the family of nations is abolished through the organization of a world order so strong that its guardians can prevent and punish international crime, and so just that all peoples will feel that they have a stake in preserving it for all future time. In the words of Pascal: " Right without might is weakness. Might without right is tyranny. We must therefore combine right and might, making what is right mighty and what is mighty right."

There is little reason to suppose that this goal can be attained simply by defeating the ruthless and cruel aggressors who are attacking and seeking to enslave the United States and all other free nations. Neither is it likely to be reached by new alliances or by a restoration of the old League of Nations. If the peace is to be won, as well as the war, the free peoples of the world will be obliged to act together, in some form or other, to build a World Union of the Free through which justice can be administered and law can be enforced all over the planet. Such a World Union may take the form at the beginning, as Clarence Streit and many other people have urged, of a greater United States of all the English-speaking peoples. It may take the form of a European-Anglo-American-Pan-American Federation. It may take the form of a new and stronger League of Nations, with effective authority and world-wide membership in fulfillment of the vision of Woodrow Wilson. Or it may take a form which no one now can foresee. It must grow not from paper blueprints but from the experience and the suffering, the wisdom and the imagination, of all the peoples of all the United Nations.

In the days to come, as Lincoln said in 1862, " We shall nobly save or meanly lose the last best hope of earth." In the days to come, the American dream will either fade and flicker out or be rekindled as a flaming beacon of hope for all the peoples of the globe. Success in war and peace alike will be gained if all people of goodwill turn their minds and hearts, even in the midst of battle, to the task of finding the good way toward the reordering of the world. Nothing less than victory in this quest can justify the anguish and bloodshed of today. Nothing less than victory in the vast enterprise of creating a Free World Order can keep the faith with those who are giving their lives for freedom.

Victory will dispel the darkness and grief which today hang heavy over the human spirit. Victory will bring tomorrow to all mankind a new dawn of liberty under law. Victory will give life to a new vision of economic security and creative work wherein all peoples are assured a future of peace and freedom. Victory must mean, if it is not to be a purpose twice betrayed, that all men and women everywhere will henceforth be protected in their enjoyment of equal rights and equal opportunities and will find their self-realization in contributing, from each to all, whatever their talents and their hearts' desire enable them to give to the common civilization of a world at last united. That world must henceforth remain one and indivisible for the days of glory and the years of promise that lie ahead. The winning of that world and the building of that future are the tasks which challenge all Americans and all other free peoples to the supreme adventure of the twentieth century. Those who see the goal will do what must be done to crush the evil forces of our age, to foresee and cure in time the evils of tomorrow, and to make the dream of human brotherhood come true.

III. How does this war differ from other American wars?

MAX LERNER

Max Lerner is one of those rare persons who sees things in the round. He is professor of political science in Williams College. He has taught at Sarah Lawrence College and at Harvard. Formerly an editor of the 'Nation,' he is one of the contributing editors of the 'New Republic.' He is the author of 'It Is Later Than You Think,' 'Ideas Are Weapons,' 'Ideas for the Ice Age,' and many articles in recent and current issues of magazines.

The question which this chapter poses can be answered most simply in a single sentence: For the first time in American history America is fighting a war for world stakes, on a genuinely world-wide scale, with weapons which we have not chosen for ourselves but which have been chosen for us by the nature of the world today. Thus, even more than was true of the war of 1917–18, this is in fact a World War.

But this seemingly simple answer is really far less simple than it seems. It is the purpose of this chapter to break it down into the parts that compose it, and to translate it into concrete terms. And in doing that we shall see more clearly how intricate and complex, and how demanding of our best brains and energies, this war will be.

A WAR FOR WORLD LIBERTY AND ORDER

The first American victim of this war has been the traditional American idea of isolationism. Those who settled our
country felt they were sending down roots into a New World,
and they had a sense of release from the corruption and decay
of the Old World. We fought our first war, the American
Revolution, for independence not only from Great Britain
but from the Old World as a whole. We fought the war
with Tripoli, the War of 1812, and the Mexican War to establish our stature as a new nation, and to round out the boundaries
of what we considered at the time our " manifest destiny."
The Civil War was a clash between two economic systems, the
industrial economy of the North and the plantation economy
of the South; but it was also a war over the issue of national
unity and the idea of the basic dignity of all the common people, whatever their color. In the Spanish-American War we
reached out for the first time, although in a fumbling way, for
our place as a World Power in the sun of world empire. The
First World War was, so far as America's role was concerned,
a struggle against the German ideas of militarism and au-
tocracy; but it was also an effort on our part to prevent Germany from upsetting the established " balance of power " in
the world, and particularly from destroying the " Atlantic system " whereby the combination of British and American sea
power assured the freedom of the seas in trade for all nations.

There were many in America who felt after the First World
War that the idealism of Americans had been betrayed by the
craft and cynicism of the Old World. They and others felt
that the real motives in modern wars were economic and " im-
perialistic " rather than idealistic, and that all wars increased
militarism. As a result the movements for pacifism and isolationism — the feeling that all wars are wicked and that America

should stay in its own back yard and not go off on foreign ad-
ventures — increased among many Americans. This crippled
our efforts in preparing for the present war, while the German
military and political leaders, who knew very well what they
wanted, planned a world war on a scale never before witnessed
and with all the weapons of modern warfare. Finally, under
the sheer pressure of events from 1935 to 1941, Americans have
begun to learn some of the lessons of the modern era: that a
nation cannot survive by pacifism while other nations are preparing war; that America cannot isolate itself from the rest of
the world; and that a nation cannot survive today unless it un-
derstands the nature of what has been called " total war."

Just what does " total war " mean as applied to the war in
which America is now engaged? Several years ago C. Hartley
Grattan wrote a book with the title *The Deadly Parallel*. The
parallel he sought to describe was that between the First World
War and the present one. In spite of external similarities between the two, there was a deep fallacy in the idea. And the
fallacy lay mainly in the failure of the author, like most other
people at the time, to see that the Nazis were planning and waging a total war — a war in which every energy in the nation was
directed to the single purpose of military power and no notions of liberty or decency were allowed to interfere with it;
a war in which every weapon known to science, military art,
economics, politics, diplomacy, and psychology was marshaled
to this purpose; a war without the slightest shred of truth or
scruple; a war not to obtain for Germany a better place in the
sun or a greater share in the balance of power, but a war to destroy the whole idea of the balance of power and bring the entire world under Nazi domination in a single world empire; a
war fought not merely to change the distribution of power
among nations but to wipe out the very idea of a nation and of
an international community; a war, finally, which was — as

Aurel Kolnai has put it in the title of his great study of Nazi thought — a *War against the West*, against everything that the civilizations of Europe and the Americas have arduously achieved in the course of the centuries.

That is basically what makes this war different for America from every war in which America has fought. The Nazis have told us that it is a question of " we or they," of the survival of their world or ours: and we must take them at their word. At the same time that we are fighting for our own liberty we are fighting also for the chance for liberty in the world as a whole. At the same time that we are fighting to preserve our democracy we are fighting also to preserve the ideas and traditions all over the world within which the growth of that democracy has been made possible, and within which America and other nations can go on to finish the unfinished business of democracy.

A TOTAL WAR

But this is not only a war different from others in the world scale of the stakes that are being fought for. It is also different from others in the conditions under which it is being fought. And the principal difference here lies in this fact: that this is not only a war, it is also a revolution. The revolution lies in the attempt of the Nazi adventurers to exploit to their own purposes the instability of social systems and the unrest of nations which have been a feature of the past quarter-century. Hitler and the group about him have sought, through appeals to racial pride and racial hatred, through promises of economic overturn and reconstruction, through the evoking of the martial spirit and national ambitions, through the mystical dream of a breed of cruel and ruthless supermen in the world, to take advantage of men's unrest and their dissatisfaction with the existing system. He has spoken of the " New Order " that he was creating. As we witness what he has already done in the conquered portions of Europe, we must agree with President Roosevelt that it is neither new nor is it an order. It is rather, in Carl Becker's vivid phrase, the " old disorder " — a throwback to lawlessness, a return to the cave. The " totalitarian state " itself, which has been widely advertised as the Fascist contribution to politics, is in reality the old tyranny with a new thoroughness. It means that the state extends its power over every aspect of a man's life, to every nook and cranny of his personality, leaving no area of it which is not at the mercy of the ruling gang.

But while seeing this, we must also see that even reaction can be revolutionary. As Archibald MacLeish has put it, the Nazi revolution is the " revolution *against*." And for a while it looked as if it might be successful, not because of any merit it possessed, but simply because the Nazis had been willing to agitate and promise and act while the democracies had not, and because the Nazis had prepared for war and the struggle for world power while the democracies had relied on the attempt to appease them. In one other aspect the Nazis were revolutionary: they had studied the military lessons of the First World War and had availed themselves of the most daring new inventions in the military arts. They mastered the principles of mobile warfare, putting their armies on wheels, and the principles of tank warfare. General Charles de Gaulle had sought to convert the French General Staff to these new methods even before the Germans developed them, but to no avail. Similarly, long ago, the American " Billy " Mitchell had unsuccessfully urged our own country to make air warfare the core of its fighting strength, only to be court-martialed for his insistence; whereas Germany eagerly took up the idea of air warfare and developed its powerful sky force, the Luftwaffe.

Thus in several respects it is not too much to say that the

Nazis were able to make their movement seem revolutionary largely because the democracies were caught unprepared, because they did not act in time, because they did not act strongly, because they did not act together. This was not the fault of democracy itself, which is a system of government far superior to dictatorship in any form. It was the fault of those who were directing policy in the European democracies, and who did not see that democracies would have to be strong and tough in order to survive in this revolutionary era and in the face of world aggression. In general we may say that there is nothing that a dictatorship can do which a democracy cannot do better — provided that its leaders have the will and the strength and provided that its people are taught the facts.

This war, along with the period of depression and the rise of Fascism which preceded it, has taught the democracies some valuable lessons. It has been given to our generation, as to no generation before it, to sit in the schoolroom of the world and to watch the swift enactments of history unfold before our eyes as by a rapid-motion movie. Things have happened in our generation that formerly took centuries to happen. Things have happened in a decade that formerly took generations. Things have happened in a year that formerly took decades. It has been given to us to see nations like France collapse of inner weakness and outer aggression; of the lack of fighting faith in its people and the adherence to Fascism among its leaders; of inertia and betrayal. We have seen Hitler plunge his sword hilt-deep into the heart of Europe, and have seen a whole continent come under his sway. We have seen England gather its strength after Dunkirk, and at the moment when it seemed most prostrate we have seen it rise to its full stature and repulse the strength of the Luftwaffe, with English morale emerging undiminished from the rubble of shattered buildings. We have seen China fighting for years almost without arms against the superior training and equipment of the Japanese. We have seen the Russian armies retreat before the German divisions, scorching the Russian earth as they went, and then — when the German strength had begun to spend itself — surge forward again and hurl the invaders back. Adam Smith wrote a book in 1776 called *The Wealth of Nations,* a book that has been the Bible ever since of a civilization that has been primarily economic, and has measured its values in economic terms. But we have seen, as Peter Drucker has put it, the " end of economic man." We have watched the breaking of nations and the resistance of peoples. This war differs for us from every other war because it has taught us to replace the idea of the *wealth* of nations with the idea of the *strength* of nations.

SOURCES OF DEMOCRATIC STRENGTH

What is it that makes a democracy strong in this time of world crisis? If we can spell out the answer to this question, we shall have the answer as to how we shall win not only the war but the peace after it.

One answer is that a democracy in a time of world crisis must have an efficiently organized economic system. This involves two basic questions: first, how big a pie of total national income there is available for cutting up and distributing; and second, how well it is distributed, so that ordinary people have the purchasing power with which to buy the products of the machines and thus keep them busy and the man power employed. There can be little doubt that a democracy has within its reach a knowledge of how to make the economic machine function at full efficiency — if only we have the will to apply that knowledge. Recent years have taught us that part of the answer lies in government action to dislodge monopolies and enforce competition; that another part lies in strengthening the more weakly situated farmers and workers, so that they will have what Justice Holmes called an " equality of bargaining power " with the corporations; that still another part lies in the role of the Government as a great lender and spender; and that somewhere along the line it is necessary for the technical people — whether they come from management, labor, or Government — to get together and plan with forethought as to using the economic resources of today for the economic needs of tomorrow.

A good administrative system is just as necessary as a good economic system, and just as subject to abuse. During the past quarter-century the people of the United States have learned that next to leadership the most important thing about government is administration. Despite a lot of bitter criticism — much of it justified — about our " bureaucracy," and despite the ridicule cast on the " alphabet soup " of our administrative agencies and on our " brain trust," the fact is that we have made a good start in developing a new type of government servant, very different from the baby-kissing and back-slapping politician of old, trained in his technical job and more or less independent of partisan politics. James Burnham has recently written a book called *The Managerial Revolution* in which he says that in every important country these technicians and specialists form a new " managerial " class and have taken over power. It is, however, much too soon to think of them as a separate class, and in a democracy — whatever may be true of Germany, Japan, Russia — they are as completely subject to the law as any other person.

In addition to a strong economic system and a strong administrative system, the third element of a strong democracy in time of crisis is an efficient military machine and a wide-awake military leadership. There has always been a tradition in the United States that held a strong standing army in suspicion. This goes back to early colonial times when the King's Army was an oppressive weight on the American colonists; and there are provisions in our Bill of Rights against the quartering of troops in homes and for the right of the ordinary citizen to bear arms. Largely because of this and because of our pacifist leanings, the Army career has not enjoyed very high prestige, and the men of ability have tended to go into business and the civil professions rather than into the Army. Until recently we have not felt this weakness seriously. But we have now come to understand that without a strong army always ready to act in an emergency and equipped with the latest military inventions, a democracy — no matter how just its practices and no matter how high-minded its citizens — may fall a prey to a stronger and more ruthless Power. Our young people are coming to understand this also. And it is a safe prophecy that in the future a military or naval or aviation career will rank as high as any other in the country.

The present war is a test of how well we can put these things to work in a great war crisis. For everything that has happened so far in the war — to the United States as well as to other countries — shows the need of a highly planned and keenly alert military machine, inside of a highly efficient administrative machine, inside of an economic machine that is running on all cylinders and making the very best use of all its resources. This is, of course, a counsel of perfection. But the closer we come to achieving this ideal, the more certain will be victory in as short a time as possible.

ORGANIZING OUR CIVILIAN STRENGTH

The elements described above are, of course, put to a more arduous test in wartime than at any other. This is the first war we have fought in which our economic efficiency has been of such crucial importance. It has become a rather familiar saying that modern war is a war of machines and factories. Yet, although familiar, it is none the less true. For every soldier on the firing lines there are approximately sixteen men and women needed behind the lines as workers, farmers, technicians, to feed and clothe and equip him and keep him going. What we call the " rate of obsolescence " — that is, the rate of getting worn-out and old-fashioned — is so high now among war machines that the airplane or submarine or tank that is superior in one year of the war may be outstripped by the enemy the next year, and we must keep pace.

Moreover, the quantities in which these machines must be produced are now enormous. President Roosevelt has issued " directives " for our war economy according to which we are to produce 60,000 planes in 1942 and 125,000 in 1943. This means mass production, or assembly-line production, after the fashion in which for years we have been producing the standardized automobile. But this means also new machine tools; large quantities of raw materials, including aluminum and steel and rubber; the enlargement of the capacity of our plants even beyond the 100 per cent capacity they have had at their peak in the most prosperous peacetime years; and the conversion of peacetime industries such as the automobile industry to wartime uses such as the production of planes.

All this involves a " war economy." Such an economy is not easy to set up or to keep going, especially when time is so important and every minute counts. All sorts of peacetime activities are torn up by the roots. Factories producing peacetime commodities have to shut down, and their men are thrown out of work. The capital has to be reinvested in wartime industry, and the workers have to be retrained for new skills. War machines, like others, are mainly an assemblage of parts, and some way has to be found of " farming out " these parts so that each of them can be produced in quantity by some factory, and then some way of assembling the parts. This in-

MANY WORKERS ARE NEEDED
TO SUPPLY ONE FIGHTING MAN

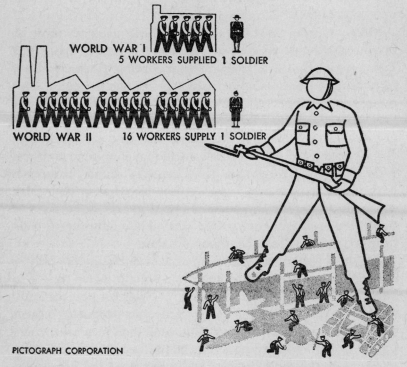

IN NAPOLEON'S TIME

1 WORKER SUPPLIED 2 SOLDIERS

WORLD WAR I

5 WORKERS SUPPLIED 1 SOLDIER

WORLD WAR II   16 WORKERS SUPPLY 1 SOLDIER

PICTOGRAPH CORPORATION

War is more than a death struggle in the front line. Many men behind the lines — in field and forest and factory — are needed to keep one man properly equipped at the front. In lathes and drill presses, hoes and combines, crosscut saws and tractors, America has an immense advantage. But this productive capacity must be geared to war to supply our fighting men.

volves a highly difficult plan for meshing together all these operations. Methods have to be found also for letting contracts,
for determining " priorities " (that is, who shall have first claim
upon the available raw materials and transportation and labor),
for setting up an over-all " procurement " system whereby the
Army and the Navy and the Air Force can make their purchases of supplies without overlapping or getting in one another's way. And all the time there are problems to be met of
fixing prices so that they will not zoom sky-high, of preventing " profiteering " by unscrupulous businessmen and mer-
chants who take advantage of the war emergency, of levying
taxes and selling bonds to pay for the costs of the war, of preventing strikes and settling labor disputes which may do great
harm to the rate of war production. All of these problems of
the war economy are discussed in later chapters in greater
detail.

ORGANIZING OUR MILITARY STRENGTH

Thus we have been seeking to meet the problems of a war
economy and a war administrative machine. The problems of
a military machine, as they have thus far been forced upon us,
are similar. This war, like no other war in American history,
is a war of surprise and a war of swift maneuver. The Fascist
nations have been showing for years that they do not believe
in declarations of war. They waged undeclared wars in Manchuria, Spain, Czechoslovakia, Poland. Similarly, when Japan
made war upon us, by agreement with Germany, the attack
came suddenly as a surprise air attack upon Pearl Harbor in
the Hawaiian Islands. Such a war of surprise requires a military force that is always on the alert. Unfortunately, according to Secretary of the Navy Knox and later according to the
commission of inquiry headed by Justice Owen Roberts, our
forces in the Hawaiian area were not " on the alert."

Modern warfare is "timetable" warfare, in which there must be complete co-operation between the various branches of the armed forces. According to the report of the Roberts committee this co-operation did not exist at the time of the attack on Pearl Harbor, despite the fact that orders from Washington had given warning that some Japanese surprise attack might be expected somewhere.

Here too America is moving forward and learning in a very short period of time from the mistakes of other nations and from its own past mistakes. Not only are the High Commands of our various military services learning to act together, but President Roosevelt, along with Mr. Churchill and Mr. Stalin and Generalissimo Chiang Kai-shek, the leaders of our principal allies, has taken steps to unify the commands of the various countries fighting together in this war. In each theater of warfare all over the world this sort of unified regional High Command has now been established.

But perhaps more important than anything else in this military phase of the war is the "career open to talent." Sir Stafford Cripps, recently British Ambassador to Moscow, who has had a chance to study the successful Russian Army at close range, said in an interview that one of the causes of its success was the practice of giving ample opportunity for younger officers to rise rapidly to the top ranks. Observers of the successful Royal Air Force of Great Britain have pointed out that its quality has improved since the bars of wealth and social distinction were let down and admission into its ranks was opened for any qualified young man. Observers of the German Army, such as Joseph Harsch, the American foreign correspondent who spent some time in Germany and wrote a book, *Pattern for Conquest*, out of his experiences there, point out that even though the Germans hate democracy, they practice in the Army the principle of opening the officers' ranks to young men regardless of wealth or social standing. Because of America's long democratic tradition, the idea of the " career open to talent " in the armed forces should have deeper roots here than in any other country in the world. We have learned that it is one of the conditions of warfare today. That is another reason why a democracy should be able to fight modern warfare even more successfully than a dictatorship. These problems of military organization and of co-operation with our allies are discussed more fully in the next four chapters.

WAR FOR THE CONTROL OF MINDS

So far we have considered only the military phases of war, and the kind of economic and administrative machines that are necessary for those phases. But modern war differs from previous wars in still another respect. There is an important branch of modern warfare called " psychological " warfare, having to do mainly with the " morale " of soldiers and even more of civilians, and with ways of strengthening your own morale and weakening or undermining that of the enemy. As will be pointed out in some detail in Chapter XIII, the Nazis have for some time been waging this sort of war by their use of elaborate " mass espionage," in which they have forced large numbers of their " nationals " living abroad to spy for them, and also by their use of " fifth columns." The term " fifth column " has an interesting history. It came out of the Spanish Civil War, of 1936–38, when General Mola, one of the leaders of the Fascist troops of General Franco, boasted that he was marching on Madrid with four columns of soldiers and that there was a " fifth column " of civilians within Madrid that was working for him and that would meet him when he entered the city. But the term did not become popular until the German invasion of Norway, when it became apparent that the Nazis had an elaborate system of " fifth-columnists " or

"Quislings" within Norway who had helped deliver the country over to them.

Moreover, the Nazis have also developed the system whereby their diplomatic and consular offices in every country became nests of spying and sabotage; and many of their traveling businessmen and commercial men did the same work. This has been particularly true of Nazi activities in the Latin-American countries. And they were able to build up in most countries, including the United States, fanatical antidemocratic groups who used the slogans of Americanism and pacifism and religious hatred in order to break down our democracy and help the forces of Germany.

But these are all the negative side of psychological warfare. There is an affirmative side as well. The British and the Russians showed the enormous power of civilian morale (to be discussed more fully in Chapter XIV) during the dangerous periods of the war when London was under heavy air attack and when Moscow was almost captured by German armies. The civilians kept their heads, went on producing war materials for their armies, set up a system of putting out fires and fighting off aircraft and caring for the casualties, and after each attack were more determined than ever to win the war.

There is one sense in which the idea of democracy can itself be one of the most powerful weapons in winning the war. For if it is true that civilian morale is one of the great factors in modern warfare, then it follows that the democratic idea can be used to strengthen our own morale and weaken that of our enemies. If we can show our people, especially our young people, how efficient and yet how just and humane democracy in action can be, even in wartime, then we will be helping them to get a "fighting faith" in democracy which will overcome every obstacle. Democracy in action means that we fight the war without sacrificing the important civil liberties guaranteed to our people in the Bill of Rights. It means that we do away as far as possible with hunger and poverty and racial discrimination. It means that we take to heart President Roosevelt's great message in which he defined our war aims as " the four freedoms " — freedom of speech, freedom of worship, freedom from want, and freedom from fear — and in which he pointed out that we are fighting for these freedoms not only for ourselves but for men and women everywhere.

The best type of psychological warfare is for America to show the whole world that it can put the four freedoms into real practice in its own country. Then we must use every resource of the radio and the printed page to bring this message to the people of Germany and Italy and Japan, and even more to the people in the conquered and occupied countries of Europe: that we are not fighting this war for booty or for more territory or for imperialism; that we do not intend to destroy other peoples, but only to destroy the idea of Fascism; that they will be given a chance in the postwar world to build their own democratic systems. If we do and say these things, we can make out of democracy an idea winged with fire, to capture the imaginations of the young in mind and spirit all over the world.

iv. How is the Navy organized to fight the war?

PAUL SCHUBERT

Paul Schubert is a graduate of the Naval Academy at Annapolis, and for five years was an officer in the United States Navy. He has traveled in Africa and South America, and for eight years lived in Europe, spending time in all parts of the Continent. He has written a number of books on naval history, and articles and short stories for 'Collier's,' 'The Saturday Evening Post,' 'The American Magazine,' and other periodicals. Since the outbreak of the war in Europe in 1939, Mr. Schubert has been a naval analyst for the Mutual Broadcasting System, and has discussed 'The War at Sea' over Station WOR, New York.

AMERICA'S SEA POWER

The main striking force of our Navy is the United States Fleet. Virtually all the Navy's seagoing fighting, or combat, ships are included in this organization, so that if they should all at any time be included in one vast armada going out to do battle, each ship would have a definite place and duties, and be ready to play its part in fleet combat.

Under the usual distribution of ships, however, the fleet is divided into several combat units, operating in widely distant parts of the world. The Atlantic Fleet operates from the East Coast of the United States, and in the present war is active in co-operation with the British Navy in guarding the movement of munitions, oil, and food across the North and South Atlantic, and also in fighting active warfare against Axis submarines and raiders, and against Axis aircraft at sea.

Neither Germany nor Italy is strong in naval power. The Atlantic Fleet is therefore not at present so much concerned with the possibility of a major fleet battle as with countering the raids of small units of Axis ships, such as that made into the Atlantic by the powerful German battleship *Bismarck* and the cruiser *Prinz Eugen* in May, 1941.

The Pacific Fleet operates in the Pacific Ocean from the West Coast of the United States. Its principal offshore operating base is at Pearl Harbor, Hawaii. Ordinarily, this is the most powerful of the battle fleets we keep at sea. It is maintained to prevent the powerful Japanese battle fleet from dominating the Pacific.

Our third fleet, the Asiatic, is the farthest from home, and in the present war is a fleet of co-operative alliance with Netherlander and British naval forces in Far Eastern waters. It is usually made up of a group of cruisers, several groups of destroyers, and a considerable number of submarines, but under war conditions it may be strengthened to meet situations as they arise. For many years our Asiatic Fleet has used Cavite, on Manila Bay, and Olongapo, on Subic Bay, in the Philippines as its bases. Loss of these bases, however, does not endanger the fleet, as our alliance with the British and the Netherlanders makes it possible to fall back upon secure harbors in the Netherlands East Indies, and if necessary to fall back farther still to bases in Australia and New Zealand.

Besides the three fleets, the Navy usually operates a number of lesser combat forces — normally a squadron in Central American waters, often a small group of ships in the Mediterranean or in the South Atlantic, wherever it is essential that

United States sea power make itself felt. In time of war the Navy also takes over the ships and duties of the Coast Guard (which is under the Treasury Department during peace) and also enrolls many yachts and motorboats for patrol duties; passenger liners and cargo ships likewise become useful "auxiliaries" of the wartime Navy.

The force called "sea power" is broad and complex. It includes all the numerous elements by which a nation extends influence over sea areas.

Sea power is strongly affected by geography. When we study the globe, we see that some nations are more favorably situated than others, in terms of sea influence. Places where waterways are narrow — straits, canals, channels — so that ships are forced to pass close to the land lend great power to the countries which control them. The Panama Canal, the Suez Canal, the English Channel, the Strait of Gibraltar, the Malacca Strait, are typical strong points of sea power.

Islands are naturally strong in sea power. Good harbors are important. Nations with long seacoasts, many harbors, and high industrial development naturally become maritime nations. Inland nations like Switzerland or Bolivia cannot be sea powers, but must depend on the sea power of others.

Sea power is dependent in part on a large mercantile marine made up of ships for the transport of cargo and passengers. Without the co-operation of cargo-carrying ships in peace and war, the strongest navy in the world cannot guarantee the benefits of sea power. Naval might is merely sea power's striking force, while the merchant marine is needed for carrying exports and necessary supplies.

In the same way, the Navy's battle fleet may appear to be its most spectacular part, but the battle fleet would be helpless without the host of auxiliary naval vessels and the large shore establishment — navy yards, supply depots, radio stations, train-

ing stations, schools, factories, and administrative headquarters
— which serve the fleet. In time of war the United States
Navy employs over 500,000 officers, sailors, and Marines on active duty, and a large force of civilian workmen, specialists,
officials, and clerks.

Sea power, in all its manifestations, is one of the most important forces we have to wield in winning wars, and one of
our most important guarantees of prosperous existence during
times of peace. Throughout our history, from the days of
John Paul Jones down to the present, our Navy has kept up a
great tradition of gallant fighting and victory in battle.

THE NAVY'S JOB

Four-fifths of the earth's surface is covered by salt water.
The seas belong to no nation, but in peace are free to be sailed
by all men. Beyond a three-mile zone along the coasts, the
open oceans are now, as they have always been, a wide expanse
on which crude strength and human skill are the ruling powers.

The seas are highways of a tremendous world trade. In
the great manufacturing and trading era in which we live, a
certain percentage of almost every article in daily use, the
clothing on our backs, the cars we ride in, the furniture in our
homes, the food we eat, has as " raw material " been brought
in on the highways of the seas. Notable examples are rubber,
coffee, wool, tin, bananas, and silk.

Cargoes valued at between 5 and 8 billion dollars normally
enter and leave United States seaports every year. To protect
this valuable trade on its sea voyages, and to guarantee its safe
arrival without capture or molestation, is one of the chief reasons for the existence of the United States Navy.

Another principal mission of the Navy is the protection of
our soil and our people from attack and capture or injury by
any overseas nation. We can, of course, defend ourselves by

fighting on land after an invasion has been made. But since any invasion from overseas must cross the ocean, either in ships or in planes, it is preferable to stop it before it so much as touches our shores.

The third, and one of the most important of all reasons, for maintaining the Navy, is for use as a means of attack, to destroy the sea power of any nation with which we are at war, and for supporting and taking part in any military action against another country, such as an invasion and military engagement necessary to defeat enemy fighting forces. When the United States sent an expeditionary force to France in 1917 and 1918 to aid France and England against Germany, it was our naval power and that of our Allies which made possible not only the movement of troops across the Atlantic, but thereafter the steady stream of munitions, supplies, and food necessary to help supply both our armies and those of our Allies. In the present war, in which the principal Axis Powers, Germany, Italy, and Japan, are all overseas nations, the Navy must move troops and weapons for the Army as well as carry on its own offensives directed at the enemy's sea power.

For special duty in overseas land operations, the United States Navy maintains a fully equipped, compact " army " of its own, the United States Marine Corps. These " soldiers of the sea " specialize in such difficult operations as landing on enemy beaches, and occupying hostile seaports. Every large ship carries a detachment of about 80 Marines.

Attack on the enemy's sea power is not confined to attack on naval forces. The first and one of the most important objectives of sea-power attack is the wiping out of the enemy's foreign trade. Without foreign trade, no nation on earth can exist. Sooner or later, the essential reserves of key raw materials will have been used up, and the result will be the " starvation " of factories and commerce.

When a navy commands the sea so effectively that vessels belonging to a hostile nation cannot cruise abroad without immediate risk of capture or destruction, that nation is said to be "blockaded." Under the conditions of the present war, Germany, Japan, and Italy are all blockaded. Their ships are confined to waters relatively close to their own coasts, within the protection of their own fleets and fortifications. Beyond that zone the foreign commerce of those three Powers is wiped out. As far as world imports and exports are concerned, Germany, Italy, and Japan were "blockaded" on the day war was declared, and placed in a virtual state of siege. Blockade is one of the most powerful and most effective uses of sea power — and sea power is one of the most valuable assets of the United States and our allies of the United Nations.

Because of our strong sea power, we ourselves have not been blockaded, and cannot be blockaded unless our sea power is destroyed. We have continued to exchange goods and supplies with other nations, and to move our troops and weapons from one part of the world to another. The Axis Powers, however, have resorted to "raider" warfare, and from time to time send out submarines, aircraft, and occasionally surface ships such as cruisers or fast battleships, to attack and destroy our cargo vessels wherever they can. These raids sink a varying percentage of our cargo ships, but neither during the First World War nor during the present war have they sunk enough to justify the name "blockade" — nor, in spite of brief periods of heavy attack or attack with surprise methods such as "wolf packs" of several U-boats operating together, have they really threatened our defeat; each surprise has soon been met by effective counter-tactics.

THE PARTS OF A BALANCED FLEET

The principal weapons of naval warfare are the gun, the torpedo, and the bomb (including the mine and the depth charge). All naval combat vessels and aircraft are constructed with a view to specializing in one or another of these weapons. The purpose of all three weapons is the same: to deliver destructive quantities of explosive upon the enemy's ships or upon his naval or military land forces, whenever the needs of war require such a blow.

The most important gun-fighting ship is the "ship of the line of battle" — the battleship. Modern battleships (sometimes called dreadnoughts after the British ship *H.M.S. Dreadnought*, completed in 1906 and the first battleship to mount an "all-big-gun" main battery) have a greater sustained fire power than any other type of ship. The *U.S.S. North Carolina*, mounting 9 16-inch guns, can belch out a full broadside oftener than once a minute. Each broadside hurls nine tons of metal and explosive through the air, well aimed to hit any target within sight of the ship. By catapulting a plane into the air to act as "spotter," a battleship can even fire at targets over the sea horizon as far as twenty miles away.

Besides the tremendous punch of the heavy turret guns, a battleship mounts a secondary battery of 16 or more 5-inch guns which either can be fired at ships (such as enemy torpedo craft) or can be pointed high for antiaircraft fire. There are also antiaircraft batteries of smaller, quick-firing "pom-poms" and machine guns.

The modern battleship of the *North Carolina* class is a giant vessel 750 feet long; as she floats, she "displaces" 35,000 tons of sea water. She is able to steam at a full speed of more than 27 knots (better than 30 land miles an hour). Her sides and decks are armored with thick plating of the finest steel, and

THE NAVY

Submarines use mostly torpedoes. On the surface they can travel at about 17 knots. Submerged, their greatest speed is about 8 knots. Submarines carry antiaircraft guns and also lay mines.

Motor torpedo boats are very small and very fast. Their principal weapons are torpedoes, which they discharge ahead of their passage. They cannot travel far and they have little protection, but they can strike quickly.

Destroyers use the torpedo for offense. They also drop depth charges (underwater bombs) and are equipped with guns. Destroyers are small ships of very high speed—up to 39 knots.

Cruisers are large and they can go up to 35 knots. The heavy ones scout far in front of the fleet, aided by large patrol bombing planes. Light cruisers steam all around the large "capital ships" to protect them. Frequently cruisers can also fire torpedoes. Their armor is not as thick as that which protects battleships.

The battleship is the most important gun-fighting ship. It can hit targets as far as 20 miles away. Its maximum speed is 27 knots. Its decks are protected from bombs by heavy armor. Its gun turrets are protected from enemy guns by armor of a foot and a half thick. Inside watertight compartments and double bottoms protect against torpedoes.

PICTOGRAPH
CORPORATION

The aircraft carrier is not only a scouting vessel, whose planes spot hostile ships. It has become a supertorpedo-boat, able to fly torpedoes to their destination in planes. For protection carriers have fighter planes and antiaircraft guns. Carriers make about 30 knots.

The principal weapons of naval warfare are the gun, the torpedo, and the bomb (including the mine and the depth charge).

her bottom and interior are specially designed to keep her afloat, if possible, even after several torpedo hits. To the 1,500 men who form the crew, such a vessel is almost a living thing. Her men sail the seas with her, master storms and gales, sometimes fight and beat off hostile attacks — they come to regard her as their home and their fortress.

It takes from three to four years of labor by thousands of skilled craftsmen, at a cost of about 100 million dollars, to build a modern dreadnought. These ships are not " unsinkable," but dozens of combats during the present war, under all manner of conditions, have shown them to be the stoutest and most nearly unsinkable ships that man can devise. Their victories have far outnumbered their defeats.

On January 1, 1942, the United States Fleet's strength in battleships was divided between a sturdy group of some 13 older ships built from twenty to thirty years ago, and a growing force of magnificent new vessels either recently commissioned or still in process of construction and fitting out.

The old ships ranged from the 1912 *Arkansas* to the 1922 *Colorado*. Many of them saw active duty in the First World War, including service with the British Grand Fleet in European waters. All the older vessels of this veteran group have been modernized and given additional deck armor and torpedo protection to fit them for modern combat.

The long battleship-building holiday which followed the Washington Conference of 1922 resulted in no new additions to the fleet battle line until the *North Carolina* and the *Washington* were commissioned in 1941. These ultramodern vessels are to be followed by 15 more new battleships, several of which will be commissioned in 1942, bringing the total of our 1942 battle line strength to between 15 and 19 ships of the line, with others being hurried to completion.

Some of these ships of the future will be giants displacing

between 50,000 and 60,000 tons, with gun batteries of greater fire power than any earlier ships. They will be the mightiest men-of-war which have ever taken the seas.

The battleship, or " ship of the line," was originally conceived as a vessel so stout that it could cruise anywhere unchallenged except by other battleships. As long as guns were the sole weapon at sea, the battleship did remain supreme. But in the last three decades the increasing effectiveness of the torpedo has had a profound effect upon naval warfare.

When the aircraft-carrier first came to sea just after the First World War, it was considered to be more or less a scouting vessel, which would send its planes on long reconnaissance flights in all directions, to notify the admiral if hostile warships were sighted. The aircraft-carrier, with its relatively small landing deck, is not a good operating base for heavy bombing planes, both because they need a long take-off to get a large bomb load into the air, and because their wingspread is too great for practical stowage aboard a carrier.

The development of the dive bomber and the torpedo bomber, however, made the aircraft-carrier one of the most important offensive units in the fleet. In effect, the aircraft-carrier has become a super-torpedo-boat, able to shoot its torpedoes at targets two or three hundred miles away by flying them to their destination in planes.

Not all a carrier's planes are torpedo planes. It is equally important for her to have strong squadrons of fighter planes to beat off enemy air attacks on the fleet. And dive bombers are essential for attack on hostile cruisers and torpedo craft, and on the lightly armored upper decks and superstructure of enemy battleships.

The United States Navy operated, early in 1942, 7 aircraft-carriers, with 11 more building. Each of them stows about 75 planes in her large hangar decks. When stowed, the planes' wings are folded back. Giant elevators lift them to the flight deck, where they can be prepared for take-off in the shortest possible time. For protecting convoys, some merchant ships have had special flight decks built so that they can carry a smaller number of planes.

The aircraft-carrier and the gun-fighting ship, acting together, form a most powerful fighting team. Neither one of them is supreme at sea. Each has its own strengths, and its weaknesses. But co-operating, their mutual support is something like teamwork between the line and backfield of a football team. The battleship is excellent for "bucking" and "blocking." The carrier has a powerful "forward passing" attack.

But battleships and carriers do not, by themselves, make up a fleet. Modern warfare finds special duties, in both defense and attack, for a number of other types of combat ships, including cruisers, destroyers, submarines, and motor torpedo craft.

As a protection against surprise, all large vessels, or "capital ships," are customarily surrounded by a double screen of light ships whenever they go to sea during wartime. The inner screen is made up of destroyers and light cruisers, which steam to both sides and also ahead of and behind the capital ships. The outer screen of light cruisers is farther away, with some destroyers well ahead as a vanguard, and others thrown out to the sides, or flanks.

Far in front of the fleet, a scouting force of heavy 10,000-ton cruisers and destroyer flotillas combs the sea. Aircraft scouts — large patrol bombers — likewise scrutinize the ocean for hundreds of miles around the fleet-operations area, and an aircraft screen in the sky above the battle line is a guarantee against surprise from the air.

The United States Navy had, early in 1942, about 40 cruisers, all relatively new vessels, and about 50 more were being built. The outstanding characteristic of cruisers is large size and high speed — they make up to 35 knots ("knot" is the nautical term for one sea mile per hour). For armament they mount 6-inch or 8-inch batteries; some of them are also equipped with torpedo tubes.

Destroyers are much smaller than cruisers, varying in size from 1,200 to 2,100 tons, but they are tough seagoing ships, very fast, and useful for a great variety of naval jobs. Their heavy offensive weapon is the torpedo — some of our newer destroyers have a broadside of 12 torpedoes. The United States Navy operates about 175 destroyers, and is building another 175.

It takes all these various types of ships and aircraft to make a balanced fleet — a fleet equipped to give and take any sort of naval blow.

But the combat navy would be more or less helpless without the services of a large number of lowlier ships which do little or no fighting (though they carry guns for self-defense). There are naval tankers, for instance, which spend their entire seafaring lives carrying fuel oil from the United States to wherever the fleet is operating, and pumping it into the oil bottoms of the combat ships. Other vessels carry food and supplies (the Navy nicknames them "beef boats"). Others are "mother ships" to submarines or to squadrons of seaplanes, while others are floating workshops equipped to do a variety of emergency repairs. There are ships which tow target rafts for target practice, ships which sweep up enemy mines — and ships (some of them submarines) which venture far into enemy waters and lay mines there, or which go out close to our own fleet bases and set up mine fields so that hostile ships, unacquainted with the safe channels, will not be able to come close. There are hospital ships which follow the fleet, staffed with doctors and nurses to take care of the sick and wounded. There are even lowly barges that steam around the fleet anchorage with fresh water, and others that collect refuse. All these many ships, large and small, are needed to make up the Navy.

The aircraft operating with the fleet are also highly important to naval combat operations. Besides those based on carriers and carried aboard battleships and cruisers, there are other aircraft based on shore flying-fields and seaplane bases. These shore-based planes have become tremendously valuable as defensive weapons for command of the sea for long distances away from our coasts. Heavy bombers, torpedo planes, and all other types of military and naval aircraft can be used to make it difficult for hostile ships to come in and attack us.

Some of this protective work is also carried out by the Army Air Force, where the Army has flying-fields near the coasts. But much of it is the province of naval aviation.

Naval aircraft operating from shore bases make routine long-range reconnaissance flights, keeping a constant watch on all the ocean areas important to our naval movements. In these and dozens of other services, the " Navy that flies " has become just as great an asset to the admiral charged with protecting our shores, as the " Navy that floats."

BASES AND SHORE ESTABLISHMENTS

Sooner or later all ships, and all aircraft, must return to the land for food, fuel, and munitions, for necessary repairs, and for recreation for the personnel.

The harbors used by the Navy are known as "bases" — repair bases, operating bases, aviation bases, and submarine bases. The harbors from which the fleet acts in its offensive and defensive missions against the enemy are called fleet operating bases. To be useful as an operating base, a harbor must be large, with good anchorage for many ships of all sizes. It must be well sheltered from storms and rough weather, and stoutly fortified against hostile attack by land, sea, or air. An operating base must be so located, geographically, that it is in strategic position for command of the sea in the surrounding area.

Our main operating base in the mid-Pacific is Pearl Harbor, in the Hawaiian Islands. This harbor is so well located and so strongly defended that not even the surprise Japanese attack which plunged the Pacific area into war in December, 1941, was able to achieve its intention to deal us crippling damage.

Another of the United States Navy's principal operating bases is that at Guantánamo Bay, Cuba, which covers the Atlantic approaches to the Panama Canal and the Caribbean. As for our allies, the British Home Fleet frequently bases on Scapa Flow, in the Orkney Islands, while British naval forces in the Mediterranean operate from the stoutly defended harbors at Gibraltar and Alexandria. In the Far Eastern area, the principal British base at Singapore is backed by harbors in Australia and New Zealand. Aviation and submarine bases, as their names imply, have special facilities for dealing with those naval activities.

It is taken for granted that during war operating bases may be attacked and perhaps damaged. They are too exposed to act as main repair bases in which damaged vessels can be restored to full combat value. They lack, likewise, the facilities for dry-docking all the ships of a large fleet for the bottom-scraping and painting which are necessary at regular intervals.

The United States Navy maintains a number of large repair bases called navy yards on both coasts of the United States. Portsmouth, New Hampshire, for instance, specializes in submarine repairs and submarine construction. Boston, Massachusetts, is invaluable for ships on North Atlantic patrol. A great trio of giant Atlantic Coast navy yards at New York, Philadelphia, and Norfolk, Virginia, is equipped not only to repair but to build ships of any size up to the largest. Another navy yard at Washington, D.C., maintains a gun factory in which most of our big naval guns are made, while Charleston, South Carolina, is a repair base for destroyers and cruisers.

On the Pacific Coast two great navy yards at Mare Island, on San Francisco Bay, and Bremerton, on Puget Sound, are main repair bases for the Pacific Fleet. Besides these navy yards operated by the Navy itself, there are numerous private shipyards on both coasts, which become the Navy's full-time partners when the nation is at war, and which are an important element of sea power.

THE MEN OF THE NAVY

A vast and specialized organization like the Navy carries on numerous other dry-land activities essential for the welfare of the fleet. Much of the constant training which is such an important part of a sailor's life is carried on aboard ship, but in addition a large, well-equipped school system is necessary. At Newport, Rhode Island, San Diego, California, and Great Lakes, Illinois, there are training stations in which new recruits are given preliminary instruction in the ways of the sea, while Marine training is carried out at Parris Island, South Carolina, and San Diego, California. Picked men are sent, later on, to various specialty schools where they are taught such subjects as electricity, torpedoes, radio, submarines, diving, marine engineering — even cooking and baking. The world renowned Naval Academy at Annapolis, Maryland, trains officers; its student body totals over 3,000, and its graduates, besides being commissioned officers in the Navy or the Marine Corps, receive the degree of Bachelor of Science. A postgraduate school at Annapolis conducts special courses for senior officers, while the War College at Newport, Rhode Island, teaches the strategy and tactics of naval operations to the pick of those who attain command rank. Reserve officers are trained in R.O.T.C. units at colleges and universities, or in special courses after their induction into the service.

The sailor's life today is still, as it has always been, a salty shipboard existence. The shrill piping of the boatswain calls him to stand watches on lookout or at the steering wheel, or below decks in the engineering department. He keeps the ship immaculate, drills at the guns and other battle stations, and sails the seven seas. Modern ships are so full of mechanical equipment, boilers, engines, motors, radio and electrical " gadgets," that Navy bluejackets have every chance to become specialists in almost any trade. Life aboard ship is a combination of adventure and practicality. The Navy is a volunteer service, and draws the best of a hand-picked group of young applicants. Those who make the sea a career can rise as petty officers and chief petty officers, while qualified men are eligible for appointment to the Naval Academy.

Sailors do duty on shore as well. Besides the activities already mentioned, the Navy operates a string of radio stations and maintains a number of well-equipped hospitals. Perhaps the most important of all the dry-land activities is the chain of administrative headquarters centering in the Navy Department in Washington, where more than 9,000 people keep the Navy's records and direct its work.

The Secretary of the Navy, three Assistant Secretaries, the Chief of Naval Operations, the Commander in Chief of the United States Fleet, and the heads of the various Navy Department bureaus have their offices there, in close touch with the President, who is Commander in Chief of the Army and Navy.

The coasts and territories of the United States are divided, for administrative purposes, into Naval Districts, each commanded by a Rear Admiral with a staff whose duty it is to direct the patrols and defenses of coastal waters and carry on such activities as recruiting, purchasing, and inspecting the many things, from ships to sealing wax, bought for the Navy.

CO–OPERATION WITH ALLIED NAVIES

Our naval influence, taken by itself, extends about halfway across the Atlantic and two-thirds of the way across the Pacific, and is more or less limited to the Northern Hemisphere.

We have as allies, however, Great Britain and a number of other Powers, including the Netherlands (with many East Indian possessions) and several South American nations. This means that our Navy has joined with the navies of those Powers to form a combat team in which the spirit is " All for one and one for all." We have pledged aid to each other for the defeat of our enemies and the guarantee of liberty and justice.

In addition to combat alliance, we and our allies have made our base facilities available to each other, and in the principal war areas we have set up unified commands over all our forces. British ships injured in battle can be repaired, when that is desirable, in American navy yards. American vessels fighting in the Far East can take shelter in places like Sydney, Australia, and Capetown, South Africa. Aircraft on patrol flights can spend one night in an American base, the next in a port of New Zealand, Australasia, or the East Indies.

This co-operation and alliance is one of the greatest assets of our world-wide sea power — in great contrast to the sea weakness of the Axis Powers, since Germany, Italy, and Japan are effectively cut off from one another at sea, except as an occasional furtive raider or submarine manages to elude our patrols.

One of the main objects of our naval warfare is to keep the Axis sea forces separated from each other, while we maintain the naval contact between ourselves and our allies of the United Nations. Another of our objectives is to keep the sea lanes open and our ships moving with raw materials, such as rubber. The entire opening phase of our war with Japan centers about this vital commodity, which we normally import from British Malaya and the Netherlands East Indies.

THE FUTURE OF NAVIES

War at sea is very much under the influence of the growing strength of aerial weapons. Aircraft will continue their remarkable evolution. Airplanes and seaplanes will grow larger, faster, and more powerful. Ships, likewise, will grow larger and more powerful — both cargo-carrying ships and ships of war. Obviously travel over seas will use both aircraft and ships.

The seas, as the common domain of man, either must be more than ever firmly policed, so that law and order prevail in the interests of all men, or on the other hand, if they continue to be subject to the jungle law of crude strength, we shall continue to see devastating wars.

It happens that the great naval nations, Britain and the United States, are likewise those interested in the rule of law and order. In administering their tremendous sea power, it is their duty to be both strong and wise. As one of the most powerful nations of the earth, we have created a great Navy which we are now using with all our might. That Navy will help bring us victory. Let us remember the lesson taught us so sharply at Pearl Harbor — that law, order, and peaceful existence at sea demand eternal vigilance, eternal willingness and readiness to fight for the things worth while, and a strength in the Navy that floats and the Navy that flies able to deal with any disturber of the peace.

v. How is the Army organized to fight the war?

S. L. A. MARSHALL

*S. L. A. Marshall is the military critic of the 'Detroit News.'
At sixteen he enlisted in the United States Army, where he
distinguished himself in grenade-throwing and topographical
engineering. He was in the A.E.F. in 1917–18 and became
the youngest lieutenant in the service. Since 1927 he has held
his present position. His analysis of the present war to 1940,
'Blitzkrieg,' has been highly praised by military authorities.*

On December 7, 1941, the day of the attack on Pearl Harbor, the United States Army, including the Air Corps, numbered approximately 1,750,000 trained and partly trained men. A fraction of this number, perhaps 100,000 men in all, were on field duty in such outposts as Iceland, Bermuda, and Newfoundland. The great majority, however, were on duty within the borders of the United States, where three field armies had just completed their first year of intensive training by staging the most extensive maneuvers in the experience of our armed forces.

A month after the attack on Pearl Harbor, Secretary of War Stimson announced that the Army would be doubled in size. A new draft law, which made men between the ages of twenty and forty-four eligible for duty, was promptly passed. February 15, 1942, was set as the registration date, and the Army set about preparing to receive, classify, house, clothe, provision, and train the hundreds of thousands of men who would soon be moving into the training camps.

RECEPTION AND REPLACEMENT CENTERS

Training 2,000,000 new soldiers is a tremendous task, but one which the Army is prepared to handle without waste motion, thanks to a radical change in training and administrative methods that was made in 1941. The Army was divided into two parts. One was to be trained for active service; the other was to devote itself to training new troops, and to taking care of supply and maintenance problems at home. A separate administrative corps was set up to discharge all administrative duties within the Zone of the Interior, meaning the United States. This corps has charge of all camps, posts, and stations, including the Replacement Centers where all recruits receive their basic training. The coming of war did not change the duties or responsibilities of this corps. As the field forces began to move by train and other methods of transport to the war areas in the Pacific islands, in Asia, Africa, and Europe, the training camps were drained of their man power; but at each camp there remained a permanent commander and his staff of trained personnel ready to receive and train the new contingents, which would be eventually formed into new combat divisions.

Initiated in January, 1941, the policy had been put into general practice by December. The Replacement Centers, where civilians are made into soldiers, were working smoothly. The Reception Centers, where recruits are classified and outfitted, had a year's valuable experience behind them. The cantonments, where the combat divisions had been trained, were under the management of their permanent staffs. The Army, therefore, was ready for the problems of wartime expansion.

The 2,000,000 men about to be taken into the service could be absorbed and trained without too seriously interrupting the movement of the combat divisions toward the battle areas.

THE ARMY WE SHALL HAVE

Since it will be spring, 1942, before the new drafts will be available, the organization of the Army, which will number approximately 4,000,000 men, cannot be entirely foreseen. Certain it is, however, that a much higher ratio of men will be sent to the air service, since it has been announced that this branch will be increased to 1,000,000 men. The Armored Force — that is, the tank corps — will also be likely to get a larger share to keep pace with our expanding program of tank production. The proportion of combat troops in the new Army will also be sure to be larger than it was in the first Army of 1,750,000, since the training and administrative personnel were drawn from the first Army, and the personnel will not need to be substantially enlarged.

The Army we shall have — even a year hence — will therefore be a very different Army from the one we had the day Pearl Harbor was attacked. The circumstances of war are ever changing, and to meet the changes everything pertaining to the Army must be ready for change too. The setup for both organization and administration must be very flexible; and both strategy (the over-all plans) and tactics (plans for actual movement of troops in battle) must be capable of quick alteration. Even in 1917, a doubling of the size of our Army meant largely that each unit of it would be approximately doubled in size; but doubling today means nothing of the sort, because war is very different from what it was in 1917. The fighting abroad has placed a new emphasis on aviation and on highly mobile ground forces, which get their mobility from gasoline-powered vehicles. That emphasis is reflected in our program of

ORGANIZATION OF OUR ARMY

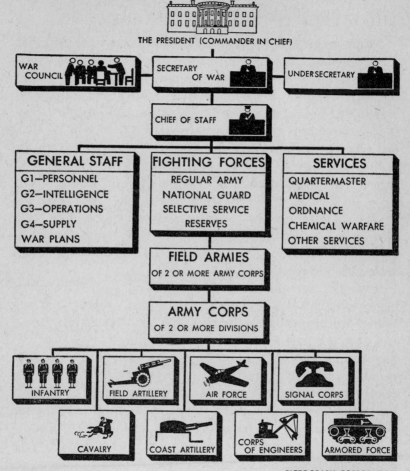

THE PRESIDENT (COMMANDER IN CHIEF)

WAR COUNCIL

SECRETARY OF WAR

UNDER SECRETARY

CHIEF OF STAFF

GENERAL STAFF
G1—PERSONNEL
G2—INTELLIGENCE
G3—OPERATIONS
G4—SUPPLY
WAR PLANS

FIGHTING FORCES
REGULAR ARMY
NATIONAL GUARD
SELECTIVE SERVICE
RESERVES

SERVICES
QUARTERMASTER
MEDICAL
ORDNANCE
CHEMICAL WARFARE
OTHER SERVICES

FIELD ARMIES
OF 2 OR MORE ARMY CORPS

ARMY CORPS
OF 2 OR MORE DIVISIONS

INFANTRY

FIELD ARTILLERY

AIR FORCE

SIGNAL CORPS

CAVALRY

COAST ARTILLERY

CORPS OF ENGINEERS

ARMORED FORCE

PICTOGRAPH CORPORATION

production of war materials, and the program, in turn, will necessarily produce changes in the organization of the Army.

THE EFFECT OF GASOLINE ENGINES

All armies are faced today with the revolutionizing influence of the gasoline engine upon land warfare, the effect of which is comparable to the changes once wrought by steam power on warfare at sea. In the nineteenth century, the building of railroads (employment of steam power on land) made it possible to move more troops and more supplies more quickly than had ever been possible before. The result was a great increase in the size of armies and an equally great broadening in strategical planning, since the High Command could depend on entirely new speed in the movement of troops. But once the troops had left the trains, the situation was little different from what it had been before the invention of the steam engine; so tactics, the actual movement of the troops on the field of battle, were little changed.

It was not until the advent of the gasoline engine that tactics began to assume new and unexpected forms. First, the invention of the airplane introduced a new arm to land warfare — and gave it a new dimension. Second, the adaptation of the motorcar to military uses vastly increased the ability of commanding officers to direct their forces in the field, led to the reintroduction of armor in land fighting, and made combat on land much like combat at sea, where the battle is fought with heavy guns fired from fast-moving and armored platforms.

The new developments in modern warfare are based largely on gasoline power and electricity, with chemistry — largely in the production of new high explosives — playing its part. These developments are bound to alter materially the nature of land warfare. Now, as always, armies are built up around the two central ideas of offensive power and defensive protection; but no army now engaged in war has yet struck a satisfactory balance between the two, especially in the organization of its motorized forces. Each is top-heavy in striking power and weak in motorized elements of protection, with the result that losses become excessive during a retreat or in a period of protracted defense. The army that first strikes the desired balance by a full motorization of its combat forces will have the greatest all-round strength. The race for this goal is on, and the enormous productive capacity of the United States ought to make it the winner.

The tank and the airplane have produced what is known as "total war." These fast-moving weapons, striking, as they do, over the heads or around the flanks of the opposing forces, have brought the battle directly to civilian populations, which, in turn, have had to find means of defending themselves and of striking back. Nowadays every highway, every means of ingress to a country, has to be guarded; every airport, harbor, factory, supply depot, and other vital objective has to be protected. Obviously, therefore, it is no longer possible for small and highly skilled professional armies to interpose themselves between the enemy and the attacking forces and thus safeguard the nation. Everybody must fight now in one way or another; that is, "total war" has become imperative. The result is a great change in general strategy, which has become so wide that it has impinged on and changed national policies. Under total war, "business as usual" — the slogan in the First World War — is absurd. And an army built on voluntary enlistments is absurdly impractical. The situation demands the giving of new powers to the national Government so that it can utilize quickly and efficiently the nation's full man power and economic resources.

Our own country was the last great nation to make the necessary adjustments. In June, 1940, there were 242,914 officers and men in our regular army, and 243,000 officers and men in our National Guard. We were still abiding by a policy that stemmed from Revolutionary War days. Putting faith, as we did, in the isolation provided for us by the two oceans, and having no powerful or covetous neighbors, we saw no need for conscription in time of peace. The Army's war plans were based on the assumption that it could expand, train, and equip itself after war came. There were in June, 1940, only three infantry divisions even theoretically ready for combat, and the only plan for a sudden enlargement of the Army called for tripling the size of this force, expanding the Army Air Force to about 11,000 planes, and strengthening our overseas garrisons in such places as Alaska, Hawaii, and the Philippines.

Germany's swift victory over France in June, 1940, rang through the United States like a warning bell. The old military policy had to be cast aside — and it was. Thereafter, the Government decided — and the citizenry approved the decision — that the American Army would be based on the citizen soldier, who would be so trained and schooled that in the briefest possible time he would be the equal of the professional soldier. The Selective Service Act, requiring the registration of all men between the ages of twenty-one and thirty-five, was passed in September, 1940, and the first 75,000 men reported at the training camps in October. As rapidly as the construction of cantonments permitted, the National Guard regiments were mustered into Federal service. By spring, 1941, the National Guard strength was fully mobilized, and the Army of the United States had more than 1,500,000 men in service.

BUILDING THE NEW ARMY

Of the old Regular Army, there remained only the names and traditions of its historic regiments. Their ranks by this time had been two-thirds filled with selectees, and three-fourths of their officers were Reserve officers but recently ordered to duty. The regular divisions had been scattered and diffused throughout the whole Army structure in the form of cadres (training and command units), which became the nuclei around which all the new divisions, those formed from National Guard regiments excepted, were to be built.

The National Guard units went to camp as a whole with their officer corps intact, and the gaps in their ranks were filled by recruits from the Replacement Centers. Thereafter, until maneuvers began in the summer of 1941, these troops were thoroughly trained in the elements of their new profession. Eventually, eighteen infantry divisions were formed out of these National Guard units.

Cadres were drawn off from the three old regular divisions, and around the cadres six new divisions were formed. Until about May, 1941, the members of the old divisions had a double job: first, they had to train many of their own members to become commissioned or noncommissioned officers, since the cadres formed of these men were of little value until the members themselves had been trained for their new jobs. Second, the men remaining in the old divisions had to train the recruits and Reserve officers who came to them as replacements.

By June, 1941, the last of the new divisions was in being, the need for cadre training seemed to have passed, and the commanding officers felt that they could look forward to a prolonged period in which their organizations could be kept intact and made ready for the field. Such was the outlook throughout the summer maneuvers. The coming of war, however, and the consequent enlargement of the Army, changed everything. The new recruits can be given their essential instruction at the Replacement Centers, but to obtain the officer and noncom staffs around which new combat regiments will be formed will necessitate a further skimming of the old divisions and a new cadre-training program.

It is one of the oldest military truths that five hundred men added to an old and experienced regiment are more valuable than a thousand when made into a new regiment, for the five hundred through their association with experienced leaders and comrades quickly become veterans. It would be desirable, therefore, to keep our combat units intact and to send trained recruits to them as replacements; but our Army simply isn't large enough to use this method. There aren't enough combat units already organized to fight a war on the scale of the present one. New units have to be formed, and they have to be formed around cadres taken from the old units. Our actual military weakness becomes clear when one considers the situation that existed when President Roosevelt said in his opening message to Congress that our Army would be sent to every theater of war where it could engage the forces of the enemy. There were then 1,750,000 men in our army, *but* of that number only about 800,000 were in the three field armies — a mighty small force in comparison with European armies. It takes fully that number to defend our own borders.

NEW KINDS OF COMBAT DIVISIONS

It is easiest to define the fighting strength of a navy in terms of battleships, cruisers, and destroyers. These are complete, self-sufficient fighting units. The smallest complete, self-sufficient fighting unit in an army is the combat division; and so by counting the combat divisions of an army, one can make an estimate of its fighting strength. A combat division is complete and self-sufficient because it is capable of carrying out all military functions; that is, it can attack, defend a position, and supply itself.

In our Army there are three kinds of divisions — infantry,

cavalry, and armored. The name indicates the kind of combat troops that *predominates* in each. No division contains only one kind. For example, the striking force of an infantry division lies mainly in its infantry regiments, but it has also its own artillery, some aviation units, and possibly attached tank units as well. In an armored division, the basic tactical unit is the tank regiment, but the armored division also contains field artillery, engineers, and some infantry. Though other units may support a cavalry division, as they do in Russia, it is largely made up of horse regiments.

We have two types of Army divisions, the old and the new. The old type is known as the " square division," and it was the basic unit of our A.E.F. in 1917–18. It contains two infantry brigades of two regiments each, and one field artillery brigade. This grouping is now considered not quite flexible and mobile enough for combat against mechanized or partially mechanized armies; but the eighteen divisions that were formed in 1941 from the National Guard regiments were square, as were the divisions in Hawaii and the Philippines.

The new type is called the "triangular division," or the "streamline," and it contains three infantry regiments and two field artillery regiments. It differs from the old square division in having one less infantry regiment. The three old divisions of the Regular Army was re-formed into triangular divisions in 1939, and the six new divisions formed from them were also triangular.

In the three field armies that we had when war was declared, there were just twice as many square as triangular divisions. These were divided into corps in a way that produced a nice balance. There were altogether nine Army corps, and each corps was composed of two National Guard divisions with a war strength of about 18,300 men, and one Regular Army triangular division with a war strength of about 14,000 men. Be-

A TRIANGULAR INFANTRY DIVISION

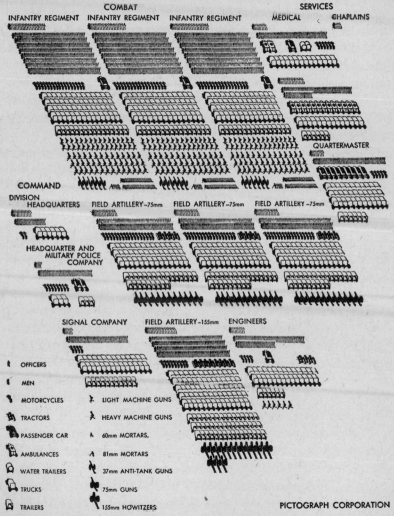

COMBAT — SERVICES

INFANTRY REGIMENT INFANTRY REGIMENT INFANTRY REGIMENT MEDICAL CHAPLAINS

QUARTERMASTER

COMMAND

DIVISION HEADQUARTERS FIELD ARTILLERY–75mm FIELD ARTILLERY–75mm FIELD ARTILLERY–75mm

HEADQUARTER AND MILITARY POLICE COMPANY

SIGNAL COMPANY FIELD ARTILLERY–155mm ENGINEERS

Symbol	Label	Symbol	Label
OFFICERS			
MEN			
MOTORCYCLES		LIGHT MACHINE GUNS	
TRACTORS		HEAVY MACHINE GUNS	
PASSENGER CAR		60mm MORTARS,	
AMBULANCES		81mm MORTARS	
WATER TRAILERS		37mm ANTI-TANK GUNS	
TRUCKS		75mm GUNS	
TRAILERS		155mm HOWITZERS	

PICTOGRAPH CORPORATION

Here is shown the complex nature of this infantry division. Note the high proportion of machines and of artillery.

sides these twenty-seven infantry divisions, the field armies included other necessary corps, Army and G.H.Q. (General Headquarters) forces, aviation, field artillery and antiaircraft regiments, two cavalry divisions, and four armored (tank) divisions.

THE ARMORED FIELD FORCE (TANK CORPS)

It is to be noted that the organization of the tank corps is independent of the field armies and operates under the Armored Field Force Commander, who is responsible for the development, maintenance, and training of tank forces and for the direction of them in combat. The Commander has his own representative on the General Staff in the War Department.

This independence has made possible the prodigious growth of the Armored Force. In the summer of 1940, we had only 3,000 soldiers and 400 obsolete vehicles in the mechanized service. One year later there were four armored divisions of 9,000 men each, and the goal then set of 85,000 men was well within reach. All the regiments had not received their full complements of tanks, but there were more than enough for training purposes. The Armored Force aspired to a personnel composed of 50 per cent highly trained technicians, and late in 1940 it established a school at Fort Knox, Kentucky, to train them. The results have been amazing. In 1939 the tank force trained only 32 specialists, and in 1940 the total was only 124. By the end of the first quarter of 1941, however, the school was returning to the Armored Force expert motorcycle and tank repairmen, radio operators, code men, gunners, topographers, and so on at the rate of 25,000 a year! The schools of the older services, infantry, cavalry, and artillery, had been long established, and the expansion of the Army required only an addition to their normal facilities. But the Armored Force was strictly a child of the war emergency and had to be newly created and developed. Even so, the Armored School has, in the opinion of many trained observers, accomplished more than all of the old Army schools organized in France in 1918 to take care of the needs of the soldiers in the A.E.F.

It is only through such schools that the Army can attain the high technical efficiency which is necessary in modern warfare. Training in the old days was strictly *military* training, devised to give the recruit a soldierly spirit, to teach him such tactics as he needed to know, and to give him a knowledge of the construction and use of arms. But now a technical corps must be created out of men with special skills, imagination, and ability to learn. It is only in a national army that a large enough number of such men can be found. Whether the national army, once assembled, can be given the necessary " professional " combat efficiency depends, of course, on the quality of its leaders and the nature of its equipment.

Nowadays about 35 per cent of the soldiers in the United States Army must be, as we say in civilian life, "skilled labor " — a higher proportion than almost any industry requires. A national army is obviously a cross section of the nation as a whole, but it must aim to bring its members to a higher level of development than the nation as a whole attains, since the successful operation of modern warfare depends very largely on the ability of a large proportion of the soldiers to make decisions. In the old days, soldiers were trained to almost blind obedience of commands, but now the emphasis is on spontaneity in action, and on the substitution of common sense for routine. This is a new psychological approach, a new psychological preparation for war. It is of no value unless the men themselves are up to it.

In the Armored Force the percentage of trained, resolute men must run even higher than elsewhere in the service, since the nature of tank warfare requires more of the individual than of the group. Tank forces, even when "concentrated" in battle, are widely separated. One tank division moving in column over a highway would extend for 90 miles. Tanks require space, and the space in which they can attain maximum efficiency is found only in a network of highways.

Communication between tanks and the command must be maintained, of course, widely separated though they may be. Speed is the essence of Armored Force operation, and communication must therefore be speedy too. Runners can't be used between tanks as they can between infantry units; nothing can be used for communication between tanks except radio. It is speedier than the tanks themselves, and it is indifferent to distance.

It can be said with complete truth that a tank unit is only as good as its radio equipment and its crew; and as the war goes on, radio is becoming more important in all combat. Many German successes, notably in the attack upon Crete, have been attributed to the perfection of the radio communication between the forces of the ground and the air. The gasoline engine has speeded up all military operations enormously, and since communication is imperative, its speed has also to be increased. Once communication is lost, all is lost — and today it is with radio that communication is largely being maintained.

Since the armored divisions are new, their organization is somewhat more experimental than that of our other divisions, and it is more likely to change with the experience of war. The German panzer divisions, upon which our Armored Force was frankly modeled, were reorganized in the winter of 1941–42 on the basis of what had been learned in Russia, with fewer tanks to each division.

As originally constituted, however, the heavy fighting equipment of an American armored division comprised 272 light tanks, 110 medium tanks, and 201 lightly armored scout cars, with supporting artillery of 24 75-millimeter (3-inch) howitzers (curved trajectory guns), 12 105-millimeter guns, and 8 75-millimeter guns. The tanks themselves are armed and armored to fight against vehicles of their own kind. Roughly speaking, one inch of armor will afford protection against a projectile of one-inch diameter. The heaviest gun on the light tank is the 37-millimeter, and the heaviest on the medium tank is the 75-millimeter; these guns give them enough power to destroy tanks with an armor equivalent to their own.

Our tank forces had not received their full quotas of medium tanks by the beginning of the war, and they had no heavy tanks. These were still to be made. When the heavy tanks are delivered, they will be formed into a G.H.Q force under the Armored Force Commander, and they will be used as break-through weapons accompanying the infantry.

THE COMBAT DIVISION OF THE FUTURE

Many Americans think that all of the infantry divisions, or at least the nine that are " streamlined," are completely motorized. Not quite. Their supply trains move under gasoline power. So does all the heavy equipment of the engineering regiments — and much of it is very heavy, since it is the business of the engineers to keep the Army in motion by sweeping all obstacles out of its path. They build bridges when bridges are needed — and blow them up when the enemy needs them, just as they destroy roads, railways, and anything else useful or necessary to the enemy. The artillery is motor-drawn too now, but the infantry still marches; its mobile power still resides in its own muscles.

There is one notable exception — the Fourth Motorized Division, which is probably the most interesting unit in the Army. It is a wholly new kind of organization, and spokesmen from the General Staff — the policy-forming group of generals under the President, the Secretary of War, and the Chief of Staff — have said that most of our infantry divisions may in time be patterned after the Fourth.

It is completely motorized, and its vehicles are remarkably independent of roads — they can cut cross-country, an independence that gives them a mobility comparable to that of the tank forces, which will make a great difference to a general planning his strategy. The infantry will still fight on foot, but they will be moved up to the battle by the " personnel carriers." An even more unusual feature of the Fourth is that its infantry has been artilleryized — that is, the motorized 75-millimeter howitzer is an infantry weapon and moves along with it instead of, as is customary, under a separate command.

Other significant changes have been made in the regimental structure of the Fourth. It has only two-thirds as many men as the standard regiment, but its weapons give it much greater fire power. Each rifle battalion consists of two rifle companies and a weapons company equipped with machine guns, light antitank guns, and 81-millimeter mortars (short-range cannon). The chief changes are in the third, or support, battalion. It is the unit that contains the company of motorized artillery, 6 75-millimeter howitzers. It also has a company equipped with 16 37-millimeter guns for use against tanks, and another of .50-caliber antiaircraft guns.

Such is the division of the future. It is a unit designed to keep up with the armored divisions, exploit fully any penetration of the enemy positions, and perhaps give the tank divisions also full defensive protection during bivouac or during periods of protracted defense. Tanks require support, and if they don't have it they are subject to the kind of extreme reverse the Germans suffered in the early winter of 1941 following the advance upon Moscow. Then large mechanized forces had to be sacrificed because the infantry was not mobile enough to cover their withdrawal from the forward areas.

The Germans pioneered the development of "fast" infantry divisions moving forward under motor power for collaborative action with tanks. The breakdown of the German offensive in November, 1941, did not prove that the structure of the fast infantry divisions was wrong; on the contrary, it proved merely that the Germans did not have enough of them. They were organized approximately on the basis of one motorized division to one tank division — and the weakness was in the ratio. Our goal is likely to be a ratio of three or four motorized divisions to each tank division. The German lack of balance in these forces wasn't due to poor planning but to lack of raw materials, especially petroleum. They could have motorized their infantry only at the expense of their air force. They had to make their choice. We don't have to. We have all the raw materials we need, and in this "war of motors" we can build whatever kind of military power it is within our genius to devise.

OUR IMMEDIATE GOALS

The organization of our vast new forces has not yet been clearly outlined, but in his first statement on the expansion policy Henry L. Stimson, Secretary of War, announced that the War Department contemplated the creation of thirty-two divisions of triangular form, and a "doubling" of the number of armored units. This statement, it can be seen, is consistent with the ratio of three or more motorized infantry divisions to every armored division. Whether the army will motorize any of the existing infantry divisions was not announced, but the statement carried the implication that the new divisions would be motorized first and that the old divisions would proceed to the theaters of war as needed, without any extensive reorganization.

The military wisdom of such a policy is evident. War is never fought with perfect instruments, and once it comes, nations are not granted time in which to shape their arms according to an ideal pattern. One's enemies do not wait, and their plans must be frustrated if one's own plans are to have a chance of fulfillment. What Major General Frank M. Andrews said about air power holds true for all military power: " Adequate air power cannot be obtained after the need for it has arisen." Our enemies won't wait for us to build an overwhelming air force, an irresistible navy, and an all-sufficient army with which to pulverize them; and we can't afford to hold the power we now have in reserve until we have made it much greater. It would be fatal to the morale of the people even to attempt such waiting, and it would be most unwise from a military point of view. There are areas in Europe and Asia where a few machine guns and a little artillery, if got to the scene of battle on time, might effect victory where there had been no chance of one. For that reason, our existing forces must proceed to the battle even though they are not all of them trained and armed according to a standard of perfection.

In general, then, we are moving toward an immediate goal of somewhere between sixty and seventy infantry divisions, about half of which will be motorized and half not, and about ten to fifteen armored divisions. As the Army is expanded, there will be proportionate increases in the strength of antiaircraft units, engineer units, and other special units. Coastal and antiaircraft defenses of the United States, heretofore estimated at 50,000 men as a minimum requirement, may absorb five or six times that number if the threat to our own borders increases. These forces operate under the Air Defense Command, which was established in 1939 and which was ready to perform its mission when the first word was received that the enemy was approaching our coast after the attack on Pearl Harbor.

Although the problems of hemisphere defense may require the retention of as many as 1,500,000 soldiers within the United States itself, a new plan will free a large proportion of that number for service overseas. The plan calls for the formation of fifty battalions of military police for home defense. This new corps will be commanded largely by First World War officers who can still meet the physical requirements. Its ranks will be augmented by Home Guard regiments, many of which are already formed and in active duty guarding defense centers.

WEAPONS OF THE NEW ARMY

Little has been said so far of the weapons the Army will use, and they can be considered here only in a general outline. The field artillery regiments still await the arrival of the 105-millimeter howitzer, a weapon with high-angle fire, intended to replace the 75-millimeter gun, which has a flat trajectory (curve of a shell in flight). The 105 howitzer is now the primary weapon of divisional artillery strength, and the plan is to relegate the 75 gun to antitank uses, but howitzer production has not yet caught up with the Army's needs. When the new gun arrives, our artillery will have much more fire power of a type much more suitable for warfare today. This footnote is worthy of attention: some of the Army's most expert artillerists recommended in 1917 that our artillery be based upon the 105 howitzer instead of the 75 gun, but in the next twenty years nothing was done about the recommendation.

Our standard infantry regiments are more heavily weaponed than in their history. Before the First World War, the rifle supplied almost all infantry fire. The change that has occurred is indicated by the following tabulation of other weapons now operated by an infantry division:

Browning automatic rifles 162
.30-caliber light machine guns 54
.30-caliber heavy machine guns 72
.50-caliber machine guns 36
60-mm mortars 81
81-mm mortars 36
37-mm antitank guns 36

By virtue of these arms, an infantry division has now attained to a fire power that enables it to operate against light tanks with some chance of success, to defend itself against airplane attack (though the .50-caliber gun is thought too light to have much effect on airplane armor), and to lay down a concentrated fire of high explosive at ranges up to 2,500 yards.   This diversity of weapons has changed the nature of infantry training, for in the heavy-weapons unit of an infantry command, each member of a gun crew is required to attain skill in the operation of three or four different weapons, so that any casualties may be immediately replaced.   The required skill is attained only by long hours of handling the guns and studying their operation; so now the infantryman, while still the marching doughboy, must also be a trained technician.

SPECIALIZED UNITS AND BRANCHES

The use of machines in warfare has resulted in a great diversity of arms, which, in turn, demands greater versatility and physical fitness in the individual soldier.   And the result is just what might be expected: teamwork, always important, is more important than it ever was before.   We are all fascinated by the newest types of combat units — parachute troops, air-borne infantry, and tank-destroyer battalions.   The specialization of modern combat units is impressive. Nevertheless, the specialization of the parts only increases the need for unity of action. The Army is one vast machine in which each bit must be properly related to every other bit if the maximum efficiency is to be obtained. The tank-destroyers, which are fast-moving artillery units designed to seek out the enemy armored forces and destroy them by the fire superiority of their guns, must look to the motorized infantry for refuge. The air-borne ground troops, which operate as infantry whether they drop from the skies by parachute or are carried to the battle area by transport plane, will gain only such success as the triumph of their own air power has made possible. They cannot maneuver successfully until their combat aviation has gained command of the air. Mutual support here, as elsewhere, is the governing principle in the relationships of all branches of the service and in the operation of all field forces.

Finally, every soldier and every branch of the service is dependent upon supply. "It is upon supply," said Napoleon, "that war is made." More armies fail from lack of supply than from any other one cause. The great Quartermaster branch of the Army has the chief responsibility for establishing and maintaining the channels (sometimes called lines of supply or communication) through which fighting materials, food, clothing, and shelter flow to soldiers at home and soldiers in the field.

The flow of supplies must never stop, and the flow of orders and information must never be interrupted. Infantry, cavalry, field artillery, coast artillery, Armored Force, and Air Corps, each has its own communications network, but the main communication system of the Army is organized and maintained by the Signal Corps. One of its important duties is the management of the radio network that keeps the War Department in touch with all corps areas and the commands overseas.

The primary task of the Medical Corps, of course, is to keep

the soldiers well and healthy, and since more men have died of
disease in every war than from battle wounds, the task of the
doctors is obviously much the same as it is in civilian practice.
About one-eighth of the doctors in the United States will be
needed in the new Army.

The Ordnance Department is responsible for the production
of all weapons and munitions with which the Army fights,
which includes everything from pistols to heavy tanks.

There are many other Army services — the Finance Department, for example, the corps of chaplains, the departments pre-
sided over by the Judge Advocate General, the Inspector
General, and the Adjutant General — but these in the main
have more to do with the administration of the Army and with
its welfare than with it as a fighting force.

THE NEW DISCIPLINE

While the fighting machinery of the Army has become more
elaborate and more complex, in one important detail there has
been no change: the groundwork of all United States Army
training is still the school of the rifle. Not only infantrymen
but artillerymen, tank men, signalers, and quartermaster clerks
get their basic training with the rifle before moving on to their
special assignments. It is rifle training that is the common de-
nominator of American soldiery. They all have training with
this weapon, and many have learned to handle the new Garand
semiautomatic, which permits a greatly increased volume of
fire, as well as the old, standard, bolt-action Springfield, the
special pet of our infantry for more than thirty years. The se-
lectee begins his rifle training almost within the first hour of his
arrival in camp, and for three months thereafter he practices
the techniques of the foot soldier. He learns how to protect
himself and to do all things in a military manner. This primary training is the common bond between all men in the land

forces. It is the basis of the discipline of the United States Army.

In other respects, however, the discipline has changed greatly since the days of the First World War. Time was when the Army slang for a recruit was " Dumb John," but to-day the Army, instead of jibing, makes it its business to relieve John of his dumbness if he actually is afflicted with it. He is instructed in the cause for which he fights, and he is told as much as is wise about military operations. In brief, he is treated as a military man instead of as an inconsequential cog in a great machine.

Relationships between officers and enlisted men are based more on the doctrine of mutual respect than they used to be. The greatest appeal is made to the soldier's loyalty. Rough-shod methods and hard-boiled language are taboo. Precept and example are employed in the training period rather than arbitrary command and " buck-passing." These are but a few of the outward manifestations of a new standard of discipline, one based upon democratic ideals, the principle of equality of citizenship in all ranks, and sincere recognition of the moral and intellectual attainments of American youth.

But don't be fooled! Lukewarm effort, argument, and in-subordination draw down the same penalties as ever. The new Army is not impractical enough to believe that obedience is of value only when based upon reason, or to agree that the sol-dier shall obey only those orders that have his individual sanc-tion — the attitude taken by many Union soldiers in the first part of the Civil War. The glove is velvetier than in 1918, but inside there is the same old iron hand. This is war, life or death, and a man can't be made fit to fight by sweet reasonableness. There must be discipline. There is — and at its heart lies the recognition that fair dealing, skill, and courage are all unavail-ing unless every man is ready and willing to give loyal support and willing service to every authority, no matter how distasteful any task may be. The beginning of all discipline is obedience; but the safeguard of morale, without which discipline soon falters, is intelligent leadership that wins loyalty by giving it.

The importance of loyalty and leadership and discipline has been neither eliminated nor reduced by the larger role the machine is playing in today's warfare. There are no short cuts to military success. Our Army has not made the mistake of stressing the value of machines to the neglect of the vital human material from which all truly great armies are formed, and upon which nations are ultimately dependent for their security. All the experience on the battlefields of Europe has simply gone to emphasize the importance of the file — the individual soldier.

Measured against all conditions of climate and geography, man remains the only perfect fighting instrument. He can move when machines cannot; he can fight when machines cannot. He generates his own power, and he has a mind of his own, which machines haven't and will never have. A well-trained man with a good rifle — there you have the real fighting man.

VI. How is the Air Force organized to fight the war?

LAUREN D. LYMAN

Lauren Dwight Lyman, assistant to the president of United Aircraft Corporation, left Yale University during the First World War to join the Army, and served overseas for two years. After the war he was first a reporter, and later aviation editor, for the 'New York Times.' He covered, among other things, all famous flights from 1927 on, and made the first passenger flight to the Philippines on Pan American Airways. Mr. Lyman was awarded the Pulitzer Prize in 1936 for his exclusive story of the departure to England of Colonel and Mrs. Charles A. Lindbergh. He is coauthor, with Captain Carl B. Allen of the United States Army Air Corps, of 'The Wonder Book of the Air.'

Nathan Bedford Forrest, the brilliant Confederate cavalry leader, is supposed to have said that battles are won by the one " who gits thar fustest with the mostest men." Nowadays, airplanes invariably get there fustest, and a large part of the Germans' success to date has been due to the fact that they have had the mostest. We haven't the mostest airplanes yet, but we will have; and, what's more, they will be the bestest.

Napoleon is credited with saying " God is on the side of the strongest battalions." In his cynical way, he was saying simply that the side which could strike the hardest was the side which would win. He turned field artillery into an attacking weapon — and won. Forrest transformed cavalry into mounted infantry, which he threw against infantry on foot — and won. Field Marshal Göring, along with a small group of fliers who fought with him in the last war, built up the present German Air Force. His motto has been " Air power is striking power."

Göring has proved with great decisiveness the soundness of his motto. Napoleon was talking about striking power, and so was Forrest; but times have changed, and with them the weapons of war. The Russians have demonstrated that cavalry still has its uses, and in the Philippines General MacArthur has repeatedly shown the Japanese what field artillery can do; but in Russia airplanes make the way ready for the cavalry, and in the Philippines General MacArthur has been at a great disadvantage because of his lack of airplanes. They are the spearhead of modern attack, and without them an army is automatically on the defensive. A navy without them is like a medieval warrior without armor; its defensive strength is so slight that it dare not move out into the open to make use of its offensive strength.

Airplanes aren't, however, merely incredibly fast weapons or, as when used with battleships, invaluable defensive armor; they are also sentries and scouts and cargo ships. Exactly as the Army posts sentries on the ground, the Air Force posts sentries in the skies; and as the Army sends out scouts to obtain information about the disposition and strength of the enemy forces, the Air Force sends out planes for exactly the same purpose. Armed with their amazing cameras, the scouting planes can, and do, bring back information infinitely detailed and absolutely accurate. Finally, in a way fundamentally no more romantic than a freight train, airplanes carry troops and supplies with great speed to the spot where they are most needed. The cargo planes made possible the German conquest of Crete, and without them General Rommel would have gone down to quick defeat before the British attack in Libya.

AIRPLANES ALONE CAN'T WIN WARS

Yet powerful as airplanes are, invaluable as they are, they can't win wars all alone. Why, everybody wondered, didn't Hitler attempt the invasion of England after Dunkirk? His air power was vastly greater than Britain's. By sacrificing enough planes and their crews — and he could have afforded the sacrifice — he might have eventually blasted the British Air Force out of the air. He could then have bombed the English cities into powder. True enough, but the English would still have been in England — and he would still have been on the Continent. He couldn't have conquered England without occupying it, and to accomplish the occupation, he had to get his troops past the British Navy. Some theorists think he could have got them past, and perhaps he could have, but Hitler obviously didn't think so — and England was not invaded.

Hanson Baldwin, a former naval officer and a leading authority on military problems, sums up the position of air power thus: " It consists in the recognition of the simple truth that air power, come of age, is more than an adjunct, auxiliary, or subordinate of surface forces but that it cannot, now or in the foreseeable future, *supplant* either armies or navies. It consists of a recognition of the fact that whereas air power must often be used to support sea and land power, it is itself capable of *independent* strategic missions in which neither armies nor navies can aid or participate, missions that may, under certain circumstances, be decisive."

Mr. Baldwin's book, *United We Stand*, in which this paragraph appears, was written before the attack by the Japanese on Pearl Harbor. The success of that attack has been hailed as proof positive that air power unassisted can carry out independent missions. The argument when based on the evidence of Pearl Harbor is obviously absurd. The Japanese planes were borne to the vicinity of the action by carriers. The carriers, in turn, were protected by a screen of submarines and probably — though we have no sure evidence of this yet — by heavily armed cruisers and destroyers. Actually, the success at Pearl Harbor merely proves once again that battles are won by getting " thar fustest with the mostest," whatever the striking force may be. In the actual fighting, the Japanese planes had the effective support of submarines and, most important of all, they had the floating base of the naval carriers from which to take off and on which to land.

AIRPLANES IN ACTION AT SEA

But we have a tragic example of how air power can be effective in an independent action. Moreover, this independent action ought to convince the most reactionary of admirals — and we still have them — that the airplane can be more than a match for even the most powerfully armed battleships.

It is altogether possible that the battle in the warm blue seas off Malaya between two of Britain's best ships and a small fleet of Japanese planes may rank historically with the Civil War battle between the *Merrimac* and the *Monitor*. The battle in Hampton Roads was in itself only a minor engagement, but it proved to the world that the day of wooden ships and iron men had gone forever. From that day on naval thinking changed, and out of the change came the " modern " navy — modern, that is, until Pearl Harbor was attacked and until the battle cruiser *Repulse* and the battleship *Prince of Wales* were sunk a few days later by attacking airplanes. The sinking of those two ships was the greatest naval loss the English had suffered in the war — and possibly it was the most instructive. Let's review the story.

Proudly these ships of war steamed forth seeking contact with the enemy. Their turrets and decks were ready for action. Keen-eyed lads manned the lookout posts. The fighting tops and decks bristled with antiaircraft guns. The latest in electric sound-detectors were tuned for duty — those marvelous man-made ears which warn that aircraft are approaching even before they can be seen with the most powerful glasses. All hands knew they were seeking battle, and all hands thought they were ready for it. Their objective was a convoy of Japanese transports bringing tens of thousands of the little brown men to the Malayan battle front.

Prime Minister Churchill has said recently that the Admiralty realized that air support was advisable, but that no carrier was available to act with the *Repulse* and the *Prince of Wales*. Be that as it may, the officers in command of the battleships certainly knew that an air attack was likely, and just as certainly they seem to have discounted the danger. There might be loss of life and some damage to the ships, but whoever heard of a battleship, properly armored and properly armed and properly manned and properly alert, being put out of action by planes? Of course, the British airplanes had smashed up the Italian fleet as it lay at anchor at Taranto, but those were *British* airplanes attacking *Italian* ships! Besides, the Italians had managed to lose every kind of fight possible on land or sea; so the sinking of their ships hardly counted. Pearl Harbor was apparently too recent to have properly impressed the British Navy command; also, at Pearl Harbor the Japanese had had the enormous advantage of surprise, while here in Malayan waters the *Prince of Wales* and the *Repulse* expected an attack — an enemy scouting plane had been following their wake for hours — and they were ready for it.

Ready for it? The reports of the battle are still confused, but this much is certain: The British ships had no screen of flyers overhead. Their flanks on the surface were guarded by destroyers and perhaps submarines, but one flank was naked — the air above them. Even the surface screen plus antiaircraft fire, which they had thought would be adequate against torpedo planes, could not save them. Down through the hot tropical skies came the dive bombers. Fore and aft they raked the decks and superstructures with bombs and machine-gun fire. From all directions they came diving through the antiaircraft fire. Simultaneously from north and south and east and west, swooping close to the waters, came the torpedo planes. Some of them burst into flames, struck by shells from accurately aimed guns. Others broke through to come within yards of the zigzagging, twisting ships before dropping their torpedoes. Having dropped their loads, the planes swept on, zooming over the doomed ships, almost grazing masts, turrets, and decks, knocking out a gun crew here and there with machine-gun fire and then turning to sweep back again.

Many torpedoes were wasted, but a few got home. The steering gear of the *Prince of Wales* was disabled, and she could no longer maneuver. The *Repulse* was struck by a torpedo, then by another one, and then by still one more. She staggered and listed and began to go down. Her captain ordered the vessel abandoned, and as those who were able donned life belts and leaped into the oil-covered waters, they saw up ahead the *Prince of Wales*, crippled and smashed and sinking.

We do not know what losses the Japanese suffered — how many planes and their crews were destroyed; but we do know that whatever they were, the loss was small for the size of the victory won. The planes had not only sunk two of the finest warships ever built; they had also sunk the legend that Singapore was impregnable because of Britain's sea power. That victory changed the attack down the Malayan Peninsula from a desperate gamble to a battle that held the chance of another victory. It proved that dive bombers and torpedo planes together could destroy the most modern warship, and it proved even more: it proved that no ship and no group of ships can sail the seas in security without control of the air above them.

If the British had been defended by squadrons of fighter planes, either shore- or carrier-based, the story might well have been different. As it was, the Japanese could disregard the air above and concentrate on the enemy below. Even a small air force can be tremendously effective. On Wake Island our Marines had twelve fighter planes, only four of which could take part in the battle at any one time, a battle that lasted for days. Without those four fighter planes it is possible, even probable, that Wake would have fallen within hours.

FIVE TYPES OF NAVY PLANES

We have wandered a little perhaps from our central theme, but in wandering we have reviewed in action two important plane types, the torpedo plane and the bomber, fighters we shall hear from again and again before this war is won. At the risk of wandering even a little farther afield, we shall review even more briefly a ship-and-air action which the air force won for the Allies, an action in which a third type of plane played a vital part.

On May 24, 1941, the great German battleship *Bismarck* sank Britain's *Hood* in an action near Iceland. The *Bismarck* then turned to escape from the rest of Britain's fleet; but before she got away, torpedo planes from the carrier *Victorious* made hits which reduced her speed from 30 to 20 knots. Even so, she apparently had made good her escape. While British ships scurried hither and yon over the ocean seeking for her in vain, she steamed steadily for home and safety. Thirty-two hours passed, and then, slipping down from the clouds, came a far-ranging Catalina, the Consolidated Flying Boat, known in the United States Navy as PBY — that is, patrol bomber. The *Bismarck* was then 500 miles west of Land's End. The Catalina sent out signals of her discovery and then proceeded to keep the *Bismarck* continuously in sight.

The British ships had used up most of their fuel in their search, but torpedo planes from the *Ark Royal* answered the Catalina's call. They succeeded in making hits, at least one of which apparently crippled the *Bismarck*, since her speed dropped to 8 or 10 knots, and she began to move in circles. Then surface vessels came up and sank her with torpedoes and shells; but if they had never appeared, it is almost certain that the torpedo planes could have finished the job. Just the same, neither the torpedo planes nor the surface vessels would ever have had the chance if a long-range scouting plane hadn't found the German ship and kept it in sight. In this action, the long-range plane proved its great value, as it has in many other actions less dramatic.

There are two more types of plane of great importance, the fourth and fifth. The fourth is a little single-engined plane, of which our Navy makes great use. When stationed on carriers, it takes off on wheels; but when stationed on battleships or cruisers, it is fitted with pontoons and is catapulted into the air. It is called the observation scout (OS) and carries only two persons, the pilot and an observer. The armament is small, but there is an efficient two-way radio. Naval aviation authorities believe surface vessels should have a veritable " umbrella " of these little planes in the skies above them. Their value to a fleet searching the seas for enemy forces or convoys is obvious.

The fifth important type of Navy plane is the fighter, a powerful single-seater, heavily armed, which performs many of the same duties of the Army pursuit and interceptor planes besides having other duties of its own. The Navy fighter must

HOW PLANES ARE USED

FOR BOMBING SHIPS

FOR LONG RANGE PATROL

FOR TORPEDO ATTACKS

FOR OBSERVATION

FOR PURSUIT AND INTERCEPTION

FOR LONG RANGE BOMBING

FOR ATTACK BOMBING AND GROUND STRAFING

FOR CARRYING CARGO AND PARACHUTE TROOPS

PICTOGRAPH CORPORATION

have a slower landing speed than its Army brother, because it must be able to operate from carrier decks. At the same time, it must have high speed in the air. While ordinarily the Army pursuit plane carries no bombs, the Navy fighter carries a small bomb load. Outstanding among Navy fighter-type planes is the United States Grumman fighter, a stubby, quick-turning, fast-climbing, deadly little machine, which throughout 1942, and perhaps throughout the war, must bear the brunt of the Navy's interceptor work.

Most of our Navy planes have double titles. We have said something about Japanese " dive bombers." The United States Navy calls these planes scout bombers. The torpedo planes are referred to as torpedo bombers and the big flying boats of the Catalina type are referred to as patrol bombers.

There is a reason for these double names. The Navy has developed its Air Force over a long period and after intensive study by the Bureau of Aeronautics. Lack of room for planes on surface vessels, the great variety of flying duties to be performed, and the wide spaces to be defended or attacked, have all contributed reasons to our Navy for developing airplanes that can be used for different purposes. Even the Navy fighter, which is a special type if there ever was one, carries small bombs. Thus every Navy airplane, as the names indicate, is a two-purpose plane; and every Navy plane, with the exception of the patrol bombers (flying boats) and the observation scouts on pontoons (seaplanes), can be used, and is being used, in land warfare.

Air war, as the Germans have amply shown, is equally important over land and sea. Over the Burma Road and over the Malayan jungle, Brewster Buffaloes, Navy fighters built for carrier duty, have competed for honors on equal terms against the enemy with the P-40's, Army pursuit planes built for interceptor duty against bombers and against other fighters over land. At Wake, the Grumman fighter operated from land, though designed for use from carriers, and wrought frightful havoc among the destroyers, transports, and troop barges of an overwhelmingly superior force of attacking Japanese. As time goes on, we are likely to see more of this use of " Navy " planes over land and of " Army " planes over water.

So far in this chapter we have considered the planes in relation to their use in naval warfare. We have seen that a navy without planes is no longer effective, perhaps useless. However, if we are going to carry the war to our enemies, if we are going to stop the enemy from bringing the war to us, we must have ships. We must have transports and naval vessels to guard these transports; we must have battleships, cruisers, tankers, destroyers, and submarines. Already submarines have been sunk from the air, but really to cope with them, surface vessels are needed.

CARGO AND ARMY PLANES

Cargo planes are coming to be used more and more in war, but aviation has not yet reached the place where the cargo plane can take the place of the surface vessel; and until that time comes, we will continue to need a surface navy, although with less emphasis than before on the big battleship. The cargo plane saved Rommel in Libya. It brought him the troops and supplies he immediately needed; but he was unable to take the offensive until he had received reinforcements and supplies brought by surface vessels. At present the cargo plane might be called an emergency carrier of great value, but surface vessels can move much larger quantities of supplies and men at much less cost. The great cargo plane has, however, already proved its worth, and like the great land bomber and the far-ranging patrol bomber of the Catalina and the Vought-Sikorsky type, it is of particular interest to Americans, for these perhaps above all other types are America's contribution to aviation and to the winning of the war.

What, you are probably asking, about our Army Air Corps? Why all this emphasis on Navy planes? Is it true, as some critics insist, that our Army planes are inferior in every way to those of our allies and to those of our enemies? Is it true that only about 25 per cent of the planes now being built are fit for modern war?

The answer to the last question is an emphatic " No." To the other questions we can give general answers, and now and then we can be specific. We are at war, and censorship frowns — naturally! — on the publication of exact information. It can be said, however, without worrying about the censor that Navy planes have been discussed first simply because it is the Navy that has borne, and must continue to bear, the first impacts.

The various types of Navy planes have been described briefly. For each the Army has a counterpart, except for the torpedo plane. In place of the Navy's scout bomber, our Army Air Corps has the attack bomber, once called merely the attack, or ground-strafing, plane. It was originated in this country. As our Navy was the first to develop the dive bomber, so our Army was the first to develop the attack plane. The development ceased temporarily a few years ago when emphasis was shifted to the fast pursuit or interceptor plane.

In this peace-loving country, the Congress, voicing the will of the people, for years held down appropriations for the Air Corps to such an extent that our air officers had to sacrifice certain things in order to find the money to develop others, and one of the models that suffered for lack of development was the attack plane. In its place we have now the exceedingly fast medium bomber and the attack bomber. Emphasis was also placed on the heavy long-range bomber, the so-called Flying Fortress, a four-engined plane, and a load-carrier with tremendous range. The Boeing Airplane Company at Seattle was the first to design and build this type. Today the basic design is more than six years old. At San Diego, California, the Consolidated Aircraft Corporation, builders of the famous PBY flying boats for the Navy, has developed the counterpart of the Flying Fortress in the four-engined Liberator, an exceedingly fast long-range heavy bomber. Boeing has continued to improve the Fortress, and Consolidated, coming along later with its design now only three years old, is putting out its third edition of the Liberator with performance improvements in altitude, range, speed, and striking power.

So far as we know, our enemies have built nothing to equal these two planes, either in striking power or in range. Germany has its four-engined Condor, designed primarily as a cargo plane and converted into a bomber. It may be the equal of our great bombers, but its performance so far over England, Africa, and Russia suggests otherwise. Neither Britain nor Russia has planes in quantity production that compare in performance with the Flying Fortress and the Liberator. Three great companies have standardized their equipment for the Fortress, and similar arrangements have been made to turn out the Liberator in quantity, but already the shadows of their tremendous wings are moving back and forth across the seven seas, above the mountains and plains of Europe and Asia, over the steaming islands of the Indies, and over the hot deserts of northern Africa. Flying at extreme altitudes, they cruise serenely along out of range of antiaircraft guns and safe from all but the highest-flying pursuit ships. It is no secret that for more than a year now these huge machines have been used in a daily transatlantic service between North America and Great

Britain; and when the final history of this war is written, the chapter that tells the story of these giants of the air will be among the most thrilling.

As we have excelled in the design and construction of the great bombers, just so we have excelled in the design and construction of medium bombers. Reports from Africa and Europe about our Martin and Douglas medium and attack bombers have been enthusiastic, as they have been about our Lockheed Hudson — a converted commercial transport that the British have found invaluable for both bombing and coastal patrol. Today, Lockheed, Martin, and Douglas are building heavier, swifter, and more deadly planes of the same general type. In addition, a fourth plane made by North American now joins these earlier three to make a quartet that we believe outflies and outfights anything of the type our enemies may have.

These medium and attack bombers are all twin-engined. To the eye of the layman, provided he isn't too close to them, they appear to be something like our airline planes. Actually they are very different. To begin with, they have more power. Two of the four have 2,000-horse-power air-cooled engines. The newer types have three-wheeled landing gear, which makes landings at high speed feasible and provides the pilot with far better control on the ground than the conventional two-wheel gear does.

Some evidence of their striking power, speed, and maneuverability can be gained from the use that the British are making of one of them. The Douglas DB–7 was shipped to England to be used as a bomber, but the British quickly converted it into a night fighter and called it, aptly enough, the Havoc. It has raised havoc, indeed, with the German night raiders on England. The Havocs go up accompanied by light, short-range interceptors, which take care of the home defense. The

Havocs themselves slip across the Channel and wait for the return of the German squadrons. When the Germans circle over their landing fields, the ground crews turn on a few landing lights to guide them down. That is the moment the Havocs have been waiting for, and they use the moment to justify their name.

The successor to the Havoc is faster and heavier, and carries more armament. It, like the new Martin and the new Lockheed, roars through the skies at pursuit-plane speed made possible by 2,000-horse-power air-cooled engines.

We now come to a discussion of the pursuit plane, which has its counterpart in the Navy fighter. While no serious criticism has been aimed at our Navy fighters, there has been much loose talk concerning our Army pursuit planes, centered mostly around the Curtiss P–40. This plane was designed to fit a new liquid-cooled engine called the Allison. The Air Corps designed the Allison in the desire to have more than one type of engine to rely on. General Motors was asked to build the engine, and although it was inexperienced in making aircraft, it went to work with a will. The outbreak of war caught the engines in the process of development, and as a result they never received the long, arduous, thorough field tests normally given engines before they are employed in action.

The British, loyal to their own planes, were critical of the new Curtiss planes with their new, untried engines. Yet, though they found the Curtiss unsuited to high-altitude work over England, they have found it useful in the Middle East and the Far East. The American volunteers in Burma have completely outfought the Japanese with them. If General MacArthur had had an adequate supply of Curtisses, the Japanese could never have landed so easily in the Philippines. The Japanese planes, so far as we have learned, are inferior to the

American, but they had a lot of them and General MacArthur had very few. The Japanese got "thar fustest with the mostest."

MORE POWER — AND FASTER PRODUCTION

War is dynamic, and no single type of plane maintains its superiority for long. Our aircraft-builders, many of them former Army and Navy men, have long been aware of this fact. They are constantly seeking to build something better. Roy Alexander, veteran military pilot and military expert for *Time* magazine, concentrated the problem into a small capsule of words: " There is no substitute for supe." " Supe " is horse power; and when it comes to power, Uncle Sam leads the world. Even while Congressmen bickered importantly about the worth of our planes, higher-powered planes were developed and made obsolete the planes the Congressmen were bickering about.

The liquid-cooled Allison and the similar engines in England and Germany throughout the first two and a half years of the war were in the 1,000- to 1,200-horse-power class. Every effort has been made to increase this rating in the race for speed and performance, until in January, 1942, the British were using in their fighters engines of 1,400 horse power and over. The Germans have probably been successful in the same difficult task. The British have been making intense efforts to build liquid-cooled engines up to 2,000 horse power, but at this writing they have no great numbers in use.

In this power race we have been more successful. Our latest Navy fighters and Army pursuit planes, just now — spring, 1942 — moving into production are equipped with engines of 2,000 horse power. For the Navy a number of companies are to build the Vought Corsair. Other companies have joined with Republic Aviation to build the Republic Thunderbolt. The United States was the first nation to get these 2,000-horse-power engines into production. They happen to be air-cooled, but that fact is not half so important as the fact that they are the most powerful in the world, that they are simple and dependable and easy to service — and that we are getting a lot of them. Both the Wright Aeronautical Corporation and the Pratt & Whitney Aircraft Division of United Aircraft are turning out similar engines, and the great Ford organization is also building the Pratt & Whitney type.

The President's Office of Facts and Figures summed up the situation in regard to our plane production in its first report, which was made public in January, 1942. It stated: " In performance, our Army Air Corps can be credited with spectacular progress. We now have four types of combat planes better than anything yet produced abroad, so far as is known. Details on air speeds cannot be given because, with the declaration of war, these become military secrets. Our new achievements in performance were accomplished not with specially built power units but with engines in regular production. This is particularly significant because of the promise of improvement of more horsepower in still larger types."

Thus, while the production men are attending to the quantity, our engineers, behind locked doors in great laboratories, are attending to the improvement in quality. Here in these laboratories the war is also being fought grimly and tirelessly. Outside them, on floors acres and acres in area, machine tools are turning night and day. Men and women, many of them novices, are working with all their strength to provide the air power that is striking power. Folks from the farms; girls from offices; boys from school and college, from city streets and mountain villages; youngsters just out of school; old men who thought they had retired — they are all there together, all playing the greatest game of their lives on the varsity team of

Democracy, playing with no time out, as consecrated to victory, and as necessary to it, as the pilots are who will actually fly the planes they, the workers, are making.

Other chapters of this book will tell more fully of these workers, but they should be mentioned in any chapter dealing with the Air Force. In peacetime it has been said that it takes about nineteen persons on the ground to keep one pilot in the air. During the First World War it was said that it took five men behind the lines to keep one soldier at the front. In the present war both these figures have been succeeded by others that are almost incredible. A modern air-combat unit at the front today requires something like 106 men on the ground to keep a plane in the air. Of course bomber planes have crews of from two to five and in some cases nine persons. Today the air-combat zone is a complicated factory, a transport terminal, a highly scientific laboratory dealing with aerology, medicine, physics, and other branches of science.

Armorers who know the intricacies of a complicated machine gun; propeller experts who can etch the contours of an aluminum blade, balance the whole propeller, and send it forth to the wars again — the British are repairing 90 per cent of their aluminum propellers; engine mechanics, electricians, hydraulic engineers, to work on the huge landing gears of modern planes; installation men; radio specialists; instrument mechanics with hands and eyes like jewelers or artists in mosaics; and other specialists, virtually without number — all are needed to keep a modern battle squadron in the air.

Then there are the airport engineers, surveyors, civil engineers, machine-setup men, and toolmakers; operators of drills, grinders, broachers, and other machines; riveters, welders, and others, to say nothing of guards and those who are not specialists but who are all needed in modern mechanized war.

When you hear people talk of a million pilots and planes for them to fly, stop and think of these figures.

Returning now to our listing of fighting planes, we find that the two superfighters, the Corsair and the Thunderbolt, are not alone. The Navy had its Grumman in quantity production for more than a year before Japan made its attack. We saw what this little plane did at Wake Island. Pound for pound, it is probably the most deadly navy fighter in the world. As fast as the Army fighters in its own power range, it will continue to bear the brunt of the Navy fighting throughout 1942 and will continue to have a part throughout the war. The Army, in turn, has the speedy and powerfully armed Bell Aerocobra and the North American Mustang, a new and very fast machine. The Aerocobra is of radical design, since its engine is buried in the fuselage behind the pilot. It is extremely maneuverable and outperforms anything in its class up to 15,000 feet. Then there is the Lockheed Lightning, also radically designed, twin-engined, and called the fastest military plane in the world. This machine is deadly. It attains the highest altitudes, and it will make the air dangerous for enemy bombers anywhere it is used. The Army also has in production the Republic P–43, a smaller brother of the new Republic Thunderbolt. It is a very maneuverable, fast, high-altitude pursuit plane built around a 1,200-horse-power air-cooled engine.

Wartime censorship forbids the mention of numbers of each type of plane. A few days after our entrance into the war, however, the President announced calmly that 60,000 planes, of which 45,000 would be combat types, would be built by the aircraft industry of the United States in 1942. He added, and in making the addition he was counting upon real help from the automobile industry, that 125,000 planes would be built in 1943, of which 100,000 would be combat planes.

The other 25,000 are to be cargo and training planes for the most part. Both are extremely important. The cargo or transport plane might well be listed as combat. Both the great flying boats and the big land planes have been used, and will be used, as never before to carry munitions and troops directly into battle. The Germans, of course, led the way in the movement of troops by air, and the Japanese are following the German example successfully. China's coastline, all the way from Japan to Indo-China, is dotted with air bases, stations on a military airway of the greatest importance. Hawaii and the American-controlled islands beyond it are as important to us as terminal and subterminal air bases as they are for any other purpose. For that reason, the loss of Guam and Wake hamstrung us at the beginning of the war. Without them, the movement of planes and of plane cargoes of men and munitions was slowed up tragically. With them, support could have been brought much more quickly to General MacArthur in Luzon, to the British at Singapore, and to the Netherlanders in the East Indies. Watch the transport and cargo plane as the war continues. It is already of vital importance, and that importance will grow.

MEN OF THE AIR AND MEN ON THE GROUND

The men who are to fly all these planes will be the youngest group in our fighting forces. Just what their numbers will total is still a secret, but this much is known: Our Army Air Force, including pilots and enlisted men, by the end of 1942 will number something between 600,000 and 800,000, perhaps more. Of this number, it would be safe to guess that more than 50,000 will be pilots. As for the Navy, the increase in enlistments pretty well tells the story. In May, 1940, the Navy was enlisting 100 men a month for flying; in July, 1941, it was enlisting 800; and in January, 1942, it was enlisting

2,500. If the January rate of enlistment is merely maintained, the Navy will have added 30,000 pilots to its Air Force within the year.

Both the Army and the Navy have eased the requirements for enlistment, without, however, in any way lowering the rigid requirements the cadets must meet once training has begun. Both services have relaxed the qualification of two years of college training for acceptance as a cadet, although they still continue to seek college-trained men. And both are, like the British services, creating squadrons of noncommissioned flyers. No longer is the job of handling controls to be restricted to college men or to officer graduates of Annapolis and West Point.

Physical requirements are as strict as ever for pilots, but the Army is training to be observers and bombardiers thousands of young men who haven't quite met the rigid tests for flight officers. It is hardly worth while to set down in detail the regulations governing admission to the flying services, since they are subject to constant change - so constant that they have been changed several times since the writing of this book was begun. The Army and Navy recruiting offices all over the country have on hand the fullest and latest information as to how one goes about becoming a flyer. Both services are eager for more and more candidates.

Many young men who have had ambitions to be flyers, both military and commercial, in the opinion of experienced airmen have laid too much stress on merely obtaining two years of college work. Listen to Brigadier General Ira Eaker, United States Army Air Force and coauthor with Lieutenant General H. H. Arnold, Assistant Chief of Staff and Chief of the Army Air Force, of three fine books on flying. General Eaker went to England early in the war and returned there later to command our own airmen in February, 1942. The writer of this chapter asked General Eaker what young men should do to prepare themselves for a career in the air.

Tell your readers to start in early on physical condition. Tell them to train as if for football. One of the essentials in flying is fine physical condition. Eyesight, of course, has to be excellent, but I believe that many lads who fail the physical requirements on such little things as eyesight need not have failed if they had been more careful of their general physical condition. Get sleep, lots of sleep. I repeat — train as if for a basketball or football team. Not only will physical condition be better, but studies are sure to be better and the chances of a candidate not only for passing the first requirements but for staying in through the course of training will be better.

General Eaker said that too many young men had the idea that they could build up their physiques in a few weeks, just before attempting the physical test required for admission to flying school, not realizing that a good physique is built up through years of careful living instead of a few weeks of gym or road work.

On the study side he stressed mathematics and the kindred sciences, physics, and chemistry. The pilot of the modern high-altitude plane must know a lot about navigation. Time and again he finds himself in a position where he cannot come home on his radio. Celestial navigation and the ability to make his calculations at lightning speed are everyday functions of the competent flyer.

It is hard to see how English and English composition can be important elements of a flyer's training — that is, any more important than in other professions — but they are. Wars are won and battles are won on information, among other things, and the pilot, whether he be combat or observation, and the navigator and observer are sometimes more important for the news they bring back than for the damage they do to the enemy. There are countless reports to make, countless details to see and record for those in high command — those who must make the decisions. Accuracy to the last detail in writing the report of a mission is of the utmost importance and one of the ways to attain proficiency in this particular task is to be proficient in the use of words. More often than not some quick-eyed, accurate observer who can tell his story well may be responsible for changing the whole course of a battle or a campaign.

The Army has requisitioned the best of the civilian aviation schools for preliminary training, and early in January, 1941, there were forty-one of these schools filled with cadets. Early in the same year the Army restrictions were relaxed to admit young married men. The Navy for a time continued to insist on single men and to require that they remain single for at least two years after admission, but this regulation too may be changed under the pressure of war. The Navy has sixteen Naval Reserve aviation bases where preliminary training is given. From these bases the successful candidates go to advanced schools after sixty days in the elimination courses. Then comes the hardest work of all: ground courses covering every phase of the naval aviator's life, long hours in the classroom and more hours in the laboratory, hangar, and machine shop. After six weeks of this training, the student begins the actual flying, but for nine more weeks he spends three hours a day in the classroom. The whole course takes ten months, with the proportion of time spent in the air ever increasing. Finally he is ready to join the fleet. He is a Navy flyer; he has his wings.

The Army training is similar and just as exacting. Specialization comes toward the end of the courses, with much remaining to be learned after the candidates have actually been assigned to units.

One more word for those who would serve their country in the air. When at last the war is over, opportunities to continue in aviation will be greater than ever before. First, it is hoped, the nation will never let down its air defenses. If this war is showing anything, it is showing that those defenses must be maintained. Second, the world of peace was just beginning to utilize the airplane when the war began. Thoughtful and experienced students agree that commercial airlines will use ten planes for every one in use today on our commercial airways, and they estimate that international airlines will actually use thirty for one. Good pilots, they believe, will be in great demand. Fifty pilots should find employment for every one that was on active duty in 1941.

Just as in the war, the airplane in the days of peace after the war will have a place in our lives far beyond the belief of all but the most daring dreamers in those years we knew before Adolf Hitler set the world aflame.

VII. How can America co-operate with its allies?

HAROLD M. VINACKE

Harold M. Vinacke is a specialist in international organization. He is now professor of international law and politics at the University of Cincinnati. He spent one year on the faculty of the Nan Kai University, Tientsin, China, and has spent some time in Japan and a year in Europe. His books are 'Modern Constitutional Development in China,' 'Problems of Industrial Development in China,' 'A History of the Far East in Modern Times,' and 'International Organization.'

A certain man had several sons who were always quarreling with one another and, try as he might, he could not get them to live together in harmony. So he determined to convince them of their folly by the following means: Bidding them fetch a bundle of sticks, he invited each in turn to break it across his knee. All tried and failed; and then he undid the bundle and handed them the sticks one by one, when they had no trouble at all in breaking them. "There, my boys," said he, "united you will be more than a match for your enemies; but if you quarrel and separate, your weakness will put you at the mercy of those who attack you." Union is strength — Aesop's *Fables*

No one has remembered this fable more continuously than Adolf Hitler, and most of his success has been due to his skill in putting a reverse English on the moral. Knowing that union is strength, he has sought from the beginning to see that there was no union among those who opposed him. He has never wanted to attempt breaking a bundle of nations; instead he has carefully kept the nations apart so that he could destroy them one by one. With one twist of his fingers he could snap little twigs like Poland and Denmark and Norway and Belgium and Holland, but if even such little twigs as these had been tied firmly into one single bundle he would have been forced to use up a good deal of his power to break them. They weren't tied, however. His fingers moved; there was a series of cracks — and those little nations were gone.

Even France and Britain were not really tied together; they did not work as a single unit, and so early in the war Hitler was able to separate them and defeat France. Britain bent under the terrible force exerted upon it, but it did not break.

Now a new bundle of national sticks has been collected and tied together. Some of those sticks, such as the Central American states, are very tiny twigs indeed; and some of them, such as the United States, Britain, Russia, and China, are hickory branches as thick as your arm. That bundle won't break if it remains a bundle. Certainly Germany, Italy, and Japan can't break it — and if they try long enough, they will destroy themselves with trying.

The nations that go to make up this formidable bundle are called allies because they are formally bound together to wage war against the Axis. They have a common purpose, and on January 2, 1942, they signed a pledge in Washington, D.C., to make war in common and never to make a separate peace.

The common aim is not enough to make the nations into allies; there must be the formal agreement, the mutual pledges. In the First World War, for example, the United States entered the war against Germany, but it did not ally itself with

Britain, France, Russia, Japan, and Italy, who were already waging war against that country and its allies, Austria-Hungary, Bulgaria, and Turkey. The United States called itself an "Associated Power," a phrase that made quite clear that it was independent in action. That independence revealed itself sharply at the peace table. The war aims of the United States were not entirely the same as those of the nations by whose side it had fought, and so, of course, it wanted a different kind of peace treaty.

In this Second World War, however, the United States is a part of an alliance of twenty-six nations, and since it is potentially the most powerful member of the alliance, its co-operation with the other states is of the utmost importance. It must not only fight but give, and where and how it gives will have as much to do with failure or success as where or how it fights.

WHO ARE OUR ALLIES?

It is not at all easy to describe accurately our allies. Britain, China, and Russia have governments that are operating from their homelands in fighting the war. Czechoslovakia, Greece, Yugoslavia, Norway, and Poland are governments in exile; that is, governments of nations that have been conquered by Hitler and consequently are not in control of the homeland or of colonies. Some of our allies, like Costa Rica, can send neither men nor much other help overseas. It is important, however, that their harbors and airports be open to our forces and closed to those of Germany and Japan.

There are other governments which cannot be listed in any of these groups. There is the Netherlands, for example, which is a government in exile, since Hitler conquered Holland and forced the Queen and her Government to flee to England. But Holland is only the heart of the Netherlands; the other members remain free and are actively engaged in fighting the war, especially after it spread to the Pacific. Belgium likewise, defeated though it is in Europe, still exercises authority over its African possessions.

France as an ally is peculiarly difficult to define. The French Government officially recognized by the United States is at Vichy, France. That Government is, as it puts it, " collaborating " with Germany, our archenemy. Britain, our sworn ally, however, does not recognize the Vichy Government; instead it recognizes the government in exile of General Charles de Gaulle, which he calls the Government of Free France. Since some of the French colonies also recognize De Gaulle's government rather than that of Vichy, the diplomatic situation is almost impossibly confused. The De Gaulle government is an ally of Britain, but it is not officially an ally of the United States.

The British Dominions are important members of the alliance. Four of them having complete Dominion status — Canada, Australia, New Zealand, and the Union of South Africa — have authority to declare war by their own governments and to wage it independently. They are our full-fledged allies, not mere followers of the British Government in England. India and Burma, on the other hand, are not Dominions, but by the authority of Britain they are in the war, and they cannot be disregarded in the plans of the United States for full co-operation. The Irish Free State has insisted on remaining neutral and thus is not one of our allies.

After the Japanese attack on Pearl Harbor, all the Central American and Caribbean states declared war on Japan or Germany and Italy or all three. They too are our allies. The South American states — with the exception of Argentina and Chile — and Mexico have broken off diplomatic relations with the Axis Powers. Their resources are to be pooled with those of the United States for war purposes. Thus for all practical purposes, except in the actual waging of the war, they will have to be treated as if they were our allies. Their economic needs, as well as our own, must always be taken into consideration — and the need to protect the South American coastline from Axis attacks must never be forgotten. Treating the South American states as allies will enable the often proclaimed " hemisphere solidarity " to be maintained and strengthened.

NEEDS AND AIMS OF OUR ALLIES

China has been at war longer than any other of our allies. Since 1937, when Japan first launched its totally indefensible attack, China has stood up under a seemingly endless series of merciless assaults. It has lost most of its great cities and much of its rich coastal area. Its railroads are largely in Japanese control; its original industry has been either destroyed or seriously interrupted. It has retreated, but has never surrendered, though some of its great armies have been wiped out and untold numbers of its civilians slaughtered. China's one aim, of course, is the defeat of Japan, and with the aid of the allies it can defeat the aggressor country. China is rich in man power, but it needs planes and offensive weapons immediately. Given these, China can defend itself and also make an adequate return for them in its contribution to the general war effort.

When the Japanese made their attack on Pearl Harbor they instantly made their war with China a part of the war in the West. There were no longer two wars, the European war and the Sino-Japanese; there was only one war, the war that ringed the world. The two wars were definitely merged into one when Germany and Italy, in fulfillment of their obligations to Japan, declared war on the United States. China, in turn, declared war on the Axis. Then Japan attacked British and Netherlander territories in eastern Asia, which led to declarations of war from those two countries — and both of them were already at war with Japan's allies, Italy and Germany. It is obvious, therefore, that the contributions we may make to China must be decided upon with European problems constantly in mind.

Those European problems are pressing and overwhelmingly important; nevertheless, the Far East is of equally great importance to us, not only because it provides us with some of our essential raw materials, such as tin, rubber, hemp, and quinine, but also because for forty years we have followed a definite policy in regard to eastern Asia. We have insisted on the Open Door for trade — a trade, incidentally, very valuable to us — and we have sought to protect the integrity of some of the Far Eastern countries. We have no intention of changing those policies, as Japan has at last discovered.

A great many Americans were, to put it mildly, startled to find their country an ally of Russia, the Union of Socialist Soviet Republics. The United States (like Britain) was suspicious of Russia and its Communism, and Russia was equally suspicious of the United States and its capitalism. We resented intensely Russia's earlier efforts to spread Communism over the world, and it can be safely said that a very large number of Americans would have liked nothing better than to see Russia and Germany destroy each other. Yet our immediate aim is now the same as Russia's — the defeat of Germany — and we are allies. Through the Lend-Lease Act we have been sending aid to Russia, and we plan to continue sending it. Like China, Russia has adequate man power but inadequate supplies of munitions, and it is part of our job, at least, to make up the lack.

There was some resentment in the United States because Russia did not declare war on Japan after the attack on Pearl Harbor, but when the attack was made, the Germans were at the gates of Moscow, and Russia had all it could handle in the

West without taking on Japan too in the East. Russia's hostility toward Japan, however, is long-standing; its Eastern armies are still in position; and if the opportunity comes for it to settle its score with the Japanese, it is not very likely to let it slip by unused.

The Netherlanders in the East Indies need ships, planes, and munitions from us, but they need more; they need our Army and our Navy. We were co-operating with them even before we were a belligerent; we were selling them planes and other military equipment so that they might be better prepared to repel a Japanese attack. In return the Netherlanders gave us access to the vital raw materials of the East Indies. They also gave us base facilities in their American colony, Dutch Guiana.

The Netherlanders, having a government in action as well as a government in exile, pursue a double war aim. In the East they want to defeat the Japanese and retain their valuable Asian possessions; in the West they want to defeat Germany and regain their homeland. We, of course, are in sympathy with both aims and expect to aid in their attainment of both.

Britain, which is perhaps our major ally, has stood off the Germans and Italians and, with our help, expects to continue standing them off while taking on Japan too. Britain's empire is world-wide, and so for it the war is also world-wide. It has, as the orators like to say, been the bulwark against aggression; it has saved democracy from Fascist domination. True enough, but Great Britain has done what it has done primarily for the sake of preserving itself and its empire. There are Americans who feel that Britain's instinct for self-preservation is very selfish. They insist that Britain ought to be fighting and sacrificing and dying for something nobler than its own interests. One is inclined to ask sarcastically why America was at peace before the attack on Pearl Harbor. The nobler purpose existed, and we were quite capable of fighting for it.

To a degree, however, the sarcasm would be improper, because there is some justice in the condemnation of England's selfish course. Britain followed the weak policy known as " appeasement " before the war, and it continued to follow that policy in the Far East after the outbreak of the war in Europe. Britain made no move to lead the League of Nations into action against Japan when Manchuria was stolen from China in 1931–32. Britain shadowboxed with Italy over the conquest of Ethiopia, but backed down completely when Italy threatened war if oil sanctions were imposed against it. Britain established the policy of nonintervention which enabled the Fascist Franco, with German and Italian aid, to overthrow the Spanish Republic. Britain stood by idly when Hitler stole Austria, and — this, perhaps, above all — Britain weakly knuckled down to Hitler at Munich and permitted him to take over Czechoslovakia. Britain seemed to have a definite policy of sacrificing anyone in order to keep the British Empire out of difficulties. That policy offended many Americans deeply, and some of them still look with suspicion upon England as an ally.

Those people should examine the American policy. What did we do for China or Ethiopia or Austria or Czechoslovakia? We did nothing whatever, and we did nothing because we felt that it would be against our self-interest to do anything. We called our evasion of responsibility " minding our own business," and we called the British evasion of responsibility " criminal selfishness." After Pearl Harbor a good many Americans realized with a suddenness that was a shock that our own appeasement policy had hatched from its innocent-looking eggs the same kind of snakes that the British policy had hatched. At that moment the pot began to mute its criticism of the kettle. After all, they were both hopping over the same hot fire, and most Americans now realize clearly that if they don't hop together and in step, they are more than likely to find themselves not over the fire but *in* it.

Another argument commonly advanced against full co-operation with Britain is that if past history is to be trusted, Britain will gain undue spoils at the peace table. It is possible that it will. Britain is accustomed to making participation in wars as profitable as possible. But if we aren't capable of looking out for our own interests when peace comes, we can hardly expect Britain to look out for them for us. And even if, as some obstructionists maintain, this actually is a war of competing imperialisms, what essential difference does that fact — if it is a fact — make in the need for full co-operation? Britain certainly wants to save its empire, but we haven't gone to war to save it for Britain. We've gone to war because we must, and if victory for us means the salvation of the British Empire, we'll have little to complain about. We have lived at peace with Britain and its Dominions; we are never likely to live at peace with empires that are dominated by the Fascists.

Besides, Britain's record in its empire is better than the haters of Britain will admit. The Dominions are loyal enough to go to war when the mother country is attacked, and that loyalty hasn't grown out of injustice or tyranny. If the Dominions can give their faith to Britain, and the governments in exile can give it their faith, surely we can suspend our suspicion long enough at least to save ourselves with Britain's aid. Perhaps that statement is unduly sarcastic, but certainly our own record does not permit us properly to assume the holier-than-thou attitude that many of us are so fond of.

CO–OPERATION, AND WHAT DOES IT MEAN?

Co-operation, in the fullest sense of the word, is not simple to understand and is extremely difficult to attain. The Japanese, who frequently twist words out of their true meaning,

actually mean " dictation " when they speak of " co-operation " in their New Order policy. The Nazis, who are experts
at word-twisting, seek " co-operation " with the countries they
have conquered; that is, they hold a gun at the captive's head
or a lash over his back and snarl: " You do what I say or I'll
tear you apart. You *co-operate* — or else! "

True co-operation involves understanding by *both* parties
of the problem to be attacked, and willingness to act together
by *both* parties. Mere agreement on a certain action to realize
purposes defined by one of the parties is not enough. Agreement under such conditions hints at dictation, and even the
hint of dictation arouses distrust.

Since some of the parties to the co-operation under discussion at present are nations and some are governments in exile,
the assumption is that they have equal voice in the making of
decisions. There is among them, however, a great disparity in
power, and that means a great disparity in what they can contribute toward winning the war. The existence of the actual
disparity in the face of the theoretical equality makes the problem of co-operation extremely difficult and delicate. The
stronger Powers, especially the strongest Power, will have to
show almost infinite tact in dealing with the lesser Powers if
charges of dictation are not to be heard. Once such charges
are made, the necessary unity of purpose and action is bound
to be disrupted.

The United States at this moment is definitely the strongest
Power, and it will have to exercise the greatest tact. Under
any circumstances its power is potentially the greatest; but
under the present circumstances it is actually the greatest. It
has entered the war after much of the strength of the other
Powers has been dissipated in battle. Its war machine and its
industries are untouched, and, it must be remembered, they
are untouched partly because the other Powers have been

fighting. In one sense, those Powers have been co-operating before we felt the need for co-operation. China, for example, in standing off Japan since 1937 has made the Japan that attacked Pearl Harbor a far less formidable foe than it would have been if China had surrendered. If large bodies of Japanese troops were not now held in China by China's stubborn resistance, our difficulties, great as they are, would be far greater.

The British and Netherlander forces in the Far East have attempted to hold positions, such as Singapore and Surabaya, considered invaluable to us. Britain's defense of its islands and of North Africa, together with Russia's resistance to the German invasion, have made it possible for us to face the Axis in the West, not alone but with allies already strongly established in defensive positions. Our allies conserved our strength for us before they were our allies. They need our strength and need it badly, but their need should not be our excuse to attempt dictation. Neither should their experience and their losses justify them in any attempt to dictate to us. Dictation must be avoided. Equals must act together as equals.

Under these circumstances, we can most effectively co-operate with our allies by avoiding any attempt to determine how much of the war is ours and how much of it, or what part of it, is theirs. Problems will never be solved by any such method as that. The war must be looked upon by all members of the alliance as what it is, a total world war, which involves the maintenance of fronts in Europe, Asia, Africa, and possibly in both Americas. Each member, therefore, must devote its complete military and economic strength not only to the task of defeating its own particular enemy or enemies but also to that of defeating the Axis Powers viewed as one enemy. In other words, all the members must fight all the war with all their resources everywhere all the time.

Planning is necessary if this maximum strength is to be used with maximum effect — and planning demands organization. Mr. Churchill came to the United States in December, 1941, to initiate the planning and the creation of the necessary boards of strategy. Obviously, the grand strategy must be decided upon by the heads of the co-operating governments — in personal contact, so far as that is possible. The contact is possible only at intervals, and so the method used at Washington, Moscow, and Chungking, of heads of governments consulting with high representatives of the other governments, will have to be employed.

From the outset it will be of the utmost importance that all who are parties to the alliance shall be drawn responsibly into consultation — and that the consultants shall be as close as possible to the heads of their respective governments. Otherwise we shall suffer such embarrassments as that which occurred when the Free French occupied the islands of St. Pierre and Miquelon. Compulsion was immediately applied, especially by the United States, to cause a withdrawal, because the presence of the Free French in those islands interfered with plans of the allies of which the Free French, who are allies of Britain, apparently knew nothing. Finally, the consultants must be key persons in their home governments if the plans evolved are to be put into motion with adequate speed.

It must be recognized that the plans reached in general consultation will have to be executed individually by the member nations. If action is determined upon by a single nation before an agreement is reached with the other nations involved, it is naturally going to be both harder to reach the agreement and harder to put it into effect once it is reached. If, for example, Mr. T. V. Soong, the Chinese Minister for Foreign Affairs, should make his headquarters in Washington, if that is the place where the central planning is to be done, a general plan involving China is not so liable to be interfered with by plans made in China, and action is bound to be much faster than if Mr. Soong remains in Chungking and acts here through the Chinese Ambassador. There will be one less intermediary between Chiang Kai-shek and President Roosevelt. Similarly, since Mr. Churchill cannot himself be in Washington, it is fortunate that the British Ambassador is also a member of the British Cabinet, possessing both the information and the authority that a Cabinet position gives.

The central board will make plans, but the course of events will sometimes upset the plans and make new decisions necessary. The British, for example, had to allocate materials to Russia, though they needed those materials themselves and the loss of them weakened their forces in the Far East and in the Middle East. The loss had to be taken, however, because the front most in danger of immediate disaster had to be bolstered — and that was the Russian front. We ourselves bent before the power of circumstances even before we entered the war. We had to prevent the collapse of Britain as a fighting power, and so we gave it priority on our production over the needs and demands of our own forces.

Such situations will undoubtedly arise again, but, forced decisions aside, we shall have to balance the needs of China for arms and reinforcements against those of Russia, of Britain and the Netherlands against our own. True co-operation will require that each nation offer only tentative demands for aid, and that the final decision of what aid is given to each claimant be made by the central board. Each nation will understand its own needs, but it will not know of the needs of others until the board meets and the claims of all are presented. If America, which will do most of the giving, attempts to make the decisions, there is sure to be dissatisfaction, and the accusation of dictation is sure to be made. The dissatisfaction would be bad for both morale and co-operation, but even worse from our point of view would be the responsibility put on our shoulders for the failure of individual nations.

SPECIFIC PROBLEMS

One of the most immediate problems that must be solved is the allocation of shipping. In this war, as in the last one, transport is one of the greatest difficulties in the way of carrying the war to a successful conclusion. The demands on shipping are bound to become heavier and heavier. Men, supplies, and munitions must be shipped to all parts of the world — and at present there aren't enough ships available to meet the pressing need. A general shipping plan will have to be made, and tonnage allocated where it will do the most good.

The problem can be solved co-operatively in either of two ways: All the tonnage available can be pooled under the control of a board composed of representatives of all the nations contributing tonnage, or of representatives of all the allies; or each nation can retain control of its own tonnage, allocating such surpluses as may be available after its own estimated needs have been met. This surplus tonnage could then be employed under the authority of a common agency. Of course, if the second method were employed Britain and the United States, the two great shipping Powers, would have to cut their own needs to the bone in order to free ships for the general war effort, which involves transporting large bodies of men and immense quantities of materials over tremendous distances. At present negotiations are under way between competent British authorities and the United States Maritime Commission to find the most satisfactory method of making the most efficient use of the shipping available.

Winning the war also requires the total use of the productive capacity (agricultural as well as industrial) of all of the United

Nations. This requires the pooling of all resources and their allocation for war purposes according to a common plan. Canada and the United States had reached agreements for the co-ordination of production even before the United States entered the war. Britain and America have more recently established a co-ordinated supply service, together with a joint advisory council of military men to plan allocation of war materials. Decisions taken at the conference at Rio de Janeiro look toward a pooling of the productive resources of the American states. Thus co-operation in the industrial effort necessary for the winning of the war has been instituted.

In the general military effort, American co-operation requires that its full military, naval, and air power be used in concert with that of the other United Nations. Unified commands in the various theaters of war have already been established. At the conferences held in Washington it was decided to establish unified naval commands in the North and South Atlantic. There, and in conferences held at Chungking, a similar decision was made for the area comprising eastern and southeastern Asia. The British General Sir Archibald Wavell was selected as the Commander in Chief of land and naval operations in the entire area. An American, Major General George H. Brett, was made Deputy Commander in Chief. All naval forces in the area were first placed under the command of an American, Admiral Thomas C. Hart, presently succeeded by a Netherlander. All forces operating in China are to be under the command of Generalissimo Chiang Kai-shek. Netherlander and Australian claims to a share in the direction of the military effort have been advanced, and are being met.

The problem of co-operation with those of our allies whose territories have been occupied completely by Germany and Italy is, of course, practically unsolvable. We can't give supplies to the conquered peoples; but we can help them to keep up their morale. If the governments in exile are treated as true allies, their people at home will realize that they still have a government — a government with powerful friends. We can help these exiled governments in their propaganda activities, and we can also help to arm their small forces that have escaped the conqueror. Poland, for example, has a real little army still actively engaged in the war, and a larger one training in Russia for action on the Russian front. And above all, for their present and future morale we can co-operate with them and permit them to co-operate with us in the formulation of peace aims. Such co-operation is their right. No one is more closely concerned with those aims than they are.

These plans have already been put in motion. On January 2, 1942, twenty-six nations signed the pledge to make the war and the peace in common. They accepted as the basis for the peace the Atlantic Charter,[1] as it had been written and proclaimed by Prime Minister Churchill and President Roosevelt. The Declaration of the United Nations [1] gives to all these nations the assurance of American co-operation in the establishment of a satisfactory peace as well as in winning the war. For the governments in exile, in particular, it gives assurance of American co-operation in their restoration to their respective countries. For them, as well as for the other United Nations, it gives assurance that the United States will co-operate until totalitarianism throughout the world has been destroyed, and in its place the four freedoms have been established — the freedom of speech, the freedom of the press, the freedom of religion, and the freedom of the seas.

[1] Reprinted in Chapter XIX.

VIII. What are the farmers doing to help the war effort?

CLAUDE R. WICKARD

Claude R. Wickard was an Indiana dirt farmer well known in agricultural circles long before he was made first Undersecretary then Secretary of Agriculture (September, 1941). The man in control of agricultural production now has been saying ever since the beginning of the war 'Food will win the war and write the peace.'

Eager to do their part in helping to win the war, the farmers of the United States are tackling the biggest job ever placed before the farmers of any nation. As this is written, some forty-five days after Pearl Harbor, it is doubtful if anyone fully appreciates the size of the task which lies ahead of the nation's food-producers. The job has grown so rapidly and to such tremendous size that it is almost beyond imagination.

In less than one year's time, the major problem of American farmers did a complete about-face. At the beginning of 1941 farmers were asking " Where can we sell what we're able to produce? " By the beginning of 1942 the problem was " How can we produce enough to meet the needs? " Farmers individually are only beginning to realize the complete change in the situation, and even the best-informed person cannot do more than guess at the size of the demand for American farm products before the Second World War is over.

Specifically, the job of the American farmers is to produce enough food and fiber and forest products for the armed forces and the civilians of the United States; for the feeding of a large percentage of the population of the United Kingdom; for some of the food needs of the Russian people; and for others among our allies.

Without minimizing the importance of wool, tobacco, cotton, leather, wood, rosin, and other nonfood crops, it is safe to say that the most important job of the farmers is to produce food. It has been said many times that this war, any modern war, is a war of production. Victory will go to the side which produces most abundantly of the things that it takes to win wars, and delivers them where they are needed. It takes planes and tanks and guns and ships, of course; and it also takes food, tremendous quantities of food. Food is just as much a munition as gunpowder, time fuses, oil, or steel. If one side has enough food while the other is reduced in food supply, the side with plenty of food has a tremendous advantage.

Hitler has kept up the health and strength of his armed forces and workers by draining off the food supplies of the nations he has conquered. The fighters are always well fed; workers in the industries essential to winning the war receive more food than other civilians. In the countries which Hitler's armies have enslaved, food is used as a means of forcing production of important war goods; the workers in these industries receive extra food, while those in other parts of the country, or in relatively unimportant work, are reduced in their food supply and driven to eat foods they would ordinarily scorn. An increase in tuberculosis and the so-called deficiency diseases is reported from many countries; people are staying in bed an hour or two longer each day, in order to conserve their strength. We hear of people in a given area being deliberately starved of minerals and vitamins so that their resistance will be weakened in order that their German overlords can better control them.

The efficiency of the Axis war machine in Europe is maintained by using food supplies as skillfully as men and guns and planes and tanks are used. The supply of food is so small that it must be used skillfully if the greedy, grasping aims of the Nazis are to be served. The actual and potential food resources of the United Nations are much larger, which gives our forces a definite advantage; but these larger supplies must be used with equal skill. Furthermore, the food-producing plants of the United Nations must be made even more productive, and the food must be distributed in such a way that there will be no shortage at any place.

GRAND STRATEGY IN FOOD

When the grand strategy of the United Nations is completely worked out, the armies and navies of all the nations will be directed as one fighting force, each element doing the part assigned to it in the total, world-wide plan of war. The supplies of the nations, too, will be shared, and those which have more than is required will share with those which have less. That means food as well as actual armaments. The United States, having probably the greatest capacity for producing food, must be ready to share food with the nations fighting by our side, to bolster their diets and make them more effective fighters and producers. We have no way of knowing how great the demand may become, but we do know that as shipping facilities become available there will be need for all the food American farmers can produce.

Every nation, of course, meets some of its own food needs, but it also depends upon other nations for certain foods. England, for example, produced only a little more than enough for one-third of its food needs before the outbreak of the war in 1939; it depended upon the continent of Europe for much of its dairy products, bacon, eggs, and vegetables, while its grain and beef came from all parts of the world. During the war, production at home has increased somewhat, and the intake of food has come down, but even so fully half the food eaten by the people of England must be shipped across at least one ocean.

The story of how the United States has helped to fill the gaps in the food needs of the people of England is one of the most dramatic episodes of the war thus far; but it may be overshadowed by the work yet to be done.

The United States, while producing supplies of many foods beyond the demands of our own people, also imports many other foods which are not produced in this country, or which are produced in amounts below our needs. All our coffee and cocoa for example, are imported; much of our sugar and a substantial portion of our vegetable fats and oils are brought in from other countries. Some of these commodities come from war zones, and the supply may be cut off, or at least seriously reduced; American farmers must change their production to fill the gaps, in order that our own people may have plenty of food to keep up health and strength. Beyond that, if American farmers are to make their proper contribution to the food supply of the United Nations, there must be increases in the production of some important foods here in the United States. The total job of producing the foods that will be essential in 1942 and in later years looms as a tremendous task for the farmers of this country.

Before looking at the details of the job ahead, it might be helpful to consider the agricultural situation in general, and some of the problems agriculture has faced in the last quarter-century.

WHY AMERICAN AGRICULTURE CAN PRODUCE

We are lucky in this country that we still have a great deal of fertile soil, though we have wasted soil prodigally until recent years. More than a billion acres of land are included in the 6 million farms of the nation. Of this billion acres of land, about 340 million acres ordinarily have been used in recent years to produce crops; the rest is in grass or trees, although more than 130 million acres of the grassland can be plowed if necessary.

With such a wide range in temperatures and rainfall as exists in the United States, the nation's farmers can produce many different crops and produce them well. We have claimed to be the best-fed nation on earth. It is true that much improvement still needs to be made in the nutrition of large numbers of the American people, but on the whole we've had plenty to eat. If we haven't eaten the right things, it's a result of three influences: poor eating habits, not knowing what to eat, and, with many people, being unable to afford the kinds of food which make for good nutrition.

EACH REGION HELPS FEED US

Each part of the country makes its contribution to our national supply of agricultural products. The Northeast produces large amounts of milk, eggs, fruits, and vegetables; the Southeast is important for cotton and cottonseed, tobacco, and peanuts; the middle section of the country is called the Corn Belt, and here are raised the bulk of the nation's hogs; a large share of the beef cattle raised on the grasses of the plains of the West receive a fattening finish on Midwestern corn. Out of the Middle West, too, comes the great share of the nation's butter, cheese, evaporated milk, and other dairy products, and a good share of our egg supply. Wheat and beef cattle are important contributions of the prairie and mountain states, ranging from the Dakotas south to Texas, and west to the Coastal Range. In the irrigated lands of the Far West are produced much of the nation's fruits and vegetables. The Gulf and Southwestern states provide us with oranges, lemons, and grapefruit. Milk, eggs, vegetables, fruits, meats, and feed crops are produced to some extent all over the United States, some for use only in the local areas, some for shipment to other parts of the country.

It's a big food-producing plant, the farm land of America. The 6 million farms range in size from the small part-time poultry farm of a factory worker in New England to a tremendous wheat farm covering thousands of acres of Kansas plain, to Texas cattle ranches measured in hundreds of thousands of acres.

On the nation's farms live about 30 million men, women, and children. Taken together, they form probably the most skillful group of farm operators in the world. In the eighteenth century, four-fifths of the people in America had to live on farms to produce enough food for themselves and for the other one-fifth of the population. But improvements in farm machinery and farming methods have increased the efficiency of farming so that less than one-fourth of the population now can provide food for itself, food for the other three-fourths, and a large surplus for export. The farmers of America have 1.8 million tractors, replacing several times that number of horses and mules, thus making it possible to use millions of acres of land for production of human food instead of animal feed.

PUBLIC AID TO FARM RESEARCH

The people of the United States decided many years ago that the farm producers of the nation should be given help in

improving their farming methods, and so the Department of
Agriculture was created, in 1862. In the same year, a system
of agricultural colleges, one in each state, was established.
These are known as Land Grant Colleges because Federally
owned land was given the states as an aid in starting them.
Later, a system of agricultural experiment stations was attached to the Land Grant Colleges, to supplement the work of
the Department of Agriculture in developing better varieties
of crops, finding better fertilizers and ways of using them,
ways of controlling insects and diseases, better methods of
feeding livestock and poultry, plans of breeding for more efficient production of livestock products. Just before the
First World War, Federal aid was given for an educational
system known as the Extension Service, which takes the latest
developments in scientific agriculture to the farm people, and
educates and informs them on all the public farm programs.

With the advances in agricultural science, the output of each
person on the farms gradually increased, so that the nation
could be fed and clothed by a smaller proportion of its people.

During the First World War, the United States had to assume the task of feeding the Allied nations. Farmers plowed
up some 30 million acres of new land and seeded it to wheat
and other crops. We fed the Allies, but soon after the war
ended, our food was no longer needed abroad, and this nation
had a food-producing plant that had been expanded beyond
the needs of this country; or at least, it had been expanded to
the point where it could produce more food than the people of
this nation could buy at prices fair to the producers. Prices
for farm products dropped suddenly to very low levels, and
many farmers, having bought land and equipment at high
prices, eventually were forced into bankruptcy.

All during the 1920's farmers had to take low prices for the
things they produced, while the things they bought sold at

high prices. The general business depression which started in 1929 dropped prices of almost everything down to low levels; although prices of things farmers bought fell rather sharply, prices of farm products fell even lower.

THE NEW DEAL IN AGRICULTURE

The New Deal of President Franklin D. Roosevelt set out to revive the nation's entire economic system. The job of aiding agriculture was assumed by Henry A. Wallace, who was appointed Secretary of Agriculture in 1933; he held that office until 1940, shortly before he was elected Vice-President.

The New Deal for agriculture had several objectives. One was to adjust the production of agricultural commodities to domestic consumption and actual requirements of foreign markets. A steel mill, controlled by a small organization of officers, produced only enough steel to fill its orders; if less steel was needed, the plant produced less steel, and fewer men had jobs. But more than 6 million food-producing plants operating independently could not adjust their production up or down to meet the demand with nearly as much flexibility as a steel mill. Some means needed to be found to enable operators of these food-producing plants to work together; if it could be made profitable for farmers to adjust their production, then agricultural production might be guided to meet the needs of the nation, and farmers might be aided in getting prices which would provide a fair return for their labor and investment. The best means of developing this sort of program was through the Federal Government. To accomplish this objective, the Agricultural Adjustment program was started, and approximately 90 per cent of the nation's farmers have taken part in it ever since.

The price objective for agriculture, as established by Congress, is calculated not in actual dollars and cents, which vary in the amounts they can buy, but in terms of purchasing power of farm goods. The desirable purchasing power of agricultural commodities is called " parity." When a bushel of wheat or a pound of cotton will purchase as much of things farmers buy as it would during a base period (usually 1910 to 1914), the price is at parity. Purchasing power below or above parity is figured in terms of percentage of parity. The price-maintaining efforts of the national farm programs are based on parity for agricultural commodities.

Another objective of the New Deal for agriculture was to put a halt to the erosion of land by wind and water. Under the agricultural conservation program, 30 million acres of land have been taken out of crops which tend to wear out the soil quickly; another 29 million acres have been protected against erosion by contour cultivation, listing, strip-cropping, or other practices; farmers built 55,000 miles of terraces in a single year to keep the soil in place, and in the same year seeded 41 million acres of new legumes and grasses.

Many people living on farms needed assistance in becoming skilled farmers and in getting the equipment to make a satisfactory living; a new branch of the Federal Government came into being to help these people become self-supporting, through loans of money, through information and guidance on better farming and homemaking methods, through co-operative medical aid, and through other types of assistance. The agency to do this is the Farm Security Administration.

In the 1930's the United States was a nation which had so much food that many farmers were " going broke " as a result of low prices; and at the same time millions of town and city people were hungry because of reduced purchasing power. To help correct this situation, a government organization was established to purchase food from the farmers and aid in its distribution to needy families. This agency, the Surplus Marketing Administration, developed the Food Stamp Plan, and aided in a program providing hot lunches to school children.

Remembering the story of Joseph in the Bible, and how he stored up reserves of food and feed during the seven good years in order that the people of Egypt might have enough to eat during the seven lean years, after the droughts of 1934 and 1936 Secretary Wallace urged Congress to establish what he called the Ever Normal Granary. By this plan, in years of big crops the Government loans money to farmers on their crops at a rate which is established by Congress. The crops are stored and if the farmer wants to take back his crops, he pays off the loan. If he does not care to do so, the corn, wheat, cotton, or other crop becomes the property of the Government. This reserve of farm products in storage may be put on the market by the Government at any time; it is a national asset in time of emergency.

Further details of the national farm program could be given, but the important thing to keep in mind is that from 1933 to the present, during the years of the general economic depression, farmers worked together and with the Federal Government to develop a national farm program that would (1) conserve the soil; (2) take the products of the farms to a larger number of people who needed food most; (3) make more efficient producers out of low-income farm families; and (4) adjust agricultural production to demand in order that farmers might receive fair prices.

THE LEND-LEASE ACT

For years, farmers had produced abundantly, for markets at home and abroad. The outbreak of war in Europe in 1939 cut off the market for tobacco, cotton, wheat, apples, pork products, and many other commodities which American farmers ordinarily sold in England, France, Germany, and other countries of Europe. For a year and a half, it seemed that American farmers would have very few customers outside this country. Then in March, 1941, the Lend-Lease Act was passed, making possible the shipment of goods to Britain and to other nations. The British wanted not only planes, guns, and other weapons, but also American food, to fill the gaps in their diet. At first, the British requests for food through the Lend-Lease arrangement looked like merely a new and welcome market for American farm products already produced or well within the limits of the producing ability of American farmers. But it so happened that the things the British needed most from the United States were commodities in which we have not had an overly abundant supply. The things most desired were meat, cheese, evaporated milk, eggs, and some vegetables and fruits. If the British needs were to be met without reducing the supply of these foods for home use, farmers would have to produce much more of these things.

The Department of Agriculture was given the job of buying the needed food supplies and seeing that they were assembled at seaport warehouses, ready for shipment to Britain as space was available in the boats. The surest way to get increased production of any farm product is to offer a price that will make it more profitable for farmers to produce that commodity than to produce something else; so under authorization by Congress the Department of Agriculture offered to buy pork, cheese, evaporated milk, dry skim milk, eggs — both fresh and dried — and chickens at prices which would ensure farmers against taking a loss if they produced more.

At the same time, the supplies of corn in the Ever Normal Granary were offered for sale at prices which would make it worth while for farmers to feed their pigs, dairy cows, and chickens generously, and thus increase the total production of pork, milk, and eggs. Without the reserves of feed in the Ever

Normal Granary the prices could not have been kept to such reasonable levels. If both these things — supporting minimum prices for the food products and keeping moderate prices of feed — had not been done, American farmers might not have been able to produce enough of the important foods in 1941. But actually the production of eggs and milk reached new records in that year, and the total production of all agricultural commodities was the highest in the history of the nation. So great was the production of American farms that a million long tons (2,240 pounds each) of concentrated American food were unloaded in Britain before Christmas of 1941, and at the same time the American people had more food to eat than they had consumed for years.

PRODUCTION GOALS

During the greater part of 1941 the American farmer had the job of producing to meet the needs of the United States and Britain. The British needs for food are great, and their requests for American food have increased from time to time. It became apparent that even the high rate of American farm production would not be great enough in all commodities to meet the combined needs. So some of the staff members of the Department of Agriculture set to work during the summer of 1941 to calculate as exactly as possible how much of each important farm product the United States should produce in 1942 in order to meet all the needs. They took into account the needs of both the United States and Britain, and the limited amounts that could be sold through regular export channels, and then they added another item: a reserve supply to be used after the war to feed the hungry peoples of Europe. The figures were totaled, and estimates were made as to how many acres and how many animals would be needed.

The goals established in September, 1941, called for increases in the production of milk, eggs, pork, and vegetables, so that there might be enough to meet the British needs without reducing our own supply. It seemed that we had enough tobacco, wheat, and cotton on hand, so the acreage of these crops could be held down to a very low level, even below 1941 production. It seemed that we would need no increase in the acreage of corn or other feed grains. However, it would be advisable to produce more peanuts and soybeans for oil, just in case something happened to reduce the amount of oil that could be imported. It looked like a rather difficult job, but a canvass of farmers over the nation showed that farmers felt they could meet the goals.

Then came Pearl Harbor, and the United States was plunged into war. Soon came the alliance of the twenty-six United Nations, and it was obvious that American farmers could no longer plan for production to meet the needs of only two nations; there might be needs to be met in many nations. So the original production goals were reviewed carefully, and many of them were revised. Needless to say, all revisions were in an upward direction. In some instances — milk, for example — it seemed that the goal set in September, 1941, was as high as could be achieved, and so there would be little point in asking farmers to shoot at a mark beyond their reach. But many other commodity goals were raised sharply in the light of the new situation brought on by the war.

The production goals for 1942 constitute a blueprint of what farmers are doing to help win the war. Reaching these goals is the way in which the farmers of this nation can use their producing ability to meet the needs of the United Nations. A summary of the goals may not reveal to the person unfamiliar with agriculture just how big a job the farmers are undertaking, but to anyone who has lived on a farm they represent a tremendous task. Compared with 1941, milk pro-

OUR FOOD PRODUCTION

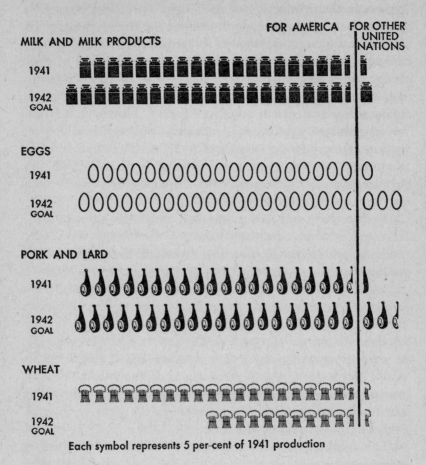

FOR AMERICA | FOR OTHER UNITED NATIONS

MILK AND MILK PRODUCTS

1941

1942 GOAL

EGGS

1941

1942 GOAL

PORK AND LARD

1941

1942 GOAL

WHEAT

1941

1942 GOAL

Each symbol represents 5 per-cent of 1941 production

PICTOGRAPH CORPORATION

The third year of the Second World War finds American farmers preparing to produce the biggest crops in their history. To an increased home demand has been added the responsibility of providing much food to Great Britain and others of the United Nations. Notwithstanding increased export needs, more food will be available for home consumption.

duction needs to be increased by 7 per cent, with only 3 per cent more cows to produce the milk; egg production needs to be raised by 11 per cent, so America's hens will produce 4 billion dozen eggs in 1942. We shall need more egg-drying plants, and more cheesemaking equipment, and more milk-evaporating and milk-drying plants, to handle the milk and eggs.

Hog-raisers can increase their production rather quickly, and it is reasonable to expect that they will be able to market 14 per cent more hogs in 1942, bringing their marketings to 83 million head. Cattle production moves much more slowly, and beef-producers are being asked to market more animals rather than to increase the production of calves.

During the fall months the demand for tobacco increased, and shortages of long-staple cotton developed, so, in spite of the fact that the nation has large quantities of cotton and tobacco on hand, moderate increases over the 1941 levels in the acreage of cotton and tobacco are anticipated in the 1942 goals. We are asking increases in the acreage of peanuts to two and a half times the 1941 acreage, and in soybeans to a planting 54 per cent greater than last year. The acreage of flaxseed also should be increased by 34 per cent, to help make up for the loss of oil imports ordinarily received from the South Pacific and other areas involved in the war.

One major food commodity in which the United States has been far from self-sufficient is sugar. Ordinarily, cane and beet growers in the United States proper produce only about one-third of our total requirements for sugar; the rest must be brought from offshore areas, some of which are involved in war and will be unable to supply much, if any, sugar in 1942. Part of the offshore sugar production is needed to make industrial alcohol for war purposes; and out of the sugar available, we shall share with Britain, Russia, and others of the United Na-

tions.   Sugar-growers in this country are being offered induce-
ments to increase their acreage of sugar beets and cane, but the
increase that can be expected from home production will not
be great enough to make up for the loss of sugar from outside
the continental United States.   In a few words, it seems that
sugar is one food which is going to be scarce, as compared with
our normal supply, during 1942 and perhaps afterward.   However, the amounts available per capita are ample and then some
— for health and strength, even if not for humoring the national
sweet tooth.

Canned tomatoes and canned peas are important in plans for
food production during 1942, and canners and growers are being asked to turn out 32 per cent more canned peas and 18 per
cent more canned tomatoes than last year.   Dried peas and dry
beans are two other crops scheduled for important increases.

All in all, farmers are being asked to produce more of every
commodity except wheat.

CAN FARMERS DO THE JOB?

It is fair to ask " Can farmers do the job? "   It's a tremendous task, and farmers themselves know it.   The resources of
the Department of Agriculture are being used to give every
possible assistance in meeting the production goals that have
been set.   Farmers are assured of a fair return on most of the
important commodities, by government promises to buy the
produce at stated prices or to loan money at rates which have
been announced to farmers.   We will do all we can to keep
feed prices at moderate levels, for abundant production of
livestock, dairy, and poultry products is impossible without
ample supplies of feed at reasonable cost.

But there are many handicaps in the way of boosting production as far as is necessary.   For one thing, many farmers'
sons and hired men already have been taken into the Army or

the Navy or into defense industries, and even more will go during 1942. This means that the farmers will have to look elsewhere for labor. Some of the work probably will need to be done by women and boys. During 1941, high-school boys in many areas did part of the work of harvesting crops. All prospective farm workers are being asked to register with the local offices of the United States Employment Service. It is our hope that the supply of available farm labor will include many high-school boys who are able-bodied and anxious to be of service, but are too young for military duty or for work in industry. There can be no more healthful type of employment, and no work that will be more useful to the nation.

The public services can give some help by these and other expedients. But ultimately, the extra man power which will be needed to replace the draft of the armed services and the war industries on farm labor will come mainly from longer hours for the farm family itself. And a lot of the man power will be woman power. The farm wives and daughters in this war, as in every major war, will be called on for some of the greatest of the personal sacrifices that are asked of citizens. The women of the farm household will have to carry on their usual home-making job under the handicaps of smaller supplies of materials and gadgets than in peacetime; and on top of that they will have to do a lot of work in the field and the barnyard normally done by the men who are no longer available. Additionally, they will be expected to help the family keep up morale by providing for family good times in the place of the commercial recreation for which they won't have time (or automobile tires to travel on). Farm women, legions of them, will be among the heroines of this war. I hope they won't go unsung. It seems to me our press and radio operators might make a special effort to report to us the achievements of this key group on the home front of the war.

War industries need steel and other metals, and so the supply of new farm machinery will be much smaller than farmers would like to have. They'll have to keep their present machinery in good working condition, and perhaps exchange equipment among themselves in some instances. War industries need some of the same chemicals that are used in fertilizers and in spray materials to control insect and disease pests. This will tend to reduce the average yield of some crops, unless farmers can make up for it by the use of legumes, cover crops, animal manures, and more thorough cultivation. The shortages of rubber for tires of tractors and trucks may offer some handicaps, and certainly farmers are going to be inconvenienced by the shortage of burlap to make feed bags.

The needs of the farmers for materials to increase their production are presented to government agencies having charge of supplies for wartime production by a branch of the Department of Agriculture. In fact, the entire department is organized on a wartime basis, with a United States Department of Agriculture War Board in every state and every county, composed of men from all the branches of the department and co-operating agencies. These War Boards will administer the many phases of the public farm program with the purpose first of all of helping farmers reach the production goals.

HOME FOOD PRODUCTION AND CONSERVATION

There are many things that individual families, in cities and on the farm, can do to aid in making food count most for victory. Farm people, as a rule, can do more to provide their own year-round food supply than city people, because producing food is their business. They have the land and the "know-how." It is the hope of the Department of Agriculture that 1.3 million more farm families will plant home vegetable gardens in 1942, and that the food which cannot be consumed fresh will be stored, canned, dried, or otherwise preserved for use during the winter.

Food produced and preserved at home does not need to be transported, and transportation may become one of the bottlenecks in the war effort; home-produced food does not drain the supply of tin, one of the exceedingly scarce metals; and it does not require the facilities of canning plants, which probably will be taxed to the limit during the production season.

There is nothing in the food-supply situation to warrant a hysterical campaign for city home gardens, which might result in plowing up lawns, parks, and athletic fields for growing vegetables. Commercial vegetable production for fresh consumption and for canning is to be expanded to meet the needs of the American people and to fill the ships with as many canned vegetables as they will be able to carry.

School and community gardens may be important contributions to the food supply for such things as hot lunches for school children and relief distribution. But gardening projects of this type need to be carefully and thoroughly planned to provide the foods that can be used to best advantage; and the garden needs to be supervised by a competent and experienced person, so every ounce of seed and every pound of fertilizer and every hour of labor results in the greatest possible production of food.

The national supply of seeds will be adequate but not overly abundant; fertilizers, especially nitrogen sources, will be limited in supply; new tools will be relatively scarce. In short, these materials which are needed to produce vegetables should be used where they will do the most good, and this means on good soil and in the hands of experienced farmers or suburban gardeners.

Urban homemakers may find it to their advantage to buy fresh vegetables and fruits when the supply is plentiful and the price is low, and preserve them at home, when it can be done successfully.

By using fresh vegetables when they are in season, dry beans and peas, cured and smoked meats instead of canned meats, and other foods which are not packed in tin, every family can help overcome shortages of that critical metal, tin, and make it possible for a larger share of foods packed in tin to go into shipments to our armed forces and to our allies.

IT WON'T BE EASY

The United States is fortunate that it has on its farms a group of nearly 30,000,000 men, women, and children who are accustomed to difficulties, who are used to working hard, and who are firm believers in the American way of life, the thing for which we are fighting. As has been noted their job of producing more farm products than ever have been turned out in the history of this country will not be easy. The farm people know this; they know it will mean longer hours, harder work, and hardships and sacrifices on the part of every individual. But the 6,000,000 American farm families undertake the task, asking for nothing more than the co-operation of every other group of American citizens, and a fair break from the weather man.

IX. How are we organizing our industrial machine to outproduce the enemy?

ALVIN E. DODD

Alvin E. Dodd is president of the American Management Association, an organization that exists to make possible an interchange of information on management problems among many of the leading companies of American industry. He was the organizer and first head of the Distribution Department of the United States Chamber of Commerce. Following that he was assistant to the president of Sears, Roebuck and Company and later vice-president in charge of merchandising of the Kroger Grocery and Baking Company. As chief executive of the American Management Association, Mr. Dodd is in touch with hundreds of business executives throughout the United States and Europe.

In America we have used our machines well. Our standard of living, in terms of useful articles and luxuries in the hands of the average citizen, is higher than that of any other nation. For example, compare our standard of living with that of average European countries. According to figures prepared before the war, the number of people per motor vehicle in the United States is 5; in France, 22; in England, 23; in Italy, 109; in Poland, 1,284. The number of people per radio in the United States is 5; in Denmark, 6; in the United Kingdom, 7; in

Russia, 90; in Bulgaria, 354. The number of people per telephone in the United States is 8; in Denmark, 10; in the United Kingdom, 20; in France, 33; in Russia, 200. In many countries the electric refrigerator is a rare thing, an electric washing machine a wonder to behold; many simple devices about which we do not think twice are either unkown or can be possessed only by the wealthy.

Yes, the American economy was built to make living good. We have been a peaceful nation that has made large use of our resources, our technical knowledge, and our machines — for peacetime goods. How was it possible to do this? Because in America men are free — free to work and to live as they please. But now this freedom is threatened.

WE FACE MACHINE WARFARE

The German Army, the world realizes, is no ordinary army that fights from trenches and from behind barbed wire in the fashion of the First World War. This army moves. This army *rolls. It is an army of machines.* It strikes swift, stunning, punishing blows and strikes again before the adversary can recover. It has stabbed like a chain of lightning through the peaceful cities and countryside of Europe, leaving smoking destruction and dead men behind.

Here was a machine with which to kill and destroy. A machine of deadly efficiency, for the Nazis had built it well. Each well-oiled part performed smoothly under the direction of its overseer-soldiers. It seemed unconquerable. But it would have to be conquered, and until it was, the normal ways of life would have to be suspended.

We too had to build a war machine, one greater and more efficient than any that existed. We had to start turning the vast stream of energy that we were putting into the manufacture of peacetime goods into the manufacture of munitions.

OUR STEEL INDUSTRY
OUTPRODUCES THE ENEMY

U. S. A.

GERMANY
AND CONQUERED COUNTRIES

U. S. S. R.

GREAT BRITAIN

REST
OF WORLD

Each ladle represents 10 million tons of ingot capacity

PICTOGRAPH CORPORATION

In steel, America leads all others. But while Germany has for years gone " all-out " for war, America's steel was largely used for machines of peace, everything from automobiles and houses to cans. Even in 1941 hardly one out of every four tons of steel was used for war purposes. Can we produce enough of this basic war metal to fill our military needs as well as those of the United Nations?

What did we need? Principally these things: airplanes, airplane engines, heavy guns, light guns, trench mortars, tanks, shells, machine guns, automatic rifles, regular rifles, rifle ammunition, fighting ships, merchant ships, camps and cantonments, airplane factories, tank factories, smokeless-powder factories, trucks, shell-loading factories.

The President himself in his message to Congress on the State of the Union on January 6, 1942, outlined our program as follows:

To increase our production rate of airplanes so rapidly that this year, 1942, we shall produce 60,000 planes, 10,000 more than the goal set a year and a half ago. This includes 45,000 combat planes — bombers, dive bombers, pursuit planes. The rate of increase will be continued, so that next year, 1943, we shall produce 125,000 airplanes, including 100,000 combat planes.

To increase our production rate of tanks so rapidly that in this year, 1942, we shall produce 45,000 tanks; and to continue that increase so that next year, 1943, we shall produce 75,000 tanks.

To increase our production rate of antiaircraft guns so rapidly that in this year, 1942, we shall produce 20,000 of them; and to continue that increase so that next year, 1943, we shall produce 35,000 antiaircraft guns.

To increase our production rate of merchant ships so rapidly that in this year, 1942, we shall build 8,000,000 deadweight tons, as compared with a 1941 production of 1,100,000. We shall continue that increase so that next year, 1943, we shall build 10,000,000 tons.

WHAT HAD TO BE DONE

We faced many problems, too many to be even listed in the brief space of this chapter. But let us consider the most important of them.

Our enemies had a head start — a big one. While we had been making peacetime goods, for years they had been busily manufacturing munitions. Further, the United States had no munitions industry as such. After the First World War we scrapped most of our munition plants. We believed there was no need for them. The reaction against war that followed 1917–18 would not permit their existence, and taxpayers did not want to support them. But virtually every European Power had a munitions industry — France, Germany, Czecho-slovakia, Britain — and all these industries, with the exception of those in England, ultimately fell to Germany to become new sources of supply for its war machine.

The need to create this multi-billion-dollar war industry in the quickest possible time led to another problem — shortages. These shortages have taken two main forms. First, there were shortages in needed materials. America is rich in natural re-sources and has developed great industries with which to ex-tract them from the earth, the forest, the fields, and the seas. But the demands of the munitions program are so great that even these resources are being taxed. Then there are certain key materials which are required in the manufacture of nearly all munitions, such as copper, steel, zinc, and lead. Then other materials which do not abound on this continent must be im-ported, and certain imports have been cut off — for example, rubber, aluminum (bauxite), and hemp.

Second, we faced shortages in skilled labor. America has a potential working population of roughly 49,000,000 people. This is our real power, and the fact is better appreciated when it is realized that the entire population of England is only 46,-000,000; that of France, 39,000,000; that of Germany, without its captive populations, 70,000,000. But, again, so great are the demands of this war program that even this vast reservoir of workers is being drained. It has been estimated that for every soldier on the firing line we must have sixteen workers in the factories.

Third, we had to organize business for war. American industry, despite its great power to produce, is not a simple organization. It sprawls throughout the length and breadth of the land and includes tiny machine shops in little villages and great factories covering several city blocks. To bring all this power to bear upon the production of munitions, to use all the muscles in the body of this giant, these factories and shops must be organized, and all made to take a part in the one great effort.

Fourth, America needed to be awakened to its peril. Because we were far removed from the scene of actual battles, there was a feeling of false security in the land, which was fanned by the propagandists of the Axis nations. "It can't happen here," many people were thinking. "American arms, if need be, could defend the nation easily." America needed jolting, its businessmen needed jolting, and so did its workers. The shock came on the morning of December 7, 1941, at Pearl Harbor.

Fifth, the insistence of many companies upon "business as usual" was an obstacle to all-out war production. In the early stages of the defense program it was mistakenly believed that industry could take arms production in its stride and could supply the nation with both guns *and* butter. As the war went on, however, it became apparent that business could *not* go on as usual. There would have to be severe readjustments. Indeed, it became soon plain that the lot of everyone in industry whose activities did not contribute to the war production effort would grow increasingly harder.

Sixth, not the least of our difficulties was in making peace between employers and organized labor. Before our actual entry into the war, strikes in defense industries were frequent and slowed down production greatly. The processes of collective bargaining would break down, and strikes would follow. Thus the war effort was seriously handicapped.

GETTING INTO ACTION

President Roosevelt and Congress recognized immediately that there would have to be peace between employers and workers. Strikes would have to stop. Therefore shortly after the entry of America into the war the President called the leaders of labor and management together for a conference to discuss ways and means of preventing labor disturbances. The result of this conference was a covenant between the employer representatives and the labor leaders that there would be no strikes and no lockouts for the duration of the war. The President then created a War Labor Board before which all disputes between management and labor would be heard and settled.

America set to work. In Washington agencies had to be established to distribute contracts, to control the flow of the nation's raw materials, and to speed the manufacture of munitions. One agency after another was set up. The first was the Advisory Commission to the Council of National Defense, which was followed by the Office of Production Management. The Supply Priorities and Allocations Board was then created to supervise and co-ordinate the work of the OPM.

Finally, after our declaration of war, the War Production Board (WPB) was established by President Roosevelt. The principal difference between this board and the agencies that had preceded it was that now authority over war production was vested in one individual who is responsible only to the President. The man that the President chose was Donald Marr Nelson, an experienced, able industrial executive who had been identified with the defense program from the start. Other members of the board were Douglas MacKeachie, W. H. Harrison, William L. Batt, J. S. Knowlson, Sidney Hillman, and Leon Henderson.

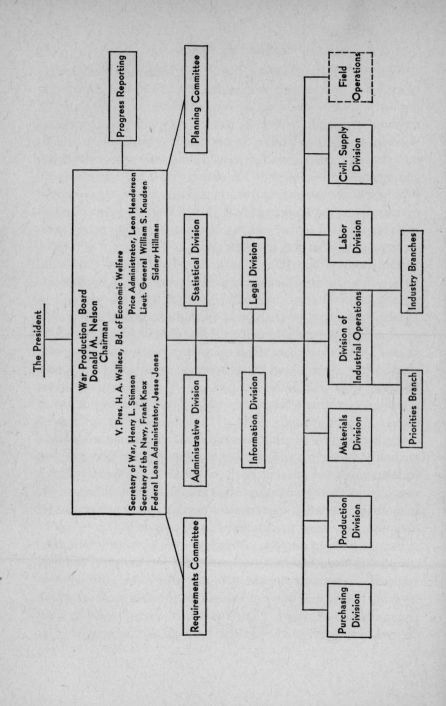

The President

War Production Board
Donald M. Nelson
Chairman

V. Pres. H. A. Wallace, Bd. of Economic Welfare
Secretary of War, Henry L. Stimson   Price Administrator, Leon Henderson
Secretary of the Navy, Frank Knox   Lieut. General William S. Knudsen
Federal Loan Administrator, Jesse Jones   Sidney Hillman

Progress Reporting

Planning Committee

Requirements Committee

Administrative Division

Statistical Division

Information Division

Legal Division

Purchasing Division

Production Division

Materials Division

Division of Industrial Operations

Labor Division

Civil. Supply Division

Field Operations

Priorities Branch

Industry Branches

The general functions of the War Production Board were to establish policies and procedures to be followed in purchasing material, in drawing up and distributing contracts, in developing specifications, in converting plants from making peacetime goods to making munitions, in constructing and financing new plants, and in controlling the supply of labor among industries. The WPB also exercised control over all supplies, both those going into munitions and those being used in manufacturing civilian goods. It was also the liaison agency between the President and the Army and Navy on all purchases and production of munitions.

The task of the War Production Board was enormous. While the original emergency defense budget in 1939 called for the expenditure of 3.3 billion dollars, at the beginning of 1942 shortly after the board was created the figure had reached 131 billion. To make good President Roosevelt's promise of 60,000 planes in 1942, plane output must reach 5,000 a month. The output of tanks and guns had to be gigantically increased. So must shipbuilding be stepped up if we were to produce 8 million tons of merchant vessels in 1942, and 10 million in 1943.

To accomplish all this the President and Congress placed virtually the entire industrial and economic resources of the nation under the control of the WPB. Its responsibility is vast. It controls a complex, intricate, and powerful machine. It must decide what materials are needed, where they can be obtained, how their production can be speeded.

In producing munitions on such a scale as is now being attempted in the United States one of the fundamental requirements is a system of *priorities*, under which needed and strategic materials will get precedence in production over those that are less important. The priorities system governs both the processing of goods and the flow of raw materials. Or-

WHAT WAR PRODUCTION WE MAY EXPECT

UNITED STATES WAR POTENTIAL IN 1940=100

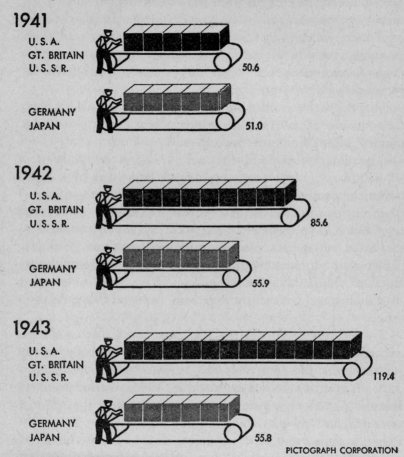

1941

U. S. A.
GT. BRITAIN
U. S. S. R. — 50.6

GERMANY
JAPAN — 51.0

1942

U. S. A.
GT. BRITAIN
U. S. S. R. — 85.6

GERMANY
JAPAN — 55.9

1943

U. S. A.
GT. BRITAIN
U. S. S. R. — 119.4

GERMANY
JAPAN — 55.8

PICTOGRAPH CORPORATION

The war found only the enemy fully prepared. As the United States shifts into war production the balance should change in favor of the United Nations. But production is not all. The Axis can still draw on tremendous reserves which they have built up in the many years in which they were planning for this war.

ders issued for military equipment have a priority rating, and if a manufacturer receives an order with a high rating he must give it precedence in his production schedule over all other orders he has on hand. Likewise, if the producer of a strategic metal receives an order with a high priority rating from a company making airplane bomb sights or some other important war requirement, he must supply that manufacturer before he supplies anyone else.

The WPB governs the priority system and also has jurisdiction over the balance between production of goods for military use and that for civilian use. As more and more energy and raw material are poured into munitions manufacture, there is a corresponding decrease in the amount that can go for making consumer goods. The production of many luxuries and semi-luxuries, such as automobiles, must halt entirely. There will also be diminishing quantities of such articles as radios, electric irons, refrigerators, sewing machines, washing machines. There are two reasons for this: first, there is not enough material, especially metals, to make these goods; second, the plants in which they were formerly made are increasingly being turned over to the manufacture of war material.

The War Production Board must see that as many factories as possible are converted into munitions plants, must integrate production so that both large and small companies are taking a part in the war effort, and must direct the construction and financing of new plants. Generally speaking, when a war is over a plant that was constructed to manufacture munitions has little commercial value. After the First World War there were thousands of these " ghost " plants scattered across the country. To their owners they were white elephants. Finally, rather than pay taxes on them, the owners demolished them and broke up the machinery for scrap.

At the outset of the defense program, American companies

remembered this experience and were loath to repeat it without assurance from the Government that their investment would be protected. In answer to this the Government offered three methods of financing munitions plants. First, plants that have no commercial value after the war will be financed entirely by the Government; they will be operated by a private company on a fixed-fee basis and will be returned to the Government after the war. It is expected that such plants will be maintained permanently by the Government. They will be closed, but their machinery and equipment will be kept oiled and in readiness to produce munitions when they are needed again. They will be similar to the " shadow " plants that were constructed in England just before the war began.

Second, other munitions plants will be built and operated by private companies at their own expense. However, during the period that the private companies operate the plants they will receive payments over a space of five years for their investment and the Government will ultimately take full title to the plants. If the war should end before the end of the five years, the Government must pay the companies in a lump sum. At the end of the war the companies have the right to buy back the plants from the Government at the original price, less depreciation.

Third, where additional facilities are added to an existing plant, the same method of financing is followed as in class two: the Government pays back the company for its investment over a five-year period. If, however, the company does not buy the addition back from the Government, the Government must demolish the addition.

Money for the financing of these plants is being furnished mostly through the Reconstruction Finance Corporation. Private financial institutions are not barred from participation, but of course must meet the interest rate of the RFC.

MASS PRODUCTION AND SUBCONTRACTING

In the months before our entry into the war, the Government let billions of dollars of contracts to industry for munitions, and after our declaration billions more were added. But giving out contracts alone does not produce the material. The money is really spent only when the material is being produced.

We wanted these munitions produced by mass production, but the secret of mass production is *preparation*, frequently long preparation. You have probably seen newspapers running in small rivers off the great presses at one of the great newspaper plants. This is mass production. Once the articles are written, set in type, the pages arranged, and all the other preparations made, the press can produce newspapers almost endlessly. Mass production of most items involves the same process. Prepare, and you can duplicate the product almost indefinitely. But newspapers are the only thing the press can make. To produce some other manufactured item a new machine is needed.

In the transition from peacetime to wartime production, industry faces very much this same problem. Our mass-production industries these many years have been making the things you and I need in our daily lives. They cannot overnight produce guns and tanks. The machines that have been making vacuum cleaners cannot make machine guns; those that have been making automobile engines cannot make airplane motors; those making cast-iron pipe cannot make bomb cases. We must build a new set of machines, and this process is called *retooling*. When it is finished we can begin the mass production of munitions. True, some of the peacetime machines can be adapted to wartime production, but many new machines have to be built.

President Roosevelt in his message to Congress on the state

of the Union on January 6 pointed out: "We must convert every available plant and tool to war production. That goes all the way from the greatest plants to the smallest — from the huge automobile industry to the village machine shop."

How was this to be done? How was it *being* done? The answer is: through subcontracting, or "farming out." This simply means that instead of using one factory or one company to make a complete weapon — a machine gun, a tank, or a mortar — the various parts are manufactured by several plants and then all assembled in one large plant.

Subcontracting is not new in the United States. Our automobile industry has used it for years. Our industrial system also had considerable experience with it in the First World War. The Germans in preparing for this war adapted the farming-out system that we had devised in 1917–18, making it even more complex than our own. The Nazis have developed an industrial system that employs thousands of small shops with co-ordination among them. Even on German farms, we are told, the agricultural workers have small lathes and electric motors with which they process some minor part of a weapon.

The military significance of such highly decentralized production is, of course, that when a country is subjected to bombardment, it is almost impossible to "knock out" an entire industry. This was borne in upon the British during the terrific aerial pounding they received during 1940. A self-sufficient factory could be put out of production with one bomb, whereas if various parts were manufactured in small scattered factories, that could not happen. The British immediately began to extend their farming-out or "bits-and-pieces" system, and that is one reason British industry ultimately did withstand the German assaults.

It has been pointed out how important it is to co-ordinate the issuing of contracts so that vitally needed war material, such

HOW TO INCREASE WAR PRODUCTION

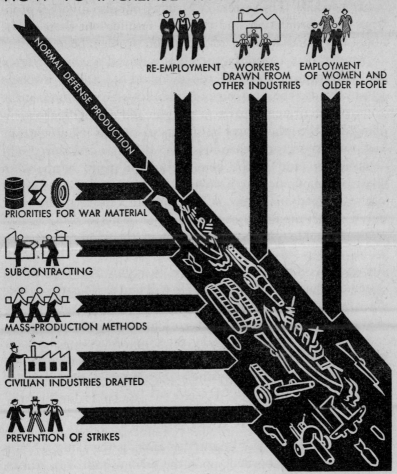

PICTOGRAPH CORPORATION

as smokeless powder, would be available in sufficient quantity when needed. The system of farming-out also involves problems of co-ordination, and the more farming-out there is, the more magnified does the co-ordination problem become.

Assume that a manufacturer has received a contract from the Government to make ten thousand .50-caliber machine guns. Under the farming-out system his factory may make some of the principal parts of the gun and do the final assembling, but the other parts he sublets to various manufacturers with smaller factories than his own. If he has, say, thirty subcontractors (and in the manufacture of many weapons an even larger number are involved), he must make certain that each " farmed-out " part is being manufactured at the right speed so that the final assembly will not be delayed for lack of some part. He must keep a continuous check on the progress of his various subcontractors, making sure that they are meeting their weekly quota of output, that they are maintaining specified standards of quality. He will find that many of them must be educated in the method of manufacture of their particular part, that they lack skilled workers, and so on.

Multiply this example many times in connection with the thousands of war materials that are being manufactured and you begin to realize the vastness of high-speed, decentralized production for war.

THE STRAIN ON RAILROADS

War production in a country as large as the United States places new heavy burdens upon the nation's railroads, trucks, and other transportation facilities. These are the arteries that carry the raw materials and the fuel from the mines and the land to the factories and the finished goods from the factories to their destinations. Greater and greater becomes the traffic, until every available boxcar is in use and the yards choked with freight. Track and roadbeds must be kept in good repair to withstand the steady pounding of the wheels of the rolling stock. Safety measures must be adhered to, lest the heavy volume of traffic give rise to costly and fatal accidents. The use of passenger trains must be available to the Army for transporting troops from one point to another.

In the subcontracting system, faithful efficient railroad service is a prime requisite. The various subcontractors on a gun or a bombsight must have steady communication with the prime contractor, even though he is several hundred miles away. For example, there are ten parts of a certain tank gun being manufactured by thirty-seven different subcontractors located all the way from Philadelphia to Davenport, Iowa. Each of these subcontractors depends on the railroads to supply him with raw or semifinished materials and to ship his finished parts to the prime contractor, who is situated in New Jersey. Now multiply this example by literally thousands of others and you begin to realize how utterly dependent is the defense program upon the country's carriers.

WANTED: SKILLED MEN

"We need more skilled workmen." Almost from the very moment that the defense program was put into effect that has been the cry of industry. Yes, we have skilled men in our industries, millions of them, but these are not enough. The defense program is big, almost too big for any one individual to appreciate. Machines need men to run them, tools need skilled hands to use them. Skilled men! There was only one answer: training for those who were not skilled.

The Government attacked this shortage from two directions: It took steps to increase the amount of pre-employment or vocational training, and it sought to stimulate training within industry — that is, training on the job.

Have you ever observed a highly skilled craftsman at work and then compared his actions with those of an unskilled or a semiskilled man at his job? The first difference you probably noticed was that, generally speaking, whereas the man of high skill performed many operations, the unskilled worker did only one or two. The labor bottleneck of our war industries is the shortage of skilled workers. If a factory is short of this kind of workman, then the whole manufacturing process is slowed down because everything must wait upon him. Industry is solving that problem in this way: The job of a highly skilled man is analyzed and broken down into simple parts. Then semiskilled men are taught how to do one or two component operations of the whole job. In some factories 80 per cent of the operations formerly done by the highly skilled men can be turned over to men of less skill. After the semiskilled man learns some of the simple operations he is taught the more difficult ones, and he is thus " upgraded " until finally he knows the whole job and becomes a master workman himself.

Recruit and train — that has been the order of the day for industry. For only thus can there be enough workers to fill the demand. As new workers are hired by companies they are given intensive training courses. They are taught to operate a machine as rapidly as possible. The length of the courses that are given in the factories depends on the relative difficulty of the jobs to which the new workers are assigned. Some courses take only a few days, others three or four weeks, and those for the more skilled jobs four or five months. The teaching in these courses is often done by already experienced workers who themselves have been given courses in how to instruct.

But with emphasis being placed upon single-purpose or simplified jobs, the length of the training period is constantly being reduced. Ultimately full use will be made of America's labor supply. As in the First World War, more and more women will be trained to jobs that were formerly done by men. Many workers now unemployed will be absorbed into munitions plants. In fact, if the experience of the United States follows the British pattern in this regard, we should have no unemployment at all when our defense production is in full swing. Before munitions production reached its peak in England, the unemployed numbered about 1,250,000, but that figure came down to about 180,000 in 1942.

PROBLEMS OF MANAGEMENT

This is a war of the factories. Much, then, depends on the skill of our industrial managers — those in charge of operating the productive facilities. Directing a large factory is the most exacting kind of work, for one mistake in judgment may cost thousands of dollars and the loss to the nation of strategic fighting equipment.

Few of the general public realize that every defense order, no matter how small, has to be priced, to be engineered, to be executed — to be produced, that is — in the most efficient possible way. Machines have to be maintained. New equipment must be purchased. Jobs have to be reorganized. Factories must be planned and erected. Materials must be purchased. There are the stockholders on one side and the Government on the other to be answered. Operations have to be financed; and so on. And each day as billions of dollars that are appropriated for defense are turned into signed contracts this load of detail grows.

In the general clamor over labor difficulties we hear little about the possible management bottleneck. But as a matter of fact, in many places such a bottleneck already exists and it threatens to spread even further. In factories steady mechanization of processes has lightened the load for labor, but no machines have been invented to replace managerial skill.

Our shortage of good managers is as serious as our shortage of skilled factory workers. And in defense industries the machinery for training managers is proceeding under forced draft. There is a revolution in middle management as younger men are being given more important responsibilities and elevated to higher jobs in their firms. Meanwhile, from lower down in the organization others are being brought up to fill the gaps. Companies report that it is not so easy now to find men suitably equipped to fill many positions as it was a few years ago.

Nor is there anything in the war outlook that would lead one to believe that this shortage of managerial talent will grow less acute in coming months. In fact, quite the reverse is to be expected. A nation at war is a nation operating at top speed. Its factories work ceaselessly; its mines disgorge their ore incessantly; men must uncomplainingly work longer hours. Nothing is permitted to stand in the way of the country's security.

Upon the declaration of war, President Roosevelt urged all companies with defense orders to go on a 168-hour, seven-day week. When a plant goes on a continuous-operation basis many problems arise. More workers are needed for the extra shifts. Vital machinery must be maintained so that breakdown will not cause a prolonged interruption in the production process. Extra raw material must be obtained and scheduled for processing.

Plant managers must make certain that every operation in their plants is being done in the best possible way known. They must see that quality of the product is not sacrificed for speed, so that the product will not fail when it is in service. They must see that adequate raw materials are on hand, that workers are paid fairly, that working conditions make for good production, that the best skill of each worker is being properly utilized, that orders are completed on schedule.

In the production of peacetime goods the United States has been supreme, the undisputed leader. Can we do the same with munitions? There is only one answer: We can and we must. Indeed, we must fulfill the promise of the President to be the arsenal for all the United Nations. Every nation that fights the Axis will be assisted by arms made in the factories of America. These arms will be used in all climates and in all continents where the enemy can be reached. This flow of weapons will create such pressure upon the enemy that it will be as though he were caught in a vise that holds him on all sides.

Yes, this conflict is costing much. We are throwing every resource that we have into the struggle — the money of our people, the labor of our workers, the sacrifices of our civilians, yes, and the lives of millions of young men. But America is rich in material things, in courage, in the will to work, in inventive genius. We fight with and for these things — fight now so that we will not have to fight to win them back again.

x. How can American labor help the war effort?

JOHN CHAMBERLAIN

John Chamberlain has, written many articles on labor, industry, and government for 'Fortune' magazine over the past six years, including 'Democracy and the Closed Shop,' in the January, 1942, issue. Mr. Chamberlain is the author of 'The American Stakes,' which argues that government must play a successful broker role in limiting the power of any and all private or public institutions if democracy is to be maintained. Mr. Chamberlain contributes a column on books to the 'New York Times' twice a week and conducts the monthly book-review pages for 'Harper's.' He is a visiting professor of journalism at the Columbia University School of Journalism.

When the workers of England say "Winnie will win us the war, and Ernie will save us the peace," they reveal a quiet confidence that Americans may well envy. For behind this trust in Winston Churchill and Ernest Bevin, there lies an assurance that British labor will not have to bear more than its share of the sufferings, the blood, sweat, toil, and tears, of the war itself or of the uneasy peace that normally follows war. Churchill is Prime Minister and Minister of Defense: Bevin is Minister of Labor and National Service. They are alike only in their dogged faith in the ultimate collapse of Hitlerism — and in an equally dogged determination that it *shall* collapse.

THE JOB TO BE DONE

Britain, which had its full share of the old, the tired, and the disgruntled who yearned for peace even at the price of the weak-kneed policy that Chamberlain called "appeasement," could never have stood up to Hitler without the full co-operation of the labor movement, which is in a position to break any wartime Cabinet. But it will take American labor to finish what the British workers began in the desperate days after Dunkirk in 1940, when every British nerve and muscle was straining to replace the war material left behind on the strewn fields of Flanders. Britain has a population of some 40,000,000 — enough to keep the Spitfires and Hurricanes flying over the Channel, enough to keep Bofors and Oerlikon antiaircraft guns firing in defensive operations, and possibly enough to hold the lines of Empire in Syria and in the Western Desert.

That much Britain can do, but it takes 90,000 man-hours to build a four-engined bombing plane, and 90,000 man-hours per plane consume the building power of a small nation like Britain at an appalling rate. Britain's war production at best is only enough for defense. If the war is to be waged offensively — and it is only by offense that it can be won — if the United Nations are to make attacks across the wide plains of the Soviet Union, in the sands of Tripolitania and the Near East, in the jungles of Burma, in the mountains of China, and, eventually, on a score of beachheads in Europe and the East Indies and even Japan, it is up to the 49,000,000 American workers to produce the tools to finish the job.

Can American labor meet the challenge? Can it produce the largest amount of military equipment ever produced in all human history? And can it produce it in time? From the standpoint of matching men to machines, whether in the fairly simple belt-line assembly operations or in the more difficult skilled

" know-how " jobs, the answer is certainly a resounding Yes. No one who has seen a ponderous Bullard Mult-au-matic turret lathe doing the work of five or more separate machines on the floor of the Pratt & Whitney airplane-engine factory in East Hartford, Connecticut, can doubt for a moment the capacity of American industry to create the needed machines. Nor can he doubt the ability of American workers to operate machine tools which the Japanese and the Germans, clever though they may be, have yet to match in speed, in complexity of work produced, and in precision.

I have seen the Ford bomber plant rising on the prairie at Willow Run, near Ypsilanti, Michigan. I have watched the Mesta rollers flatten the billets into sheet steel at Ford's great open-hearth plant at the River Rouge. I have glimpsed Chrysler's president, K. T. Keller, mulling over tank blueprints in his Detroit office. And I have visited the High Standard Arms Company plant in Hamden, Connecticut, where an inventive Swedish immigrant named Gus Swebelius is miraculously producing three thousand machine guns a month with patched-up machine tools, some of which actually date back to the 1880's. Yet without the skilled hands, the clever fingers, and the brute muscle of their labor force, Mr. Ford, Mr. Keller, and Mr. Swebelius would be as useless as a theatrical stock company without a repertory of plays.

Last spring, while making a shipyard survey, I saw giant steam shovels digging out a building basin for the so-called Ugly Duckling cargo ships on the tidal flats of South Portland, Maine. Everything was confusion behind a great coffer dam that held back the waters of Casco Bay, and one doubted that ships would actually be completed in the basin before the end of the war. But South Portland has already launched some ships for the British, and will launch many more before the end of 1942. Here the almost impossible has been done, and it would have been truly impossible without the Yankee workers of Portland and the Maine coast, those heirs to a long, and apparently dying, tradition of shipbuilding that goes all the way back to clipper days.

If marvelous machines and skilled men were all that were needed, America could say with justifiable confidence, "We can do the job." But machines are of no use without the men to run them; and men, no matter how skilled, are of no use unless they are at work. The situation facing labor in the United States is much more difficult and infinitely more complicated than the one which British labor faced and conquered. British labor was united, but American labor was split down the middle, divided into two great rival organizations, the A.F. of L. and the C.I.O. That great division was bad enough, but each organization itself was shot through with rivalries and personal feuds. Furthermore, some of the members and many of the leaders were motivated by an " if " and " but " spirit. " If we do this, we'll lose so-and-so." " If such a situation arises . . ." " We want to beat Hitler, yes, *but* our first duty is to keep what we've gained."

Neither American workers nor American labor leaders lacked patriotism, not even in the days when the United States was following a kind of appeasement policy of its own that it called " all aid short of war." And they do not lack patriotism now. Given a real conviction of danger, the Cleveland screw-machine operator, the Pascagoula, Mississippi, ship-plate welder, and the Bridgeport, Connecticut, expert in deep-drawing cartridge-brass operations, will turn to with a will every time. But the fact remains that the British labor movement entered the war in a far more mature state of mind than the American labor movement did. And greater maturity, of course, implies a greater sense of responsibility. As I write, President Roosevelt has arranged for a joint board of the American Federation of Labor (A.F. of L.) and the Congress of Industrial Organization (C.I.O.) to thresh out all wartime problems affecting the two great divisions of the labor movement. Perhaps the divisions will be blended into one, but sore spots from the long separation are bound to remain, a potential source of trouble that will have to be watched by the alert labor rank and file if we are to catch up with, and surpass, the British.

LABOR IN ENGLAND

In calling the American labor movement "immature" by comparison with the British movement, I am not putting any particular blame upon the shoulders of President William Green of the American Federation of Labor or of John L. Lewis or Philip Murray of the Congress of Industrial Organization. Nor am I blaming Joe Jones, the man on the belt line, or Jim Smith, the tool-and-die maker. The American labor movement is a product of, almost a reaction to, local conditions; it springs from an industrial situation that disappeared in Britain either during the First World War or in the period following the unsuccessful general strike of 1926.

British labor is united behind a man, a program, and a hope for a future in which, as the song has it, "There'll be some changes made." Also, British labor has an assured position in the governmental scheme. It has its own Labor party, which is a powerful shield even when the Tories are in possession of the Government. The British Consumer Co-operative Movement, largely run by manual workers, sells the basic necessities of life to union men on a nonprofit basis in twelve thousand local retail stores — hence there is little price-gouging at the expense of British labor. Free from worry about the attitude of the Government and the cost of food and clothing, British labor can face the employers with no flanks left unguarded. But the employers are not difficult to deal with. Long ago they stopped making life miserable for union men in Britain — and most employers today prefer to hire a union worker whenever possible. This preference is so ingrained that most British unions feel no need of asking for the closed shop, in which only union men may be employed. As a matter of fact, the British labor leaders do not think very well of the closed-shop idea. As in Sweden, the leaders consider that enforced membership in a union does not make for good union men. Yet despite the fact that union membership is generally a voluntary matter in Britain, few men choose to remain outside of the unions; and British employers often urge the lone wolves to " join up " merely to make things more satisfactory all around.

In Britain, then, we have a situation in which the worker has (1) security in his union membership; (2) access to cheap food and clothing through the co-operative movement; (3) the right to the benefits of collective bargaining with no interference on the part of the employers — that is, the right, in which there is power, to bargain for wages, and so on, with the employer as a unit instead of as individuals; and (4) the abstract, and seldom needed, right to refuse to join a union, or to quit a union if the leadership is unsatisfactory. (This last right, the right of individual action if desired, is typically " English," and it is worth while for the simple reason that it compels British trade-union leaders to toe the mark, to listen to minority grievances among the rank and file, and to refrain from wrangling over social theories and political isms that are foreign to a democracy operating in a capitalistic state.) So far as politics are concerned, the British worker knows that the pressure of his Labor party, even when it is in the minority, is strong enough to keep the Conservatives marching toward a goal of social security. As Gustav Stolper has recently pointed out, the National and Tory governments of the 1930's cleared slums and enlarged the whole social-security system; and 4,000,000 new British homes were built during the period between the First and Second World Wars, most of them for British workingmen and their families.

DIFFICULTIES OUTSIDE THE LABOR MOVEMENT

American labor is not girding for war in 1942 within any such advanced social condition. To begin with, American labor has no political party of its own. (It has to play politics within both the Republican and the Democratic party, which wastes time and produces enmities, even though political maneuvering is a guarantee that democracy exists. Democracy is built on the party system, but labor's lack of a party does not make our democracy more democratic.) Secondly, America has yet to produce a housing boom, whether publicly or privately financed, capable of sheltering the workers needed for our defense industries. Thirdly, the American co-operative movement, while it is sturdy enough in the agricultural districts of Indiana, Ohio, Missouri, and Wisconsin, hasn't reached sufficient proportions to assure the American worker of food and clothing at a price that does not include a profit for the retailer. Finally, if American labor is committed, as it seems to be, to a policy of forcing the worker into a closed, or compulsory union, shop, which has too much of a totalitarian flavor for my palate, the reason is not far to seek. And the reason carries with it its own justification. For American management has had a pretty black record of union-busting and union-baiting; it has admitted as much in testimony taken by the La Follette Committee. Even the passage of the Wagner Act, which guarantees to workers the right to organize and to bargain collectively through representatives of their own choosing, failed to stop antiunion practices in some quarters, and it was only a year ago that Henry Ford at last surrendered and decided to get along with the C.I.O. in the River Rouge plant. With echoes of slugging and dirty work on both sides still vibrating along the Monongahela River and in Detroit, neither management nor labor has attained a state of grace where it is willing to put much faith in the other.

DIFFICULTIES INSIDE THE LABOR MOVEMENT

As we move more deeply into full-out war, American labor is faced with a double task: it must achieve a greater measure of maturity as a movement, and at the same time direct all its energies to efficient, uninterrupted production of war materials. But can this goal be reached when the way is blocked by certain points of view? And can maturity be forced on the labor movement before labor leaders and businessmen alike have been educated to an understanding of, and a respect for, the state of the economic system as a whole? In other words, can people in positions of economic power be taught to consider the needs of the nation as a whole as of more immediate importance than their own desires? A mature labor movement is not possible as long as there are employers around who still hold to the union-busting social philosophy of 1908, or 1928. Nor is maturity possible as long as a sizable element in the unions wants to press for a class warfare designed to transform the productive system from democratic capitalism to a form of Socialism, with the Government having the final say in production. Both the employers and the workers must agree on the type of social system in which production is to continue and expand if there is to be harmony throughout the industrial machine as a whole. In Sweden and in England, an unspoken agreement was reached long ago: the capitalist mode of production — that is, with management employing and paying the worker — was to continue (subject, of course, to temporary modification in wartime), but the workers were to be assured of their bargaining rights and of certain fixed social services to be paid for out of taxes on ownership, high managerial salaries, and dividends.

The American worker's powers of possible production, then, will be formed partly by what the National Association of Manufacturers feels about the Wagner Act, and partly by what labor itself feels about pressing for social gains — including the controversial closed shop — at the expense of efficient man-hours of labor spent on the factory floor. Since the labor movement is split three ways, into the A.F. of L. and the Lewis and anti-Lewis factions of the C.I.O., the competition of three types of union leader for loyalty can result in a great deal of working inefficiency unless the President or the pressure of public opinion intervenes. In fact, interunion jealousies are the prime immediate source of danger menacing our production standards for the future. These jealousies can push leaders into making demands that ought not to be made during wartime — demands, for example, that labor be exempt from a wage ceiling when price levels are being fixed by law, or demands for a closed shop in a situation where essential union security has already been achieved, as it had been in the so-called " captive " coal mines — those owned by steel companies — which were 95 per cent unionized when John L. Lewis threatened his nationwide soft-coal tie-up if those mines were not closed to the 5 per cent of nonunion workers.

It is always boring to go into details about factional fights within the union movement; but it must be done, if only to clear the ground for understanding what labor can do for the war effort. The basic split, the great cleavage, in the American labor movement is, of course, the division of labor forces into the A.F. of L. and the C.I.O. The A.F. of L. forms its unions by crafts — a plumbers' union, a carpenters' union, a waiters' union, and so on. The C.I.O., on the other hand, aspires to take all the workers, skilled and unskilled, in a given industry into one union — the automobile workers' union, say, or the shipbuilders' union. Naturally, since their purposes are very different, the A.F. of L. organizer often comes to blows (sometimes figurative, sometimes all too real) with the C.I.O. organizer — blows which have nothing whatever to do with grievances against management. The unions aren't at such times fighting at all for the rights or the good of the workers; they are each fighting to get dominance, one over the other. Worse still, they use the strike to win their point. For the duration of the war no such fights are supposed to be held, since Mr. Roosevelt's A.F. of L.–C.I.O. war advisory board is authorized to settle all disputes as to which union has priority before the stage of strikes is reached.

The Roosevelt board, however, is powerless to close the big cracks in the labor movement, the deepest of which is the John L. Lewis-Philip Murray struggle within the C.I.O. For years, Philip Murray, now the C.I.O. president, was John L. Lewis's trusted lieutenant in the United Mine Workers. But Murray and Lewis split over the question of loyalty to the foreign policy of President Roosevelt long before December 7, 1941, and the differences between the two men were recently greatly magnified when Lewis proposed the unity — or the " accouplement," as he called it — of the A.F. of L. and the C.I.O. without consulting Murray.

To understand the importance of personal feuds and the divisions that result from them in the labor movement, we must apply a close analysis to the elements that go to make up the labor movement as a whole. American labor consists roughly of 49,000,000 gainfully employed people. There are 10,500,000 who work on farms, most of them without union organization. There are 6,000,000 self-employed proprietors and domestic workers, who also escape the union category.

Fifteen million people work in trade and finance, in the various service industries, and for the Government. And in mining, manufacturing, public utilities, construction, and transportation there are 17,000,000 more.

Every man jack of the 49,000,000 is necessary to the war effort — and there will be need for extra workers and for the re-training and shifting of old workers, too. Most of the 49,000,-000 will give to the utmost with no questions asked. It is the 10,700,000 organized workers who are the main source of difficulty, not because they are unpatriotic, but solely because one man's *organizational* definition of the patriotic thing to do commonly differs with the next man's. Is it "patriotic," for example, to ask for a wage raise in wartime? An employer, faced with rising raw-material costs and higher taxes, may think that such a request is certainly unpatriotic. Is it giving aid and comfort to Hitler to press the issue of the "union security" of the closed shop against General Motors or the National Steel Company?

By the standards of the First World War, during which the status of the unions was frozen for the duration of the armed conflict, to press such issues is at least improper. But the truth is that answers to such questions must be qualified. If prices are rising, low wages may result in inadequate diets that make for inefficiency of workers on the factory floor. And if the worker suspects that his boss is merely waiting for the end of the war to smash his union, how can the worker give his best efforts without any guarantee of union security from the Government? Washington itself must establish wise over-all price, wage, profits, tax, and union-security policies if labor is to stick to the lathe and loom without ever threatening any trouble. In default of wise direction from Congress and the President, and control by them, the average embattled union leader will continue to compete for power by promising those who follow him the best possible wages, hours, and shop conditions regardless of the needs of the war effort as a whole.

The 10,700,000 in the organized labor movement are roughly divided as follows: 700,000 in the independent railway brotherhoods (unions of railroad employees not affiliated with other unions), and 5,000,000 each in the A.F. of L. and the C.I.O. But the C.I.O., as we have seen, is itself divided between those who are for John L. Lewis and those who are against him; and the A.F. of L. is a kind of " league of nations " of semi-independent unions, in which the ruling power is not vested in any single top control. It is a loosely formed organization, with each union concerned mainly with its own interests. The boilermakers, for example, decide on their policies without any concern for, say, the policies of the machinists; and the carpenters go their own way, entirely content to let the teamsters go theirs.

While William Green, the A.F. of L. president, was one of the first labor leaders to support President Roosevelt's foreign policy, he had no authority in making his " no-strike " promise to bind the local unions or the separate national or international unions of the A.F. of L. to that promise. If Dan Tobin of the Teamsters Union decided to call a strike, Green could not stop him. Tobin, who bosses 400,000 men, is a personal friend of President Roosevelt, but not even that friendship would restrain him nor would talk about " defense " or " all-out war effort " — if the C.I.O. really pushed its campaign to lure the truck-drivers away from their independent (A.F. of L.) union into an industrial (C.I.O.) union along with the construction workers and hotel-service workers. As for burly Bill Hutcheson, who controls 500,000 carpenters (A.F. of L.), he has a mind of his own which he uses in ways that are incalculable a month in advance. John L. Lewis once knocked Bill Hutcheson down, but today John L. Lewis and Hutcheson are friends — and where that friendship will lead, no man knows.

The C.I.O. is split into the party for Lewis and the party against him. Each of those parties, in turn, is split and split again. Those splits result in a series of civil wars. Any hope of a general armistice that would make A.F. of L.–C.I.O. unity possible is a pipe dream. So long as the unions within the main organization disagree violently on matters of major policy, there isn't much chance of the main organization's developing a policy that will blend with the policy, yet unformed, of the other main organization. If one can imagine a federation of the South American republics uniting with a federation of the Balkan states, he can imagine A.F. of L. and C.I.O. uniting. Such an imagination would be wonderful, indeed.

Some of the unions are very liberal in politics, and some are very conservative. Some of those who are now supporting President Roosevelt's foreign policy are generally considered to be under the control of men who are Communist " fellow travelers " — men, that is, who are not registered members of the Communist party but who are active Communist sympathizers. Whether the accusations that are acrimoniously tossed around are true or false, it is difficult to see how Harry Bridges of the C.I.O., who has often been called a Communist, could ever get his longshoremen together in a united labor movement with Joseph Ryan's longshoremen, who hate so-called reds. Joe Curran of the C.I.O. seamen, who was against even " aid to Britain " until Hitler attacked the Soviet Union, is poles apart from Harry Lundeberg, boss of the A.F. of L. Sailors Union of the Pacific. Sidney Hillman's C.I.O. textile and clothing workers are agreed with Philip Murray's steelworkers and Walter Reuther's automobile workers in lining up behind President Roosevelt; but neither Murray nor Reuther regards Hillman with trusting eyes, and they think that the choice of

Hillman to head up the labor end of OPM (Office of Production Management) failed to give labor an adequate voice in the defense effort.

WHAT CHANCE FOR UNITY?

The rifts and crosscurrents in the A.F. of L. and the C.I.O. being what they are, John L. Lewis, who kept his promise to resign from the presidency of the C.I.O. if Roosevelt was re-elected President, has been able to play one group off against another in the effort to regain his power in the labor movement as a whole. Recently Mr. Lewis has been helping his brother Denny Lewis stage a drive to reorganize the construction workers and the teamsters — a drive that is apparently aimed at Bill Hutcheson of the A.F. of L. carpenters and Dan Tobin of the A.F. of L. teamsters. But such a drive may be nothing more than an effort to build up trading capital to be used in the game of power. John L. Lewis's recent call for "accouplement" of the A.F. of L. and the C.I.O. for the sake of war-time unity may or may not have been sincere. Certainly no such unity was possible so long as Lewis himself was busy staging raids on claims long ago staked out by the A.F. of L., as Hutcheson's and Tobin's unions were. Presumably — for the sake of "accouplement" — Mr. Lewis stood ready to call off his campaign to bring teamsters and carpenters into the C.I.O. Brother Denny's raiding party is called the Construction Workers Organizing Committee. It is more of a paper organization than a fact, but as a threat it has trading possibilities. The clever Mr. Lewis could trade it to Bill Hutcheson and Dan Tobin and thereby make himself solid with them. If the three of them joined together, they would be in a position to wield pretty powerful influence in a united labor movement.

Fear of such a power bloc as the Lewis-Hutcheson-Tobin combination of miners, carpenters, and teamsters will probably prevent labor unification for years to come. Hence the labor movement is probably doomed to go through the war divided as it is now, with its personal jealousies ready to flare up whenever anything promises to go wrong in Washington. The maturity which the union movement achieves will, then, be only temporary and artificial, a maturity forced on it by the strong hand of White House control, with Roosevelt acting here in the same capacity as Ernest Bevin in Great Britain. He will have to use authority that the Secretary of Labor does not possess. Such a control will not be equivalent to the voluntary type of labor unity they have in Britain under a Labor Minister who sits at the left hand of Winston Churchill. But it should be sufficient to keep the war production moving efficiently. The danger will come afterward, when the temporary wartime unity disappears with the removal of wartime restraints. On the day when peace comes again to this planet, the American labor movement will have to deal with its own factions and feuds if it is to have permanent organic unity.

But if it is too much to hope for a voluntarily unified labor movement this year or next, must we therefore count labor leadership out as a creative agent in war production? I do not think so. The rank and file will work, anyway — it always does when the safety of the United States is threatened. But labor leadership will work, too, in spite of its latent capacity for feuds.

CREATIVE THINKING FROM LABOR

As a matter of fact, the most effective war-production thinking to date has come from a labor leader, Mr. Walter Reuther of the United Automobile Workers. Mr. Reuther is a smart, merry-eyed, reddish-haired tool-and-die maker who once worked for Henry Ford. More than a year ago Walter Reuther decided the Number One job was to beat Hitler; and as he walked through the automotive parts plants of West Side Detroit, he was struck with the fact that both machine tools and the men who make the tools were idle a good part of the time. Putting his anti-Hitler zeal and the evidence of his eyes together, Mr. Reuther evolved the famous Reuther Plan for converting idle automobile plants to airplane bits-and-pieces production.

In Reuther's thinking, the plan for conversion of the plants to their new uses was to be administered by a board consisting of three men from management, three from the Government, and three from labor. Such a proposal naturally scared the automobile executives, who had visions of the Government stepping in to run their business by noncompetitive methods such as Hitler and Mussolini employ in their Fascist corporative states. In justice to the automobile men, it must be said that their fears had some justification: committees are notoriously inefficient, and a board such as Reuther proposed would soon have found itself dominated by the three government representatives, since they would have been called upon to break the almost certain deadlock between labor and management.

The trouble with committee-run industry is its lack of a clear " chain of command," a lack that invites seizure of final authority by those willing to pool their votes. The heart of the Reuther Plan, however, was not the proposal for a joint labor-capital board on which the Government would hold the balance of power. The real creative nub of the whole idea was to get idle equipment and idle brains and hands into effective war production by pooling the facilities of the automobile industry. When Donald Nelson finally received supreme power over production, he proceeded to adapt the essentials of the Reuther Plan to his own purpose by creating a War Production Board, with the automotive branch under Ernest

C. Kanzler. A good part of Kanzler's job is to go ahead with the pooling of tools and skills for the bits-and-pieces production which Reuther had advocated late in 1940. Reuther and the United Automobile Workers have spent a great deal of energy agitating for the adoption of his plan, and their propaganda may have been the compelling reason for the appointment of Kanzler. At any rate, Detroit labor, in the person of Walter Reuther, was in there pitching long before a majority of Americans, including most of the business executives, were alive to the issues involved.

People like Reuther are evidence that labor has a good deal to offer of a creative nature in speeding up the defense effort. Aside from such free-lance contributions of labor leaders, the government representatives of labor have been doing a man-sized job in mobilizing and training skills for the vast production effort that lies ahead of a nation dedicated to making planes, tanks, ships, and guns in an unending stream. This effort begins with the Bureau of Labor Statistics, which provides estimates of the number of men needed to fill the orders implied by the war budgeting of Congress. During the fiscal year 1942–43, 50 billion dollars will be spent for arms and military supplies. Some 15,000,000 men will be needed to translate the 50 billion into guns, tanks, planes, and uniforms. Since there were only 5,000,000 workers in the defense industries on January 1, 1942, 10,000,000 new men and women must be mobilized within the year.

A good part of the 10,000,000 will, naturally, be shifted over from nondefense industries. Instead of making automobiles, men will be making tanks; instead of nylon hosiery, women will be producing gunpowder bags and parachutes. But many of the shifted workers will have to be either retrained or " upgraded " in their skills. And at least 3,000,000 entirely new workers will be required for the completion of the program.

These new men and women can be recruited among the young people who have never held jobs, among housewives, and among those who have been on WPA during most of the 1930's.

The Labor Division of OPM, headed by Sidney Hillman of the C.I.O. Amalgamated Clothing Workers, has laid a firm foundation for the recruiting of an entirely new war labor force. Working with existing government agencies, Hillman has instituted training and "refresher" (brush-up) courses, and has provided essential information from his files. The Federal Government, in turn, has given money to the National Youth Administration and other youth agencies to train boys and girls in such basic crafts as metalworking and blueprint reading. Some 2,500,000 workers have taken training courses during the past eighteen months, and 2,000,000 more have received so-called in-plant instruction under the joint egis of management and the training-within-industry branch of Mr. Hillman's OPM Labor Division.

Mr. Hillman's methods of preparing man power for possible use in the future have not escaped all criticism. His planning, and the Government's, may not have been ideal, but the very fact that our huge shipbuilding program is ahead of schedule proves our ability as a nation to come through in the emergency. As a matter of fact, the workers of America have been doing a generally magnificent job ever since 1940: the man hours lost through strikes or elbow-leaning add up to a very insignificant total when compared with the man-hours that have gone into the making of planes, cartridge brass, "Ugly Duckling" freighters, battleships, and machine guns.

MEETING THE CHALLENGE

Now that we are actually at war on all the continents and seas of the world, however, even a small total of lost man-hours might spell the difference between victory and defeat. Strikes, therefore, must be kept to an absolute minimum — which means that both labor and management must willingly accept the arbitration of the new War Labor Board, headed by the philosophical, fair-minded William H. Davis. The main bone of contention between management and labor at the moment is the closed shop, which requires that workers belong to the union before they can be employed, or the variant of the closed shop known as the union shop, which makes the hiring of workers conditional on their willingness to join the union within a few weeks after they have received their first pay checks. Management has argued that it is unpatriotic for labor to use the war as an excuse to compel a change in union status that would not otherwise be granted. But labor has countered with an argument that "union security" is essential to the processes of collective bargaining. If a union is afraid for its life, it cannot face management across the bargaining table with anything like a proper balance of power.

The War Labor Board has the power to enforce any decision it chooses to make on both labor and management. But drastic departures from what either management or labor considers "normal expectancy" will leave a heritage of bad blood. If the WLB is to operate effectively, neither labor nor management must be stiff-necked. Labor, therefore, would do well to modify its "union-security" demand, limiting it to a request, say, for the maintenance by law of union membership for the duration of a collective-bargaining contract. Maintenance of membership, which compels a worker to remain in his freely chosen union for a voluntarily accepted stated interval, would be a guarantee that unions would not lose in strength during the war. And management, under a "maintenance-of-membership" agreement, would be free to hire an occasional rock-ribbed nonunion man if it chose to do so. Naturally, the

" maintenance-of-membership " compromise is not wholly satisfactory to either party. But war demands mutual sacrifices, and we can't afford to be partial to either labor or management when the life of the nation is at stake.

As a final contribution to wartime morale, the labor unions must do a good job of solving their own problems and of policing their own behavior. This means a war on union racketeers. It means giving a guarantee that unions shall be open to all comers, including Negroes; and it means a willingness to give up monopoly positions which are maintained by applying the apprentice system too restrictively in certain craft unions. If the unions cannot take care of their own internal problems, if they cannot guarantee internal democracy to their members, the Government will have to step in and do the job for them.

It is my guess, however, that the labor unions will not force Congress to legislation of any restrictive or supervisory nature. Alive to the need for good public relations in a period of national emergency, labor can be counted on to do its job voluntarily. In the past, both management and the unions have sometimes refused to regard each other as human beings. But war is a great solvent of prejudice and misunderstanding, and labor now has its chance to take the lead in creating an atmosphere in which the American union worker can rise to the favored status which his brothers in Sweden and England have enjoyed for many years.

XI. How can we pay for the war?

DAVID CUSHMAN COYLE

David Cushman Coyle is a civil engineer who has given his attention since 1931 to problems of public works and public finance. Among his books on these subjects are 'Brass Tacks,' 'Roads to a New America,' 'Age without Fear,' and 'Why Pay Taxes?' In 1937 he won the Harper prize of $1,000 for his article on 'The American Way.' Since 1933 he has acted as consultant to the Federal Public Works Administration, the Tennessee Valley Authority, the United States Treasury, the Defense Housing Coordinator, the Senate Committee on Unemployment and Relief, and other Federal agencies. His most recent book, 'America,' was a bestseller during the summer of 1941.

Paying for the war — or for anything else — has two different meanings. We say that we pay for something when we hand over the money and settle the bill. We also say we pay for something when we take the consequences, by giving up something else or by getting hurt. A war, like an attack of appendicitis, has to be paid for in money and also in consequences. If we understand clearly what the consequences are likely to be, we can avoid some of the worst of them, and may even get some benefits to balance the losses. And of course the way we go about paying the money cost of war necessarily has an effect on the other consequences. Wise handling of war finance can greatly reduce the real costs of war.

The money payments for war are made by the Government

to the people who serve in the Army, the Navy, or the Air Force, or who provide guns and planes and shoes and blankets for the Army and the Navy, or who work on war jobs in Washington or elsewhere. The nations that are going " all out " in this war are spending about half of their whole national income on their military expenses. If the war lasts long enough, say till the end of 1943, our Government may be spending about 60 billion dollars a year, out of a total national income of about 120 billion dollars.

WHY COSTS ARE HARD TO FIGURE

What do these figures mean? We don't shoot dollars at the enemy, and the Army can't eat dollars. The dollars are only a measure of the quantity of goods and services that we produce and sell. A total national income of 120 billion dollars means simply that in a year we shall be making shoes and bread and guns and haircuts and moving-picture performances at various prices that all add up to 120 billion dollars. When we are fully organized for war, about half of everything we produce will be bought by the Government to use in the war.

The dollar values are a measure, but they are a rubber measuring stick, because prices will go higher as the war goes on, and in 1943 a billion dollars will not represent as many loaves of bread as it did in 1940. During the First World War and the two years that followed American prices more than doubled, so that by 1920 a dollar was worth less than half as much in goods in the store as it had been worth in 1914. This time we hope to hold the prices to a smaller rise, but there is bound to be some increase. A 120-billion-dollar income for 1943, therefore, is partly a matter of prices, and may represent about as much production as 100 billion dollars would have bought in 1941.

Another thing to remember is that the money cost of the war

does not represent very closely the effort we put in. In the first place, not all the money is spent for guns and airplanes and other weapons. A large part is spent for butter and cake and roast beef and other eatables, to feed the boys in the Army and the Navy, and for shoes and overcoats and blankets to keep them warm. The boys are Americans too, who would have to eat and wear clothes even if there were no war. If they get better food in the service than some of them had in peacetime, that is not a loss to the country.

In the second place, while part of the Government's spending is used for things that are not really war at all, a great deal of the ordinary citizens' time and money will be used for the war without any pay. Many people work as air-raid wardens, others work in the Red Cross, or in all sorts of defense committees, and a great deal of this work will not have any ordinary value, only that of helping to win the war. Volunteer work that is useless except for winning the war is of course a real part of the cost of the war, but it is not reckoned in the Government's bill because the Government does not have to pay for it.

The point in taking account of all these aspects of the war cost is that we may not fool ourselves about the 60 billion dollars. The dollars may not be worth so much, because of high prices, and they may not represent the true material cost of the war, but they do mean one thing. The dollar cost of the war is a bill that the Government has to pay in dollars to the American people, and to a few foreigners who are selling materials to us.

WHERE THE MONEY FOR WAR COMES FROM

The first question, then, is how the Government is going to find $60,000,000,000 a year to pay its bills. There are three ways for a national government to find money: by taxing, by

HOW TO PAY FOR THE WAR

NATIONAL
INCOME

PRODUCTION

PAYING FOR
THE WAR
(AT HIGHER
PRICES)

MORE
TAXED AWAY

SAVINGS
BORROWED
BY GOV-
ERNMENT

NEW
MONEY
CREATED

OTHER
SAVINGS

PRODUCTION
OF WAR
MATERIAL

PRODUCTION

NATIONAL
INCOME.

PUBLIC
SERVICES

TAXED AWAY

CAPITAL
GOODS

SAVED

CAPITAL
GOODS

MORE MONEY—
FEWER GOODS

DANGER OF
PRICE INCREASE
AND
INFLATION

CONSUMER
GOODS
FOR SALE

AVAILABLE
TO BUY
GOODS

FEWER
CONSUMER
GOODS

MORE
MONEY
SPENT FOR
FEWER
GOODS

NORMAL

WARTIME

PICTOGRAPH CORPORATION

The war will greatly increase our production. But most of this production will be used in the war. With more people at work and higher wages and profits, there will be much more money to be spent for the fewer goods for consumers. To prevent prices from skyrocketing, the Government will try to get much of the money paid out back into its hands, mostly by higher taxes, and by borrowing peoples' savings.

borrowing, and by printing money. Every government in war uses all three; the main question is which to use most. There are many detailed problems of how to use taxation, borrowing, and printing for the best results.

Each one of us who has a job gets his income from either private business or the Government, and each one pays out his income, so much to the Government by paying taxes and so much to private business by buying things on Main Street. In peacetime about one-quarter of us get our money from national, state, and local governments, and three-quarters of us get ours from private business of some kind. On the average, therefore, we all have to pay about one-quarter of our money in taxes and the rest to the butcher and the baker. In war about half of us will be working for the Federal Government and getting our money from the Federal Treasury, so on the average we are all going to pay about half our money to the Federal Government, besides of course having to support our states and cities. Whatever proportion of our total income the Government takes away from us, about the same proportion of the people get their pay from the Government, so that in any case the money goes around the circle. There is a big difference between a pioneer settlement where everyone works for himself and a country like Russia where practically everyone works for the Government, but the money goes around its circulation just the same whether the employers are private or public. So now that we are going to do half our work for the United States, there is no mechanical reason why we should not tax ourselves half our income to pay for half our work.

We are not going to do it that way, but we should understand that it could be done that way without unbalancing any budgets, or bankrupting the nation, or running out of money either in Washington or in Main Street. We may have to do without automobile tires, and some other pleasant things, but that is something else. So far as money is concerned, a 60-billion-dollar budget will not drain the country of money, because the money flows in a circle, like the blood in your body.

Well, then, why not simply tax ourselves whatever is necessary, and avoid a war debt?

There are obstacles in the way of a 60-billion-dollar tax schedule. If we should use the easy kinds of taxes, such as sales and pay-roll taxes, on any such scale, the load of taxation would wreck the private business of the country by taking too much away from the poorest people. Business, especially in war, depends on the trade of workers and farmers and other people with small incomes, who buy food and simple clothes and rent small houses. For these simple necessary things are about all business has to sell at a time when luxuries must be sacrificed to military needs. Taxes, moreover, must not be laid too heavily on the small incomes, lest the mass of the people fail to get enough of the necessities to maintain their health. Many of the poorest people are overtaxed already.

The fairest way to tax the people is the personal income tax, which takes a larger proportion from the larger incomes. We need to tax away everything above $20,000 or $25,000 a year, and a large share of the rest down to $2,000 or $3,000. England already is doing just that. But the development of such a severe tax takes several years. People with comfortable incomes have habits of living, and have made promises or pledges of various kinds, that can't be suddenly dropped without upsetting our national life. It is like trying to drive a big parade float, with all sorts of tableaux on it, around a sharp turn in the road. The turn will have to be taken slowly, or we shall lose most of the scenery and some of the performers.

Then there is another trouble with taxation. A large part of our income goes through corporations on its way from the buyers to the wage-earners and the stockholders, or owners of the corporations. But the management of any corporation naturally likes to have a fat surplus, to protect it against accidents in an uncertain world. So a large slice of our national income gets stuck in the bank balances of the corporations that are booming during the war. We have to tax the corporations and get almost all of this idle money away from them. But the managers, and the influential stockholders, are apt to kick to their Congressmen, and ask to have loopholes put in the law.

For example, in the summer of 1940, some of our powerful corporations objected to the excess profits tax, though it was going to take only 50 per cent of the excess over an 8 per cent profit. The tax bill, however, allowed corporations to choose between this and another way of figuring that let some of the richest companies get away. A much more severe tax will have to be used now, but it will take time to get it passed and enforced. Meanwhile the Government has to drive ahead with the war, tax or no tax.

As soon as Congress can be persuaded to act, we need a tax system that will do two things: First, it must take away as much as possible of our money that we might hold idle in corporation or personal hoards, or that we might spend for luxuries. Second, it must tax heavily those articles which are made of scarce materials that we need for war — chiefly metals.

The rules to remember are these: A good tax system raises the most money possible with the least damage to the health and welfare of the people; and, The heavier the total tax bill, the stronger the nation will be.

But at best, our taxes are going to lag behind our war program, and so the Government will have to borrow from us the money it fails to take from us in taxes. Or else it will have to print money, or do something that amounts to the same thing. These two ways of getting money need to be considered together because of the way new money is actually created.

In the old days most Americans made all payments in cash. That is still true for some Americans, but now about 90 per cent of our payments are made by check, and only the other 10 per cent are made with paper money and small change. If the Government were to print an extra 10 billion dollars of paper money and pay it out to the soldiers and sailors, the 10 billion would be added to what we are now carrying around in our pockets. But the amount we carry is a matter of habit; we put the rest in the bank. Within a couple of weeks most of the 10 billion would be turned into bank balances, and there would be practically no more paper money floating around than before. Checks would still be used to make 90 per cent of our business and personal payments. So we can dismiss the printing of money, and look instead at the way new money is actually created in the United States.

The Government, like many people, pays its bills with checks. When the Government sells a bond to a commercial bank, the bank does not hand the Government the money in dollar bills out of the vault. The bank adds the price of the bond to the Government's deposit — the amount that the bank owes to the Government. Then the bank lays away the bonds which show that the Government owes the price of the bond to the bank. The two debts balance, but the check account is new money ready to be paid out. This is the way new money is now created and added to the total stock of money in the country — not by printing dollar bills. The effect is much the same, for there is more money loose in the market. But it is important to recognize how the new money is made, and not be fooled while keeping an eye on the mint. Money is born chiefly in banks, not in the mint.

But look at what happens when the Government sells a bond to a person or to any corporation that is not a commercial bank. When I buy a war bond, I have no government

THE RISE OF PRICES
WHOLESALE PRICES

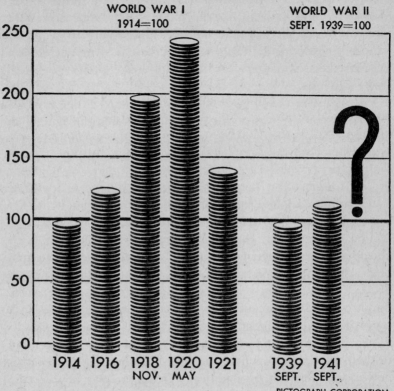

WORLD WAR I
1914=100

WORLD WAR II
SEPT. 1939=100

PICTOGRAPH CORPORATION

In the First World War the Army and the Navy sometimes bid against one another. Businessmen tried to hoard materials and speculators withheld products from the market. Prices thus began to rise. As the war program advanced, other pressures were added. There was a shortage of workers. Competitive bidding for labor increased wages, which created new buying power while goods were scarce; prices went up still higher.

Constant price increases tend to make people spend faster because they fear their money may buy less later on. They bid up the few goods that can be bought — and prices mount further.

check account to write the money into; I have to pay my own money to the Treasurer of the United States. Afterwards I have the bond and he has the money, but there is no more money in the picture than before. Borrowing from persons and business corporations does not create new money to flood the markets, and therefore does not make prices go up the way new money is apt to do.

This is why the Treasury is trying so hard to sell bonds to you and me. It wants to get the money without having the markets flooded with newborn dollars from the banks, because those new dollars are likely to increase prices and cause inflation.

THE PROBLEM OF INFLATION

"Inflation" is the word used for either a flood of new money or a severe rise in prices, or both. Actually prices are pushed from two sides. They are pushed up by an increase in the amount of money circulating, and pushed down by an increase in the amount of goods for sale. If these balance, no harm is done; prices stay about as they were. But if the quantity of goods for sale grows smaller while the people get more money to spend, you get inflation on both ends, and prices go up toward the sky. So it is easy to see why an inflation is apt to happen in a war, and why it did happen in this country from 1917 to 1920. Inflation comes when the number of goods for sale is reduced by war priorities, which take goods for defense, while the total amount of money paid to workers and businessmen is increased.

A serious inflation is bad for a country, in war as in peace, because the higher prices hurt unfairly those who do not get an increase in their incomes; they tempt businessmen to hoard materials that are needed for the war and that may rise in price; and they run up the Government's costs and so create even

HOW TO PREVENT INFLATION

PICTOGRAPH CORPORATION

more inflation. A really bad inflation could lose us the war by its disorganizing effect on our production.

How can we prevent a serious inflation? By a combination of four kinds of action. First, by taxing as heavily as possible as soon as possible, so that people will not have too much money to spend. Second, by borrowing as much as possible from those with money to spend. Third, by doing what little can be done to increase the supply of civilian goods where they don't interfere with military goods. Fourth, by having a price-control authority with power to forbid the asking or paying of unreasonable prices. We shall have to use all four of these methods boldly and powerfully if we are to keep the money cost of the war down to anything like 60 billion dollars a year.

So far as money is concerned, therefore, we can recognize that the money cost of the war will be paid first by the Government to the people for labor and goods, and then by the people back to the Government in taxes or by buying war bonds. A part of the cost, but a part which should be as small as possible, may be covered by new money, printed by the Government or issued by the banks. We really pay this, too, not directly as we ought to, but indirectly through a rise of prices, which is much more expensive than taxes.

WAR DOES NOT USE UP OUR MONEY

Some people, who were frightened by the spending of the New Deal, are disturbed when they hear talk of a 60-billion-dollar budget, and wonder whether we may not run out of money. This fear is caused by misunderstanding.

If the doctor gives you a stimulant that steps up your heart-beat, your heart will suck more blood out of your veins, but you don't run out of blood on that account. The blood is pushed into your arteries and goes jumping around the system faster, doing more work. It would be the same with our money if the Government could tax or borrow from us the same amount it pays out to us. The only slip is in the creation of new money, which is added to the stream and raises the blood pressure of the business world; that is, raises price levels and brings inflation.

No, we can't run out of money by government spending. Quite the other way, the danger is that we may flood the system with too much money. Don't worry about the country's going short of money. Worry about inflation, for it is there that we must guard ourselves or there will be trouble.

In all this discussion so far, it has been taken for granted that you know what money is, without having a definition for it. The economists are not so sure of what money is, and their definitions are apt to shed more fog than light. To you and me, of course, our own money is quite simple. It is a piece of paper or metal that we can use to buy things. If you have a dollar, it means that all the rest of us together owe you, and will give you, a dollar's worth of anything you want that is for sale. That is what money is to you, a claim on your fellow countrymen. Is money a kind of " wealth "? Yes, to you it is if you have it.

But how about the whole American people? What is money to the nation? Each dollar is a debt, owed by us all to the person who has the dollar. All the dollars, taken together, are a debt we owe to one another. To the nation, the money is not wealth, except for the metal value of the coins as junk. What is the money, then? The money is a bookkeeping system, by which we can tell who has the legal right to various shares of the total of things for sale. That explains why, though you or I may run out of money, the whole nation can't run out of money. So long as we have people who know how to do the bookkeeping, we can keep on with our bookkeeping indefinitely.

The problems of paying the money cost of the war are therefore problems of bookkeeping. They boil down to a question of who is going to have the claims on our limited stock of civilian goods at a time when the Government is claiming about half of all we can produce. The money itself is not a cost at all, only a way of dividing up the sacrifices and the benefits of our labors. If we do a good job of bookkeeping, the sacrifices will be the least possible under the strain of war. If we bungle the job, the result will be to hurt some people too much and give others a soft time, and to create confusion and lost motion. To bungle the job of war finance is to add the costs of confusion to the necessary costs of war. And too much confusion might mean losing the war, which is the greatest cost that we can imagine.

WHAT WAR REALLY COSTS

That brings us to the whole question of the real costs of the war and how we shall have to pay them. War, with all its horrors, has one advantage — it makes us see the real meaning of national strength, because war is a test of strength. Strength is not everything. A nation needs also liberty, religion, art, and all the rest of civilization. But strength is something, and it is well worth understanding. Strength is made up of material resources, and of human health and skill and courage, and of organization that works smoothly to enable us to do our work and live our lives. Here in the world of real things and real people we must look for the real costs of war.

First as to resources. The United States is a rich nation, but we are using up some of our materials for war that we could otherwise use for peace, and that is a real cost. We are losing a considerable amount of lead, zinc, copper, and other metals that we have in only limited quantities. We shall miss these metals forever. As for aluminum, we have tremendous quantities of clay from which we now know how to extract that metal. The aluminum scarcity is a temporary scarcity of plants for extracting it. And the water power to run the plants comes back again year after year. So aluminum is not a cost.

In the other World War we spent land, by plowing the plains that afterward became the Dust Bowl. Some of that land was permanently lost. That was a real cost of war. This time, though we are still losing land by erosion, the only real war cost in land is the amount that we lose by " economizing " on our program of soil conservation.

Ships that are sunk at sea, and buildings that are knocked down by bombs, represent some loss, though not as much as you might think. The steel in the ship has not much value, because iron ore is not scarce. The ship contains some valuable copper and perhaps some things in its cargo that will be missed in 1980 because they went to the bottom of the sea in 1942. As for the houses that are knocked down, the chief losses are works of art, keepsakes, furniture, and other articles that can never be replaced. The houses themselves are composed of brick, timber, and labor, and less than a year's work will rebuild England, for example, considerably better than it was. The greatest losses are apt to be in failing to protect the real treasures, such as art, science, and social progress, through a simple-minded idea that the ordinary governmental services are not part of the war.

So it is all along the line. The war cost in material wealth is made up of the scarce minerals we use up for war, and of any losses of soil, forests, or other wealth that may occur because Congress may mistake the cost of saving them for a " nonessential " and cut off the appropriations. Some of these costs, therefore, are physically unavoidable, and others are avoidable if our legislators keep clearly in mind that defending our resources is a part of national defense.

The second class of real costs is the loss of people that may come in the war. If the war continues until we have time to get in on a big scale, we shall lose thousands of strong, healthy young men in battle. But even the losses in battle are not exactly a measure of the real loss. Undoubtedly, up to the end of 1941, of the men in the armed services more were alive and healthy than would have been so if they had stayed in civilian life. In civilian life some hundreds of them would have been killed in automobile accidents, and about half of them would have been undernourished and unprotected against disease. The net loss will be the difference between the number who die because of the war and the number whose lives are saved by being pulled out of the dangers of civilian life.

As for the rest of the population, the effect of the war up to the end of 1941 was probably a net gain in health and happiness as compared with the year 1940, when there were fewer jobs. The record Christmas trade of 1941 is an indication that people were feeling pretty comfortable, even after Pearl Harbor. The American people were having to do with fewer new refrigerators, but they had more butter and meat to put in the old ones. In 1942, the shortage of tires may force us to drive under 40 miles an hour, and thus may save a few thousand of us from sudden death. Adding it all up, the American people, so far, have not had to pay much in life and health.

No such happy situation is to be found in the warring countries where food is really scarce, especially on the continent of Europe. There starvation and disease are ravaging the people, and the losses are real and fearful. In England, with bombing and food restrictions and a severe shortage of cigarettes, the population as a whole is reported to be in better health and spirits than before the war. This interesting result is believed to be caused mainly by the fact that the people now have something to do and a sense of belonging to the team, two of the best-known medicines for about half the ailments of humanity.

As America gets deeper into the war, we are not likely to suffer from lack of food. On the contrary, our poorest people will probably continue to get more and better food than ever before. We shall probably find, like the British, that war work cures a lot of nervous diseases connected with idleness and lonesomeness. But if we are not careful, we may suffer by carelessness that opens the way for epidemics of contagious disease.

In 1918, we lost more people by influenza than we had lost in battle. Part of that flu epidemic was a war cost, because we had failed to build houses for war workers, and around some of the shipyards and plants the men were sleeping in bunks crowded close together in stuffy rooms. This time, we have a big defense housing program, but there is still a dangerous amount of crowding.

Another example that may seem far away will serve to show how the world is tied together. The horrible Gambia mosquito that carries a deadly form of malaria got into Brazil from Africa by airplane a few years ago, but has now been stamped out by heroic work and organization. What if it comes again in German bombers, and gets loose? It could even make us move out of some of our Southern states. That would be a cost of war with a vengeance.

Finally, we may pay a fearful price for the war if we fail once more to organize our own country, and fail to help organize the world, to build peace and prosperity when the war is over. We may start once more to scrimp on the money, and waste our wealth and our people with unemployment. Then instead of rebuilding we shall destroy more of the real good in our country in a year of disorganization and depression than all the losses of the war put together. Peace has its horrors as well as war, and if weariness and disorganization should come out of victory, it will again be, as it was twenty years ago, a costly victory, leading to troubles without measure.

As we look to the future, we must understand what the real costs of war will be, how we shall pay them or how the oncoming generations must pay. According to the wisdom of our handling the war and the peace, the costs will be less or greater, and the burden on our children will be bearable or unbearable.

The money cost of the war will not burden us, nor our descendants, if it is wisely handled. Bookkeeping in itself is no serious burden to the nation unless it is so badly done as to get in the way of more important matters.

The war taxes, during the war, are only the bookkeeping by which we organize for all-out war work; that is, for giving everyone a job. The depression has taught those who did not know it before that hard work is no curse. True, the products are partly wasted, but that is not a money cost; it is a material cost.

FUTURE EFFECTS OF THE WAR DEBT

After the war there will be the war debt, and that also will be less of a burden than one might suppose. Future governments are not going to pay that debt to us, or to any foreign country, or even to our children. Nations seldom try to pay off their debts, and when they do try, as we did before 1929, the results are so disastrous that they soon give it up. Strong nations pay their bonds, but ordinarily they sell new ones at the same time.

Federal bonds offer opportunity to invest idle money and are used as the foundation stones in the financial structure of insurance companies, banks, universities, and other institutions of all sorts. Any serious attempt to pay the national debt would really mean taxing the holders of these bonds and paying them their own money, which would mean closing some of these institutions or reducing their activities. As it is, we can tax pretty closely the same people and pay them the interest with their own money, which keeps all in order without upsetting these useful financial structures.

There is no use being cynical about financial institutions, debts that are never paid, and interest paid to people out of their own pockets. Certainly this is all a matter of bookkeeping. But though debts and finances are only paper work, they have a real use in keeping track of the claims of people for a share in goods produced. A life-insurance policy doesn't add or subtract anything noticeable to or from the food that will be distributed in the future, but it will give certain orphans a claim on some of the food. The national debt will become more and more necessary as a backing for life insurance, as the sum deposited with American insurance companies rises from 40 to 80 to 120 billions. Since the policyholders will be much the same people as the taxpayers, the actual burden on the whole country of the interest payments will be almost entirely imaginary, but the protection of insurance for individuals will be real.

Only if the taxes to carry the interest are laid on poor people, as they were in the twenties after the First World War, will the war debt become a burden. And even then the burden will be not so much the taxes themselves as their effect in making many people unable to buy goods that need to be sold if business is to be prosperous. Here, as in every problem of public finance, the real question is not how large the public debt may be. The real question is how much we can increase the personal income and inheritance taxes, and hold down sales taxes, real-estate taxes, and all taxes resting on the poorest people.

It is near enough for practical voting purposes to put the

principles of public finance in this form: No Federal expenditure can be a burden if it causes a corresponding increase in production and income that would not occur otherwise.

Whether taxes are a burden is almost entirely a matter of what kind of taxes they are. In general, real-estate, sales, payroll, excise, and import taxes hurt business in peacetime and are a cause of unemployment and relief. Income and inheritance taxes rest easily on business and help to prevent both booms and depressions. Whether posterity will suffer grievous burdens along with the war debt will depend not on the debt but on the shape of the tax system, and that would be equally true if there had been no war.

On the other hand, the real cost of the war that we or our children must pay is the net sacrifice of resources, of life, of health, of harmony, and of happiness that may result by necessity or by error from our efforts to prevent the total loss that would come from yielding to the dictators. The future must suffer if on the whole we and our children are less healthy or less able to live happily than we should have been without the war. And above all the future will pay dearly if after the war we sit down exhausted and let the world go to pot as we did after 1919.

But if we manage wisely, and do not fear to pay the money cost of protecting our resources and our people, we can sail into the peace with new hope and new courage. We can set ourselves to build up our own country and to help build up the world, a job that will give us plenty to do if only we are boldly determined to win the peace. In so doing, we can turn the material costs of war into a job of work for human hands to do, in building a better world. And before the war came to interrupt, such a mighty job that would employ us all was exactly what we hoped and dreamed. After the war, that hope will still lie before us.

XII. How can censorship help win the war?

BYRON PRICE

A background of more than thirty years of newspaper work, coupled with broad executive experience and a knowledge of the Army in wartime, gave Byron Price special qualifications for his present position as Director of Censorship. For five years he has been executive news editor of the Associated Press, and previously he served for a decade as chief of its Washington bureau. During the World War he received a leave of absence to serve in France as a captain of infantry. He has covered many important stories, ranging from President Wilson's tragic transcontinental campaign for the League of Nations to the London Naval Conference of 1930.

It is as important for a nation at war to find out what is happening on the enemy's " home front " as it is to learn his immediate preparations for battle. Troop movements, shipping schedules, progress in the manufacture of airplanes and tanks — all this information is of great importance in planning opposition strategy.

Each nation naturally makes every effort to prevent the enemy from obtaining such material. It tries to thwart efforts of enemy agents or sympathizers to communicate with colleagues in other countries, and it tries also to stop " leaks " from innocent but careless citizens who unconsciously might give out important military or armament data.

Censorship of communications is the logical result. In this way, vital information is stopped at the nation's boundaries, and in some cases, within the country itself.

To Americans who have been reared in a proud heritage of freedom of speech and freedom of the press, any censorship is distasteful. Almost from the start of the republic, the Bill of Rights has guaranteed a cherished freedom of expression. Even in wartime, the people properly believe that their rights should be jealously guarded — that individuals should be able to criticize acts of the Government and that the public should be given all information which can consistently be disclosed.

But the people also are aware that wartime brings necessary restrictions for the good of the country as a whole. It is the responsibility of every citizen to keep information from the enemy. Not only is censorship designed to achieve that objective, but operation of the censorship system brings to the Government much valuable information about enemy plans and about possible subversive activity inside the country itself.

So essential is censorship to the conduct of a war that the United States put expert Army and Navy officers and other government officials to work on basic censorship plans long before Japan's raid on Pearl Harbor. Censorship of cable and wireless communications to and from the United States went into operation within a few hours after that attack, as did examination of mail crossing American borders.

Less than two weeks later, on December 19, 1941, President Roosevelt formally established the Office of Censorship. He signed an executive order directing that Office to censor all types of communications coming into or leaving the United States. In a statement issued from the White House, he summarized the American viewpoint toward censorship:

All Americans abhor censorship, just as they abhor war. But the experience of this and of all other nations has demonstrated that some degree of censorship is essential in wartime, and we are at war.

The important thing now is that such forms of censorship as are necessary shall be administered effectively and in harmony with the best interests of our free institutions.

It is necessary that a watch be set upon our borders, so that no such information may reach the enemy, inadvertently or otherwise, through the medium of the mails, radio or cable transmission, or by any other means.

It is necessary that prohibitions against the domestic publication of some types of information, contained in long-existing statutes, be rigidly enforced.

Finally, the Government has called upon a patriotic press and radio to abstain voluntarily from the dissemination of detailed information of certain kinds, such as reports of the movements of vessels and troops. The response has indicated a universal desire to co-operate.

In order that all of these parallel and requisite undertakings may be co-ordinated and carried forward in accordance with a single uniform policy, I have appointed Byron Price, executive news editor of the Associated Press, to be director of censorship, responsible directly to the President. He has been granted a leave of absence by the Associated Press and will take over the post assigned him within the coming week or sooner.

The censorship system established by President Roosevelt's order is an entirely different plan from that adopted in 1917–18. On April 13, 1917, a week after the United States declared war on Germany, President Wilson created a Committee on Public Information. George Creel, widely known writer and editor, was appointed chairman. The Secretaries of State, War, and Navy were the other members. Similarly, censorship of international communications was divided among a committee.

The Committee on Public Information did much more than set up a voluntary program of restricting publication of military secrets. It set about mobilizing public opinion behind the war effort by providing a mass of news stories, articles, pictures, posters, speeches, and other patriotic material. It handled government publicity. It sent news, photographs, and films abroad. It did special work in organizing women and groups of foreign-born residents for patriotic activities. Its " Four Minute Men " made talks throughout the country.

In the present war, this work has been divided. The Office of Censorship prevents the dissemination of information of value to the enemy. Certain other government agencies are charged with presenting the facts about the United States' war effort to the American people and to the world.

This chapter is concerned solely with the censorship operations. In general, these are divided into two parts: examinations of communications entering or leaving the United States, and voluntary restrictions on circulating vital information within the country. Let us see how these phases operate.

BORDER CENSORSHIP

The biggest physical work of the Office of Censorship is examining letters, post cards, newspapers, magazines, cablegrams, and radiograms brought into or sent out of the United States. There must even be a check on carrier pigeons! Communications must be studied not only to determine whether any part of the text obviously gives away military secrets but also to see whether they might contain hidden codes.

Within a month after the outbreak of war, more than a thousand men and women were engaged in this important and confidential task. Before the war ends, as many as ten thousand persons may be employed in censorship activities.

What sort of men and women should these postal and cable

censors be? Above all, they must be loyal Americans; their patriotism must be unquestioned. They must have sharp eyes and sharp minds. Many of the censors are experts in one or more foreign languages. Others are trained businessmen who can tell whether business and financial correspondence is legitimate or suspicious.

Communication of any kind with enemy and enemy-occupied countries was banned as soon as war broke out. It would not be safe to permit even the most innocent-sounding letters to be sent to those lands; every sentence might contain hidden information that eventually would be used to the detriment of the United States. Arrangements were made, however, for the American Red Cross to forward brief personal messages to families in enemy territory.

For communications to all other countries, the Office of Censorship issued instructions setting forth in general what material should be omitted. These instructions, for example, asked that mail be written in English if possible. They also advised:

Avoid use of abbreviations, nicknames, phrases or codes in place of customary reference or descriptions of any person, firm, location, or other information.

No mention should be made of defense matters, shipping, or weather conditions.

For cables and radiograms, restrictions were greater. In normal times such messages are written in amazingly few words; often the meaning is clear only to the sender and the recipient. Firms and individuals doing considerable business by cable use codes to make one word do the work of several; this is an economy practice, for the cost per word ranges from a few cents to a dollar or more, depending on the distance and the type of service desired.

Obviously, such codes — except a few made available to the public by the cable companies — could not be continued in wartime. Addresses and signatures must be written in full, and the meaning of each cabled message must be understandable to the censor.

Cable censorship requires a small staff compared to the number of men and women needed to examine the mails. Postal censorship offices are situated at the principal American ports and at border cities. To those offices sack after sack of mail destined for foreign countries or for distribution from foreign countries into the United States is brought for careful reading.

If a letter is found to contain no information of military or economic value, the censor seals it with a strip of paper and stamps it with his number. If the censor finds that a letter contains restricted information, or even if he is suspicious of its contents, it is referred to other officials for further investigation.

This censorship process is not purely the negative operation of stopping vital information from crossing the border. In the operation, the United States Government obtains much valuable information for itself. Intercepted communications may contain evidence of enemy spy activities or of plans for sabotage. In addition, material coming into the United States may contain information about the situation in enemy lands — whether there is discontent among the people, whether production is going forward satisfactorily, whether various enemy claims are true.

All this material is utilized to advantage by United States military, naval, and civilian officials. A scrap of information may be found in one letter; another scrap may turn up in a letter in another censorship station; they can be pieced together in central offices to tell a story which may deeply affect the course of the war.

PUBLIC OPINION IN WARTIME

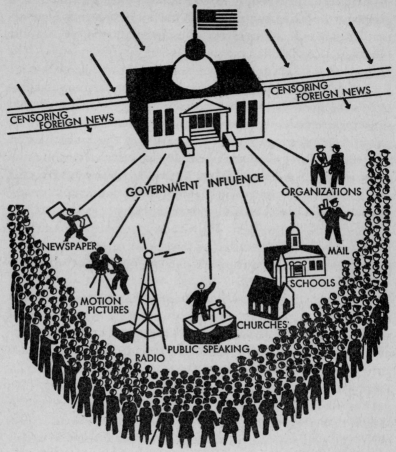

PICTOGRAPH CORPORATION

Our Government rigidly controls only a small part of communications: foreign mails. All other censorship is voluntary. Newspapers, magazines, radio, and the movies try to eliminate all news that may help the enemy. Thus even in wartime public opinion flows in two directions. The Government influences public opinion through its censorship and press releases, and sometimes through the movies and the radio. But the public also influences the Government in countless ways.

Material intercepted by American censors can be utilized in connection with information obtained by British and Canadian censors, for close co-operation is being practiced by all those offices.

In general, such nations as Great Britain and Canada have the same kind of censorship as we do. Great Britain has had to develop postal and cable censorship stations virtually around the world, because of the spread of its colonies.

Little information has been disclosed in the United States about methods of German censorship. Letters received from Germany by Americans before the United States entered the war, however, showed clearly that a thorough censorship examination had been made of the contents.

DOMESTIC CENSORSHIP

If a wall could be built around the United States so that no one could enter or leave, if the sky could be patrolled so that no enemy agent could escape in a plane or send out a message by carrier pigeon, if all communication with other countries could be stopped, there would be no need for internal censorship. But those are a lot of " ifs." Efficient as censorship of material crossing the borders may be, its operators cannot be confident that the system is perfect.

Consequently, there must be some restrictions on the military and economic information which is circulated freely inside the United States. Determining the extent of those restrictions calls for clear thinking and good judgment by men who have the welfare of American institutions at heart.

In peacetime, the American press and the American radio are the freest in the world. In wartime, the same statement holds true. It is the aim and the intention of the Office of Censorship to permit the disclosure of every bit of information which cannot be classed as vital to the enemy. There is no attempt by the Office of Censorship to prevent the people from learning the progress of the war from day to day or to curtail their expressions of opinion on the conduct of the war.

Editors and broadcasters have displayed high patriotism in their realization that harm could be caused if some limitations were not devised regarding the disclosure of military secrets. For radio stations, these restrictions necessarily must be more stringent than for newspapers. Newspapers and periodicals can be censored at the borders of the United States, but signals of hundreds of commercial American radio stations are heard thousands of miles beyond our shores. Once a statement has been broadcast, it cannot be recalled; on the other hand, a certain amount of time elapses between the writing of a news story and its publication, during which it can be edited or rejected. Still more time elapses before that publication is mailed outside the country.

To retain the democratic method in restricting military information, the co-operation of editors and broadcasters was sought for a voluntary censorship program. They readily assented, and aided the Office of Censorship in drawing up codes of wartime practices for their respective industries.

These codes cover specific problems affecting newspapers, periodicals, and radio programs. They are under the direct supervision of two assistant directors in the Office of Censorship. No censors are placed in individual newspaper offices or broadcasting stations; editors and broadcasters use their own judgment in complying with the codes. Whenever they are in doubt, they present their specific problems to the Office of Censorship and receive prompt advice as to whether certain material can be published or broadcast or whether it should be withheld.

Here is an outline of the specific information which newspapers and magazines are asked not to publish except when the information is made available officially by appropriate authority:

TROOPS: The general character and movements of United States Army, Navy, or Marine Corps units, within or without the continental limits of the United States — their location, identity, or exact composition, equipment, or strength; their destination, routes, and schedules; their assembly for embarkation, prospective embarkation, or actual embarkation. Any such information regarding the troops of friendly nations on American soil.

SHIPS: The location, movements, and identity of naval and merchant vessels of the United States in any waters, and of other nations opposing the Axis Powers in American waters; the port and the time of arrival or prospective arrival of any such vessels, or the port from which they leave; the nature of cargoes of such vessels; the location of enemy naval or merchant vessels in or near American waters; the assembly, departure, or arrival of transports or convoys; the existence of mine fields or other harbor defenses; secret orders or other secret instructions regarding lights, buoys, and other guides to navigators; the number, size, character, and location of ships in construction, or advance information as to the date of launchings or commissionings; the physical setup or technical details of shipyards.

PLANES: The disposition, movements, and strength of Army or Navy air units.

FORTIFICATIONS: Location of forts and other fortifications; location of coast-defense emplacements, or antiaircraft guns; their nature and number; location of bomb shelters; location of camouflaged objects.

PRODUCTION: Specific information about war contracts, such as the exact type of production, production schedules, dates of delivery, or progress of production; estimated supplies of strategic and critical materials available; or nation-wide " round-ups " of locally published procurement data, except when such composite information is officially approved for publication.

Specific information about the location of, or other information about, sites and factories already in existence which would aid saboteurs in gaining access to them; information other than that readily gained through observation by the general public, disclosing the location of sites and factories yet to be established, or the nature of their production. Any information about new or secret military designs, or new factory designs for war production.

WEATHER: Weather forecasts, other than those officially issued by the Weather Bureau; the routine forecasts printed by any single newspaper to cover only the state in which it is published and not more than four adjoining states, portions of which lie within a radius of 150 miles from the point of publication. Consolidated temperature tables covering more than 20 stations, in any one newspaper. Weather " roundup " stories covering actual conditions throughout more than one state, except when given out by the Weather Bureau.

PHOTOGRAPHS AND MAPS: Photographs conveying the information specified in this summary, unless officially approved for publication. Detailed maps or photographs disclosing location of munition dumps, or other restricted Army or Naval areas.

GENERAL: Casualty lists, except information about casualties from a newspaper's local field, obtained from nearest of kin. It is requested that in such cases specific military and naval units and exact locations be not mentioned.

Information disclosing the new location of national archives, art treasures, and so on, which have been moved for safe-keeping.

Information about damage to military and naval objectives,

including docks, railroads, and commercial airports, resulting from enemy action.

Information about the transportation of munitions or other war materials, including oil tank cars and trains.

Information about the movements of the President of the United States, or of official military or diplomatic missions of the United States or of any other nation opposing the Axis Powers — routes, schedules, or destination, within or without the continental limits of the United States; movements of ranking Army or Navy officers and staffs on official business; movements of other individuals or units under special orders of the Army, Navy, or State Department.

There is a sound reason for limiting each type of the foregoing information. The need for restricting reports of troop, plane, and ship movements is obvious. The reasons for curtailing information about production of war materials are equally clear when it is considered that this is a war of economic as well as of military strength. Even detailed weather forecasts might help the enemy decide when to make an air raid on American cities. Publication of casualty lists giving the units of the dead or injured men would tell the enemy what troops were immediately opposing him.

The code of wartime practices for broadcasters covers in general the same material as the press code. Several additional restrictions were found necessary, however, to prevent enemy agents or sympathizers from using broadcasts to communicate information across the borders. Broadcasters were requested to exercise extraordinary care over all programs in which the public has easy access to the microphone. In an impromptu " man in the street " program of interviews, for instance, an enemy agent might utter a seemingly innocent sentence which would contain an important secret signal. A request that a radio station play a certain musical number at a certain time might be another code. Transcripts of foreign language programs are being kept.

CENSORSHIP PRACTICE IN BRIEF

Since it is generally agreed that censorship is necessary in wartime, the question that confronted the United States Government at the start of the present conflict was: What form shall censorship take?

As put into practice by the Office of Censorship, the answer is twofold:

1. Communications crossing the borders of the United States are examined, and censored if necessary.

2. Within the country, newspapers, periodicals, and radio stations are co-operating in a voluntary censorship of material which might give valuable information to the enemy.

By this double process, the Office of Censorship believes that important information can be safeguarded and that at the same time the American people can receive an accurate and detailed picture of the war's progress until final victory is achieved.

XIII. How are we organized for psychological warfare?

LADISLAS FARAGO

Ladislas Farago, a Hungarian by birth, was for a number of years foreign correspondent for English and American newspapers. He was in the Berlin office of the 'New York Times' for four years; was sent to Ethiopia for the Associated Press; was foreign correspondent for the London 'Sunday Chronicle' and the 'News Review,' covering all Europe. He is author of 'Abyssinia on the Eve,' 'Riddle of Arabia,' 'Palestine at the Crossroads,' and is now working on a book to be entitled 'The Secret History of the Second World War.' He is also a contributor to 'Asia' magazine, the 'New Republic,' and the 'Nation,' and editor of 'German Psychological Warfare,' and 'The Axis Grand Strategy,' publications of the Committee for National Morale. He is chief editorial consultant of that committee.

Wars are no longer fought with just armies and navies, with air fleets and blockades; they are fought also with leaflets, with radio, and with " fifth columns." The fifth columns, the leaflets, and the radio are all employed to spread ideas, with the hope that the ideas will build up morale at home and weaken, if not destroy, morale in enemy countries. This battle of ideas is known as psychological warfare, and everyone — young and old, men and women, soldiers and civilians — is subjected to it. It is as omnipresent as the weather, and sometimes, as with the

Russian winter, it proves itself quite as powerful as mighty armaments.

In the old days when wars were fought by professional soldiers, morale — at least, as we understand it today — was of minor importance. Frederick the Great, for example, paid no attention to the morale of his civilian subjects and not much more to the morale of his soldiers. He concentrated on drill and discipline. If his armies could be taught to do exactly as they were told to do, they would become the kind of war weapon he wanted. Their spirit — though " spirit " does seem a strange word to indicate their emotional attitude — was known as *Kadavergehorsam,* the obedient one of corpses. Nothing could be more beautifully Prussian than such blind obedience, and it still dominated the German Army at the outbreak of the First World War. It was believed then that sound strategy would win a war if it was perfectly executed by soldiers equipped with superior weapons. The Germans — and the rest of the world — discovered that the best strategy executed by the best soldiers using the best weapons would win only battles, and, strangely, not always those. On the basis of sheer military strength, the Germans should have won at Verdun, but the French spirit, expressed so perfectly in their battle cry *Ils ne passeront pas* (They shall not pass), actually proved capable of hurling back those perfectly trained, perfectly equipped German soldiers, who had the obedience to become corpses at command. The French spirit was positive, the German essentially negative — and the positive was the stronger.

It soon became obvious that the old theories of warfare were no longer adequate. The world had changed. The battlefield was no longer isolated from the homeland. Soldiers were no longer merely mercenaries, hired and trained to do a job. Armies were so much larger that the problem of supply had become infinitely more complex, and its solution depended on the people at home — and on their morale. While the armies had grown larger, the world itself had grown much, much smaller. The enormous increase in speed of all kinds of transport had decimated the distance between the civilians and the battlefield; and when the airplane became a weapon of war, the distance was wiped out entirely — the airplane swept through the skies and brought the battlefield to the civilians. Then they became a part of the war, a very important part, and they had received no training in becoming corpses. New methods of fighting had to be found, and the most effective method proved to be mental — that is, psychological warfare.

WHAT IS IT?

What is psychological warfare? It is the systematic preparation and execution of many operations that are designed to destroy the enemy's will to fight and, at the same time, to build up will to fight at home. It has one other important function too, which is to influence public opinion among nonbelligerents. From the day Hitler rose to power, the Germans have used almost every possible method to sway all the minds and the feelings of the Germans. The first purpose, of course, was to strengthen the Nazi party, and the second to strengthen the German war effort. A continuous intellectual war has been fought with all the enemy countries, and an intellectual war, just as continuous, has been fought in the nonbelligerent countries. For years German agents and German propaganda have been extremely active in all Latin America. What's more, they have won victories that have caused, and are causing, us no end of trouble.

The field of operations of this psychological struggle is limited by neither time nor space. It is conducted where the fighting is thickest, and where there is no fighting, and where none is expected. It is timeless because it begins without a declaration of war and does not end with truces, armistices, or peace treaties. Nowadays, it is never-ending.

The Germans call psychological warfare " war in peace " or " the war between wars," which does not mean at all that it is not waged with even increased vigor during actual hostilities; but it begins long before the hostilities do, and Colonel Blau, an important official in the German High Command, has emphasized that the most important feature of intellectual war is that it must score its most important victories before hostilities begin.

HOW DOES IT WORK?

The weapons of psychological warfare are propaganda and education. In a sense, propaganda is the offensive arm of the intellectual forces, education the defensive arm. According to Blau, propaganda is a bridge leading from new ideas to their eventual realization. The object of the propagandists, of course, is to induce people to walk across that bridge. If the propaganda is effective, they have forgotten their old ideas by the time they have reached the other end — and have accepted the new ideas. Education, however, is used to build morale at home — not only that, but also to keep the people at home from crossing bridges erected by enemy propagandists.

Germany changed its strategy to meet the requirements of intellectual warfare. General Geyer, commander of a German army, advised his colleagues to cease frontal attacks on enemy positions and to attack enemy morale instead. The overpowering din of artillery fire and the shrieking, screaming dive bombers are employed to destroy enemy morale. Many soldiers have testified in the present war that the noise is much harder to bear than the possibility of death. " The aim is now," said General Geyer, " not to destroy the gun, but to paralyze the finger which pulls the trigger."

Similarly, elaborate plans have been evolved to wage psychological warfare on the largest possible scale. The object is not to destroy actual machines of war in enemy countries but to paralyze the hands that turn the war machine. The propagandists aren't after the work, but the workers. They are attempting not physical or mechanical sabotage, but mental and moral sabotage — something subtler and much deadlier. Factories and machines can be rebuilt quickly, but points of view can be changed only slowly, and lost morale can be replaced even more slowly — if at all.

The Germans believe that economic, political, and psychological campaigns are often sufficient by themselves to win a war without resorting to military action. It must be emphasized, however, that no one of these parts of the Nazi total war is an isolated weapon in itself. Each works in conjunction with the others toward the realization of some particular objective. Each has its psychological tactics woven with the tactics of the other two into one grand strategical scheme.

Political warfare, for example, is the effort to get in a strong position before war begins. Germany was making that effort all over Europe long before the first gun was fired in Poland. The gun was actually fired, of course, because this particular campaign in the political warfare had failed; but Germany had had many political successes — and the greatest of them probably was the nonaggression pact signed with Russia just before hostilities opened.

After war begins, all countries continue the political offensive. It is aimed at providing the possibility of a negotiated peace, at breaking up enemy alliances, and at scaring neutrals into giving " voluntary " help. Germany has had many such diplomatic triumphs. Hungary and Rumania are " collaborating," and so is Vichy, though not with very good grace. If, as some maintain, Japan's attack on Pearl Harbor was made as a result of Germany's political offensive, Germany scored a great victory. If, however, as others maintain, Japan made the attack contrary to Germany's wishes at the moment, the apparent victory may be actually a serious defeat.

THE GERMAN CAMPAIGN AGAINST THE U. S.

Hitler has always feared American intervention more than anything else. In his speech of January 30, 1941, he told the German people that a possible American participation in the war had been anticipated and fully provided for in his calculations. His mindfulness of the possibility of American intervention is in striking contrast to the nonchalance with which Kaiser Wilhelm treated the same danger. Even while we were technically neutral, Hitler frankly distrusted our neutrality. He agreed with the German who remarked, " America is so neutral indeed that she does not care who is going to defeat Germany."

The Germans realize clearly enough that even a quick defeat of the Soviet Union and of the United Kingdom would not get the United States out of the path of Nazi domination of the world. But getting the United States out of the path is necessary to Germany's war aims. Since the United States is at present definitely out of range of its war machine, Germany must make its greatest effort to destroy our morale. For the moment, at least, physical attack in adequate force is beyond Hitler's power, but he can wage, he is waging, and he will wage psychological war. The German submarines that are at the moment of this writing sinking American ships along our Atlantic coast are sent primarily to upset our calm and our confidence, even though they may not seriously upset our shipping.

It is important to emphasize that the beginning of Hitler's campaign against our morale did not wait for the outbreak of the present war. It started immediately upon the Nazis' seizure of power in 1933. At first it was mainly defensive, since the main purpose was to " sell " the Hitler regime to the American people, whose goodwill was considered essential to both political and economic success. The effort to sell us the Nazi ideology came later.

But even then the campaign, which was largely educational — " educational," of course, in a propagandist's use of the word — contained elements of attack. The " education " was attempted by short-wave broadcasts, Nazi lecturers in America, and every other possible method of propaganda. In Berlin it was regarded as a preparatory phase of a morale offensive to be followed by an actual morale offensive on the largest possible scale. The whole plan of this offensive was outlined in a document issued by the German Ministry of Propaganda in September, 1933. It went under the title of " General Instructions Concerning German Propaganda Action in the Two Americas," and it was sent to secret agents in both this country and the Argentine. A copy of the document was intercepted by the Second Bureau of the French General Staff, which also succeeded in establishing its authenticity.

Despite the fact that the document is now more than eight years old, it is still the best guide to an understanding of the aims and methods of the German morale offensive. In addition to this document, Schönemann's book *The Art of Influencing the Masses in the United States of America* provides us with more material on German methods of propaganda.

The principles of German propaganda aimed at the United States are these:

First, since American personalities depend on public opinion and not vice versa, the effort must be made to win over public opinion as a whole rather than to convert individuals of importance.

Second, German propaganda must be painstakingly camouflaged: it must never appear as German or as propaganda.

Third, it must be based on accurate knowledge of the intellectual, emotional, and economic trends in the United States. That knowledge must be acquired by special agents working among the American people.

Fourth, it must never try to create new issues and then attempt to " sell " them to Americans. Instead, it must detect existing issues and concentrate on twisting and exploiting them.

Fifth, it must not have a fixed, stationary policy, but one that is extremely flexible and fluid, adapted to day-by-day developments and trends.

Sixth, it cannot be conducted by remote control. While general instructions may come from abroad, their execution must be left exclusively to resident agents.

Seventh, it must utilize to full capacity the good offices of existing Fascist or prototalitarian native American organizations, with whom a working alliance must be established.

Schönemann believes that eight largely independent American institutions have a dominant influence on the formation of American public opinion. It will be amusing to some to find women classed as an American institution, but to others it will be significant. In Germany, women are neither an institution nor an influence on public opinion; they are, as they have been plainly told, bearers of Nazi children.

Here, then, is the list of institutions as Schönemann gives it: the church, the educational system, women, the press, radio, motion pictures, industry and labor — he calls them the business world — and society clubs and fraternities. With typical German efficiency, there are, accordingly, eight almost independent propaganda campaigns conducted against democracy in the United States, each one working with different methods to funnel Nazi propaganda through but one of these eight channels to the American public.

According to the investigations conducted by the American

Committee for National Morale, the agents of German psychological warfare may be divided into two groups: trouble-seekers and troublemakers.

The trouble-seekers are the members of the numerous German fact-finding agencies who ferret out what the Nazis call " kernels of disturbance "; that is, differences of opinion that divide political parties and minority groups, the frustrated ambitions of discarded politicians, racial prejudices and controversies, economic inequalities, petty jealousies in public life, and all other cleavages. These agents maintain contact with Americans of German origin and establish relations with native Americans of German sympathies and with anyone else whose unwitting assistance to the Nazi cause can be secured.

In the United States, we believe in having an active opposition to the government in power; the minority party or parties are essential to a truly democratic government. But the Nazis consider this entirely legitimate opposition among the most important " allies " of their propagandists. This fact was disclosed by the German military writer Banse:

Applied psychology as a weapon of war means propaganda intended to influence the mental attitude of nations toward war. . . . It is essential to attack the enemy nation in its weak spots (and what nation has not its weak spots?), to undermine and break down its resistance, and to convince it that it is being deceived, misled, and brought to destruction by its own government. Thus the people will lose confidence in the justice of its cause so that political opposition in those nations (and what government is without one?) will raise its head and become a powerful troublemaker. The enemy nation's originally solid, powerful, and well-knit fabric must be gradually disintegrated, broken down, rotted, so that it falls apart like a fungus trodden upon in a forest.

Most important of the trouble-seeking agencies is the German Foreign Institute at Stuttgart. For all practical purposes, it is the world's most extensive intelligence service disguised as a patriotic-scientific organization. According to its own prospectus, it is devoted to the study of the " thirty million men and women of German blood living abroad." The Institute claims to have established that there are 5,830,000 Americans of German blood, of whom 2,188,000 were born in Germany. The organization was frankly described by Dr. Richard Csaki, its director, in these highly significant words:

The German Foreign Institute stands in the service of Germandom and aims at the spiritual, racial, and ideological unification of all Germans in one great community. Within Germany, it is the most extensive gathering place of materials concerning foreigners of German origin and German nationals living abroad. The specific duty and responsibility of the Institute to State and Nazi party consists in the most appropriate exploitation of this material. The Institute is at the disposal of all German nationals abroad, as well as organizations of foreign Germans, with guidance and help. The foreign German, no matter what citizenship he may hold, finds here understanding and support by the strength of his membership in the German folkdom.

The 1939 report of the Institute emphasized that

the research of German blood in the United States is of particularly urgent importance. We have now assigned a huge staff of excellently trained experts to this special task. This is the duty of our American Research Department, which is also preparing a central map showing the geographical distribution of German-Americans all over the United States.

According to the Institute's own testimony, it now possesses the complete membership list of 43,000 German organizations functioning in foreign countries — including all German-American societies, associations, churches, schools, and hospitals — with the biographies and personal records of more than

300,000 families of German ancestry. It sends out so-called Home Letters to Germans living in foreign countries, informing them of all the events occurring in the regions from which they emigrated. Some of its regional mailing lists contain as many as 30,000 names.

The so-called fact-finding methods of the Institute are so ingenious and so efficient that they sometimes approach absurdity. To cite but one example, in 1934–36 associates of the American Research Department were sent to the United States to visit all American towns that were named after German towns. Dr. Nobert Zimmermann, an assistant director of the department, was sent to all American Hanovers, while others were sent to the Berlins, Hamburgs, Stuttgarts, and so on.

The results obtained from these costly expeditions were not at all encouraging; in fact, the " scientists " reported back home that " due to the higher civilization level of the Anglo-Saxon environment and the racial admixture of the American cities, our blood brothers in America are rapidly losing their Germanic characteristics and their ties to the old country." It was then suggested that " an immense religious work in all its details [be conducted] to prevent the final decay of our Germanic brethren in the United States." Schönemann, too, complained that America's German element was slow to become the main prop of Nazi propaganda in the United States. He came to the conclusion that the main propaganda-carriers could be found not among German-Americans, but among disgruntled native Americans who had been converted to the Nazi cause, and who believed in the wave of the Nazi future.

The German Academy at Munich, with its Seminar of Geopolitics, is another important fact-finding agency. This organization is particularly interested in the United States. Thus, during the past five years it has published papers on Alaska, on the fortifications of Guam, on Japanese-American fishery controversies, on the " German frontier " in the United States, on the Civilian Conservation Corps, on the Ukrainian minority groups, on the Japanese in Hawaii, on the maneuvers of the Pacific fleet, on American policies in Central America, on imperialism and planning in our foreign policy, on the Philippines, on short-wave broadcasts to Latin America, and on many other American problems and policies.

Of course, the German Propaganda Ministry itself is the central office of all the fact-finding agencies. Its Sections III and VII are devoted entirely to foreign propaganda. Fact-finding, however, is not enough, and its activities carry over into the group of troublemakers who are assigned to the task of actually conducting the psychological war on the actual battlefields.

So much for the fact-finding of the trouble-seekers. The duties of the trouble*makers* are manifold. They utilize the facts discovered by the trouble-seekers, exploit and publicize all kinds of frictions in order to effect demoralization and disintegration. They spread Nazi doctrine, perpetrate philosophical and material sabotage, and discredit refugees from Germany and from the countries occupied by its armed forces.

The morale offensive against the United States is not confined to German activities within this country. A network of organizations is assigned to the important task of spreading anti-American propaganda in foreign countries, particularly in Latin America and China. A violent anti-American " crusade " is being constantly beamed, via short wave, at Great Britain. British listeners to German broadcasts are told that the United States has once again resumed its " traditional role of Uncle Shylock," and that it is banking on Britain's downfall to seize all British possessions in the Western Hemisphere.

An equally violent and even more venomous campaign is conducted on the Japanese radio and by Japanese agents working feverishly in the Far East with methods copied from their

German masters without the slightest change. The Axis strategy of psychological warfare in all its phases is patterned after the German model; indeed, it is actually designed, co-ordinated, and generally supervised in Berlin so that the seemingly common aims of the Axis partners will be served. This co-ordination of propaganda within the Axis grand strategy can be met, of course, only by a similar co-ordinated propaganda campaign by the United Nations.

U. S. METHODS OF PSYCHOLOGICAL WARFARE

In the face of this concentrated attack against American morale, the United States is now developing a defense. We were not, however, caught entirely unprepared. Long before Hitler wrote *Mein Kampf*, long before Banse and Ludendorff prepared their blueprints for total war or Blau wrote his secret textbook, an American officer, Colonel (later, General) Walter Campbell Sweeney, described the changed character of modern war in a prophetic little book entitled *Military Intelligence — A New Weapon of War*.

Written almost eighteen years ago and now all but forgotten, that little book was actually the first outline and warning of psychological warfare. The following quotation will show how clearly Colonel Sweeney foresaw events to come.

While espionage is still one of the recognized agencies in the collection of military information, its field of action has been extended . . . so as to make its military phase an unimportant one. . . . It may be called War Propaganda. . . . And it is not a military weapon but a national one. It is not operated by military personnel but by civilians. Even in war the attack chiefly is directed against the civilian population in the homeland and only partially against the military forces. Its main objective in war is to weaken the enemy by destroying the faith of his people in their government. Its main object in peace is to select and prepare agencies which will be of value to it for the purposes when the time for the use of military force arrives.

The fifth column was clearly foreseen by Colonel Sweeney:

A possible method of acquiring information of value under such conditions, but one whose use would not be considered by the United States, lies in establishing within the enemy country a system whereby local resident inhabitants act as spies and agents and make their reports to representatives who pass through at regular intervals. Such a system to be effective must be one that has been built up years before the commencement of the war.

And he gave this warning:

It appears to be evident that a new agency with a new method of attack has come into existence. It was born out of the modern industrial necessities of the armies and the need for having full support of the public prosecuting a war. New methods of attack require new methods of defense. The new weapon, war propaganda, as described, has developed the new method of attack and has brought us to the point where we must create a new agency and method of defense.

The Committee for National Morale, in a report prepared for the Cabinet of the President of the United States, outlined what it considered to be the best methods of defense:

The cornerstone of all prophylactic and defensive measures must be a social and military application of the Socratic principle of self-knowledge. A searching survey of American morale, both civilian and military, must be conducted from the same point of view as the enemy survey; i.e., with the object of discovering actual or potential weak spots. This survey should be conducted under the guidance of trained social psychologists, but the conclusions to be drawn from it should be entrusted to men having a mentality and experience as nearly analogous as possible to the chiefs of enemy propaganda services: public-relations experts, publicists, politicians, and soldiers. When the outline of the Nazi plan to demoralize America is agreed upon, experts in the various fields can formulate specific recommendations, either to eliminate the weak spots or to orient counter-propaganda or censorship.

This plan, which was submitted to the Cabinet on February 28, 1941, has been translated into action by a series of interrelated agencies assigned to the various phases of our own psychological warfare. Most important among these agencies are the office of Coordinator of Information, the Office of Facts and Figures, the Office of Civilian Defense, the Foreign Broadcast Monitoring Service of the Federal Communication Commission, the Coordinator of Inter-American Affairs, and the Intelligence Departments of the Army, Navy, and Marine Corps. These agencies, manned as they are by competent scholars, publicists, foreign correspondents, publishers, advertising executives, who are ideally suited to the task, will eventually carry the psychological war back to the dictator countries, which are, by the very nature of their structure, extremely vulnerable to such offensives, waged, as they will be, by short-wave broadcasts and by leaflets dropped from airplanes.

XIV. How can individuals keep a healthy morale in wartime?

ARTHUR UPHAM POPE

Arthur Upham Pope is chairman of the Committee for National Morale, organized in June, 1940, to offset German propaganda and to develop better understanding of the issues of the war. Mr. Pope was engaged in similar efforts during the First World War. He has taught philosophy at Brown University, the University of California, and Amherst College. He is also a distinguished authority and writer on Persia and Persian art.

Morale is the spine in your back, the lift to your chin, the song on your lips, the grit in your craw. Morale is the spirit that makes you say defiantly " Is *that* so? " when you are told you aren't man enough to do something — and makes you do it! Morale gives you the heart to smile when the going is toughest; it gives you the spunk to wisecrack when the danger is greatest. When the gallant little band of Marines on Wake Island were asked what they wanted when they were assailed day after day by overwhelming Japanese forces, they radioed back " Send us more Japs." The glorious morale of those Marines gave the whole nation a thrill of pride and a feeling of brotherhood. We laughed with them; we were overwhelmingly proud of them — and we made up our minds never to let them down. Their morale stiffened ours. They did something much greater for their country than sink Japanese ships and destroy Japanese airplanes; they lifted our chins, they squared our jaws and stiffened our backs, they made us one in loyalty and pride; they gave us morale.

In the end, the Japanese will find that they were stupid when they treacherously bombed Pearl Harbor, just as the Germans have been stupid time and time again in making treacherous attacks. Even if the Japanese had conquered Hawaii before the war had actually begun, they would still have been stupid. They won something when they rained down their bombs, but they lost far more than they won.

Bismarck, who was probably the ablest German statesman who ever lived, said once that you must never forget the imponderables. By that, he meant that statesmen must never forget to take into consideration the elements in international relations that can't be weighed, such elements as loyalty, indignation, a feeling for justice, national pride, and so on. Kaiser Wilhelm forgot an Imponderable in 1914 when he invaded Belgium and another when he began his indiscriminate submarine warfare. He thought that the American people would be sensible and practical. He made a mistake!

AND THE JAPANESE MADE A MISTAKE, TOO

They thought they could get an overwhelming initial advantage if they could put Pearl Harbor and the fleet there out of commission before war was declared. They got an advantage all right, but they got the American back up at the same time. They made us mad clear through, and, most important of all, they helped make us *one*. The division that had existed in the American public before December 7, 1941, was worth more to an enemy than a dozen naval bases. We weren't thinking together, we weren't working together, and we had no will to fight. After December 7, 1941, we were an angry, determined people, and we itched to fight; we had morale at last.

Our anger and our determination are terrible weapons, but it is the feeling of brotherhood that will make them effective. Ask any football coach. He knows! He isn't putting on an act when he pleads with the student body " to get behind the team," just as the President isn't putting on an act when he pleads with the public to get behind the armed forces. The coach knows that the student body can give the absolutely necessary morale to the team, and he knows that without the morale the team isn't a team at all; it is just eleven football players. It's the morale that gives the team its spirit, its drive, its fight — its unity. He spends hour after hour training his players to act as one, but he knows he will never succeed until they *feel* one; and if they do feel one — if their morale is high — they will go out on the field and lick eleven better players. It's been done time and time again. The public calls the result an upset — but not the coaches. They know that morale won the game.

Morale, as every commander knows, is far and away the most potent weapon in the whole arsenal. Napoleon said that in war morale is to physical force as three to one; but our own Chief of Staff, General Marshall, says, " The ratio should be six, not three, to one." Six to one? The ratio was much greater than that at Thermopylae when Leonidas and his three hundred Spartans held the pass against the vast mass of Persians. The three hundred were made one by high morale, and as long as life remained in the Greeks their one was stronger than Xerxes' tens of thousands.

What kept the American Revolutionaries alive at Valley Forge through that terrible winter? Not food and adequate clothing, certainly, not victories, not superiority in numbers or equipment; not anything tangible kept those men alive, but something intangible, imponderable — morale. General Lee was theoretically defeated long before he surrendered; and he won victories after he was theoretically defeated. He was like a football captain who wouldn't be licked, who didn't even know when he *was* licked, and so he fought on, setting his bigger, stronger opponent back on his heels over and over again. Morale? Lee had it!

Why are the Italians so ineffectual in this war? General Wavell captured 160,000 of them in Libya, although his army was less than one-quarter the number and far less well equipped. Give the Italians a cause in which they believe, a leader in whom they believe, and they can fight; in other words, give them morale. They aren't cowards; they are dispirited.

Before the beginning of the war, the French Army was considered the finest in the world. In a few short weeks it was overwhelmed — not because it was incapable of victory, but because its morale was wrecked by German propaganda, by treachery at home, and by bad leadership. When the test came, it wasn't an army at all, only loose groups of bewildered soldiers, willing and eager enough to fight but lost without the unity and concentration that morale would have given them.

Thanks to the Japanese attack on Pearl Harbor, the United States entered the war with a strong morale. The morale is solid and stout because it hasn't been aroused by flag-waving or hysterical cries for revenge. The armed forces understand perfectly that they have an overwhelmingly difficult job to do, and they intend to do it. The people at home and in the factories understand that the armed forces can do the job only if they have civilian backing and civilian assistance.

Most countries *enter* wars with their morale high, but the problem is to keep it high. Sometimes, as in France, a single reverse will wreck it entirely; and sometimes, as in England, the same reverse will heighten it. The reverse scattered the French people; in England it united them. We too have begun with initial reverses, but so far they haven't touched our morale. It is possible that our morale is unbreakable — let us hope so; but it is possible, too, that we are merely smug and over-confident. When, and if, we have reason to get really frightened, the true quality of our morale will stand revealed.

CIVILIAN MORALE

In waging war, especially today, civilian morale is quite as important as military morale; indeed, the morale among the soldiers and sailors is largely dependent on the morale at home. In the last war, the morale of the German civilians broke while the Army was still able and willing to fight; but when the home morale cracked, the war was lost. Once the rhythm of work behind the lines broke, the lines broke too. In a way, the armed forces are only the façade of a nation at war. That façade must be constantly supported by the beams and girders behind it — and they, in turn, must be held in place by the strong cement of morale.

In the past, home morale was important for two reasons: first, it was essential to maximum production of the tools of war; second, it was essential to the fighting spirit at the front. When management and labor are in accord, when their eagerness to produce is high, production is high; but when management and labor disagree, fight among themselves, they destroy their own morale, and with it the rate of production. And the fighting spirit at the front, the military morale, will fade and die every time the men have reason to feel that the war effort at home is less than their own. They have to feel that the fighting spirit at home is equal to their own. After all, a man can hardly be expected to face machine guns and dive bombers if he has evidence that the people he is fighting for are whimpering because they have less sugar than usual, or because they haven't any golf balls at all.

What was true in past wars is also true in this one, but one thing more is also true: civilians are no longer merely *behind* the front. The front comes to them now, and they have to face the dive bombers too. The Chinese civilians have suffered unspeakable horrors, but in five years their morale has not cracked. If it had, the Japanese would have won the war long ago. The civilians in the bombed cities of England — and of Germany — know war from firsthand experience. With each bombing in England, the civilian morale seems to mount higher; and much as we may like to believe that the German civilian can't stand up, their morale has not cracked yet either.

ARTIFICIAL MORALE

Since morale is so overwhelmingly important, the governments, of course, do everything they can to build it up and keep it up. Sometimes their methods are positive, and sometimes they are negative. Of the positive methods we shall soon say more, but at the moment let us examine the negative ones a little.

The simplest negative method of maintaining morale consists in keeping news of defeats from the people. In the end the people must be told, but if the bad news is kept from them long enough, they can be prepared so well for the news that its shock is greatly lessened. The German people were not told, for example, that their troops were retreating in Russia. They were told instead that the troops were taking up new defensive positions, that they were preparing for the winter, that they were moving to the rear to shorten their line — and the people had accepted the fact that their troops were retreating before they understood that they were retreating by the will of the Russians instead of by their own. The feeling of discouragement must have been greatly lessened. The lies formed a psychological cushion that made the fall much easier.

From prisoners the Russians have learned, as the English in Libya have learned, that the German soldiers were not told that America was in the war. The reason for the withholding of the information is obvious: the morale of the soldiers, defeated and depressed, would have fairly nose-dived if they had learned that the most powerful nation in the world had been added to their long list of enemies.

Such negative methods of upholding morale are, at best, only stopgaps. In the end, the bad news is always out, and when it becomes common knowledge, the people are likely to be resentful. Worse, they are likely to lose faith in the authorities who kept the news from them — and when a people loses faith in its leaders, morale is gone. Our Government has promised not to keep bad news from us, and in making the promise it was wise. We Americans always want to know the worst. We can " take it," as we say; but we can't take hints and whisperings and evasions.

Our Government is also wisely avoiding artificial methods of building morale. It is not trying to whip us into a frenzy. The "Four Minute Men" who gave passionate speeches wherever people gathered during the last war are silent now. The rabble-rousers are gagged. The flag isn't being waved under our noses every minute. We aren't being exhorted to hate with every bite we eat. We are being exhorted to work, to stick together, and to take the bad news with the good — and exhortations of that kind we understand and respect.

The Germans have used the artificial methods of building morale with great audacity and success, but the success is as artificial as the method; it won't stand up under defeat, and the only kind of morale worth building is the kind that will take defeat after defeat after defeat until victory is won. At the moment of this writing, the Germans are on the run in both Russia and Àfrica, and so the old psychological tricks of inflating the national ego are no good. With enormous cleverness, Goebbels has reversed the formula. Now he is saying, " There is nothing for you but starvation, massacre, and total ruin as a nation, unless you stick by and conquer with us." The appeal toward unity is, of course, enormous, but it is an appeal to fear. As such, it is weak if it has to be held for more than a short time. Fear is such an overwhelming emotion that it can't be endured very long. Terrified people sometimes fight frantically for a brief period; sometimes they grow weak and impotent — and sometimes they stampede. Goebbels is clever, but he is lying when he tells the Germans they have to live or die with the Nazi party, and lots of the Germans know he is lying. Their knowledge can hardly improve their morale.

Lies or oratory or flag-waving may create a temporary confidence, a passing hysteria that will seem like high endeavor or a will to win; but they never will create the kind of morale that lasts under adversity, and they will never create, either, the kind of morale that grows out of teamwork or — and this is equally true — the kind of teamwork that grows out of morale. The importance of teamwork is being stressed every day, and it can't be overstressed. It is important twice over: first, teamwork gets things done, as everybody knows; and, second, it builds morale as almost nothing else will.

There is an excitement and a satisfaction in doing things in time and in tune with others that can hardly be described. In its simplest form, we experience that satisfaction and excitement when we march in step — and the more there are who march in step, the greater the satisfaction. There's a thrill in watching a regiment pass in review, but there's an even greater thrill in being part of the regiment. Singing is fun, but singing with a group is much more fun. Moving a railroad tie

alone is exceedingly hard work; but let someone take hold of
the other end of the tie and swing it in rhythm with you —
then the hard work becomes a pleasure. It's a heave and a ho
— and give us another tie! A group can make a picnic out of
a difficult, nasty task; and whereas a nation can't make a picnic
out of a war, and doesn't want to, it can, if it marches in step
and works together, accomplish miracles and accomplish them
with a satisfaction that at times attains the highest exaltation.
And when there is that kind of exaltation in a land, the morale
is unbreakable. But if there is strife, if groups are out of step,
if — but why continue? Everyone knows what will happen.

WE HAVE SOME WEAK SPOTS

We have, we believe, a very clear idea of what we are fighting for in this war. We aren't interested in conquest or glory;
we're interested in just one thing — our right to live as free
men. We are free, and we intend to stay free. We aren't going to be slaves to Adolf Hitler, as the peoples he has conquered are his slaves, and we are going to protect ourselves
from Japanese aggression. Prime Minister Churchill and President Roosevelt stated our war aims in the Atlantic Charter,
and the base on which those aims were built has become known
as the four freedoms: freedom of speech, freedom of assembly,
freedom of the press, and freedom of worship. We believe de-
voutly in these four freedoms, and our belief in them is the
foundation of our morale.

Those four freedoms, we often say — and pretty glibly, too
— are our heritage; and we are likely to take the heritage for
granted. We hardly know where it came from, and certainly
we seldom realize that we have it only because our forefathers
fought for it. To appreciate the heritage properly, to draw
the strength from it that we should, we must know how we got
it. In other words, we must know our history if we would

know ourselves and understand our obligations. Knowledge of the past is the only index to the future; and if the knowledge reveals anything to us, it will reveal that we are not the end of history but only a chapter of it; and it will reveal that we are not heirs but trustees, trustees of freedom.

Well, then, what kind of trustees are we? We are going out to fight for freedom. How well have we nurtured freedom at home? Have we kept the faith?

Not very well — not well at all. We're true enough to freedom as an ideal, but our practice might well make us squirm, and if we squirm hard enough we may eventually confess the truth to ourselves. When we do, we shall have built a stronger morale, because it will be built on the truth, however shameful, instead of on lies and evasion.

We say glibly that in the United States of America all men are free and equal, but do we treat them as if they were? Far from it. There is religious and racial prejudice everywhere in the land, and if there is a greater obstacle anywhere to the attainment of the teamwork we must have, no one knows what it is. Hitler is so well aware of the disrupting influences of prejudice that he sent his agents to the United States to foment anti-Semitism, and for a time they were very successful. The agents told preposterous lies, but people are ignorant, and the lies made them feel superior; so they swallowed the lies eagerly and did the disrupting work the Nazis wanted them to do. They forgot their American ideals, though they would have passionately resented any suggestion that they were un-American. But they were just as un-American as they were ignorant and gullible. The Nazi agents are silenced now, and many of the Americans have regained their natural decency.

No Nazi agents were ever needed, however, to make many of us suspicious of citizens more or less recently arrived from other countries. The word " immigrant " is commonly used as an epithet of scorn and contempt — as if every last one of us wasn't descended from immigrants! But the date of the immigration; that's the important thing, you say. If one's ancestors were immigrants in the seventeenth century, one is very proud of them; if they were immigrants in the eighteenth century, one certainly isn't ashamed of them; if they were immigrants in the nineteenth century, the less said the better; and if they were immigrants in the twentieth century — well, then, they're immigrants right now, they're " foreigners," they're beneath notice. Of course, descendants of seventeenth-century immigrants are eager and proud to entertain Thomas Mann and Albert Einstein, both immigrants, both Germans, with Einstein a Jew into the bargain. They are very distinguished men, it is true, but most of the people who scorn other immigrants are no more distinguished than the immigrants they scorn. Thousands upon thousands of the sons of those immigrants are proud American soldiers; thousands upon thousands of others are invaluable workers in our mines and factories; dozens are important leaders, Knudsen and Sidney Hillman, for example; thousands more are students in our colleges — they seem to produce most of the best football players — and thousands more have become so much a part of us that they can be marked out only by their names. These people are loyal; they want to walk in step with us and work in step with us. Our prejudice is a hindrance; it is stupid and smug and un-American; it is false to our heritage; and it is a danger to our morale that is as great as it is unjustified and unjustifiable.

As for our treatment of the Negroes — what can one say of that? We announce to the world that we are ready to fight to the death for the rights of minorities. We say, and we say truly, that there can be no real democracy if minorities are accorded less than full respect. We expect the Negroes to serve in our fighting forces — and we see to it that they do serve

—but we don't expect them to serve as equals. The less said about our treatment of them as citizens, the better. When great numbers of them are deprived of the right to vote, our pride in our democracy seems false, and our conduct seems hypocritical beyond any defense. Ill-treatment of minorities always makes for bad morale; so does prejudice and hypocrisy; and so does faithlessness to a trust. Our Civil War soldiers sang " As Christ died to make men holy, let us die to make men free." They meant what they sang, and proved that they meant it. We are proud of them. They would be ashamed of some of us.

History would show us too that good morale depends upon some qualities that are entirely unspectacular and absolutely indispensable: patience, thoroughness, goodwill and confidence toward one's associates; and the tenacity to wait through strain and inactivity, to stand up to the wear and tear of a dull, corrosive routine. In times of stress and danger such qualities are beyond price, and it is hard to develop them and maintain them without an understanding of the ultimate purpose which they serve. The English have revealed those qualities magnificently because they understand the ultimate purpose. As Sir Charles Wilson said with complete conviction: " Every Englishman today would rather die and see his family die and his home destroyed than yield to the shame and misery of enslavement to a brutal enemy; this, they see with perfect clarity, is a humiliation worse than death; indeed, a shameful death-in-life which is worse than extinction." As a people, we haven't that understanding yet, but if danger grows imminent, we will get it.

POSITIVE METHODS

Work itself is a great morale-builder. Spirits rarely flag when people are busy, especially when they feel that their busyness is helpful, even essential, to victory. People must work — and they must relax. President Roosevelt has recently said that he thought professional baseball should continue right through the emergency. He knows that sports and fun are morale-builders. Human beings can't be kept permanently at the peak of strain, and they can't work their best unless they have periods of pleasurable rest. There are organizations devoted entirely to entertaining the armed forces. They are morale-builders. And the soldiers sing. A singing army is the right kind of army. When it no longer sings, its morale is low, its fighting spirit is weak. Work, hard work; exercise and play; song and laughter — these are an unbeatable combination.

Morale is dependent, too, on a recognition of the facts. Nothing weakens morale so subtly and effectively as evasion. Until Dunkirk, the English evaded, and their morale was not good. Then came immediate danger, danger that could not be minimized or escaped by any evasion. That danger was like a rough, brutal hand shaking England awake. Once its eyes were open, it looked squarely at the facts for the first time, really faced them — and overnight the morale became magnificent. It has stayed magnificent because the English haven't closed their eyes again. It is less dispiriting to be confronted by almost any danger than it is to wonder uneasily if there really is danger. If you know what danger threatens, you can go to work and prepare to meet it; but if you don't know, you can only feel futile and uncertain and unprepared.

There is, obviously, nothing that will build morale better than confidence — confidence in the leaders, in the technical equipment, in the training the armed forces are receiving, in the unanimity of the workers, in the loyalty of all the citizens, in the efficiency of the general management. The dismissal of a leader who has proved himself incompetent gives an immediate lift to the morale of everyone, because the dismissal is concrete evidence that if a leader doesn't prove himself the best, he isn't going to be permitted to lead. Immediately after the disaster at Pearl Harbor, the commanding general and admiral were relieved of their commands. The whole country applauded the act and felt better — more confident. Morale that might easily have been weakened was immediately restored.

Just as it is wise to continue professional baseball for the sake of the relaxation of great numbers of people, so it is also wise, almost essential indeed, that our great organizations should continue — our churches, our universities, our schools. The more the normal life of a nation is dislocated by war, the more danger to its morale. Routine is always a steadying influence, and breaks in it are emotionally disturbing. If schools and churches closed, parents would suffer great distress, since they would know that their children were losing invaluable time. Bombed England still runs its schools; its churches still hold services — and at present there is certainly little to fear for either our churches or our schools.

In a lesser way, minor organizations are also important to the maintenance of high morale, partly because they offer the relaxation mentioned earlier, partly because they keep our way of life living and important to us, and partly because they keep our humanity warm. We need our museums, our games, our movies and theaters, our clubs, our friendly parties. There is much we shall have to give up — automobile tires, for example, and perhaps the automobiles above the tires. Very well, we can give them up without any harm to our spirit, personal or communal; but we can't give up clubs and similar group associations without definite harm. Even the Germans, dedicated to war though they are, haven't given up such associations. The war lords know that they mustn't be given up if the war effort is to be held at a peak.

INDIVIDUAL MORALE

Still the question to which this chapter is devoted hasn't been answered — how can individuals keep a healthy morale in wartime? The question hasn't been answered because in wartime the individual doesn't count as an individual; he counts only as part of the nation. If he remembers that fact, forgets about himself, and dedicates himself to the good of the nation as a whole, his morale through his very dedication will be as high as morale can well be. If he works hard, he isn't likely to be frightened; and if those about him are frightened, he can cleanse himself of fear by calming them. He can keep his ears open for rumors — and he can keep his mind open to the danger of rumors and of rumor-carriers. He can keep a firm hand on the cowardly, so that the hysteria of one will not have an opportunity to pass like a devastating plague among the many.

And best of all, perhaps, he can keep his sense of humor in active working condition. Laughter is not only the finest morale-builder known; it is also one of the most powerful weapons in the world, especially against such humorless peoples as the Japanese and the Germans. That wonderful message from Wake Island, " Send us more Japs," must have dazed the Japanese just as much as the guns of the defenders themselves did. During the First World War the Germans thundered across no man's land their hymn of hate — *Gott strafe England,* which they were sure would dismay and terrify the listening English. No German, however, can understand the English people's unfailing sense of the ridiculous. The Tommies promptly learned the tune and roared it happily back at the

Germans, just changing the words a bit to "*Gott strafe Stick-ler!*" Who was Stickler? The manufacturer of a particularly gummy kind of jam that was being served to the Tommies at that time.

Our morale will be under multiple assault. The facts themselves are likely to be bad enough. The Germans and the Japanese will use every method of propaganda to confuse, deceive, and discourage us. Agents will try to fan dissension, set neighbor against neighbor, group against group. They will try to split political parties, labor and capital, white and Negro; they will try to break our national unity in every way they can — and their weapons will be lies and rumors and whisperings. The individual must be always on the alert. One hundred and thirty million individuals make up the nation. Each must think of the others first.

We are urged to "keep 'em rolling," to "keep 'em flying." We must — and we can if we keep our aims clear, our determination steady, our loyalty unwavering, our steady beat of marching feet and marching workers regular and unbroken. We'll manage it all, and our morale will take care of itself if we work as one people dedicated to a single task — and we'll work better and last longer if we whistle while we work.

xv. What are the scientists doing?

WALDEMAR KAEMPFFERT

For more than thirty years Waldemar Kaempffert has been writing about science and engineering. He was managing editor of the 'Scientific American' for eighteen years, and of 'Popular Science' for five years. He was the first director of the Museum of Science and Industry in Chicago, founded by Julius Rosenwald. At present he is science and engineering editor of the 'New York Times,' for which he writes editorials on those subjects. He also conducts a weekly Science Department. His books include 'A History of Astronomy,' 'The New Art of Flying,' 'A Popular History of American Invention' and 'Science Today and Tomorrow.'

It was not until gunpowder was introduced that what we call science was introduced in war and the mechanization of armies began. It was the discovery and military use of gunpowder that started the great growth of science and technology. If an explosive is to hurl a projectile, there is clearly need of a suitable weapon. The need was met by the cannon and the musket. The first cannon were of bronze, a copper alloy much too expensive for use on a large military scale, yet the only metal that could be used in the beginning for lack of the proper skill and knowledge. Iron is cheaper and more abundant than copper. The change from copper to iron marked the beginning of not only a great military but a great social change. It was made about 1410 somewhere in western Germany, eastern France, or Belgium. And the first successful makers of iron cannon were the foundrymen of England.

Until these English foundrymen began to make their cannon iron had always been smelted with charcoal. But even in Queen Elizabeth's time England's forests had been all but exhausted. A substitute had to be found. That substitute was coke, which, like coal, was heated in a chamber to drive off undesirable organic compounds and leave fairly pure carbon behind. A tremendous demand for coal and coke arose. Miners who tried to meet the demand dug coal in open pits. Springs were struck. To drain off the water pumps were necessary. Accordingly the steam pump was invented. James Watt greatly improved it by the invention of a device called a separate condenser. With his invention, the outcome of military necessity, begins the modern factory system.

HOW MASS PRODUCTION BEGAN

The early cannon and muskets were made by craftsmen. That was a slow process, and the products were not uniform. So as early as the sixteenth century the demand was such that specialization was necessary. Even then women were engaged in making some parts of muskets, though the idea of interchangeability of parts that makes mass production possible still had to be supplied. By the end of the sixteenth century the musket-makers of Augsburg, Germany, offered to the Duke of Milan nine hundred " hand tubes," all designed to fire shot of the same size. By 1540 calibers — that is, the relation of bore to length — were standardized and by 1773 all firearms fired standard projectiles. In other words, it was discovered nearly four centuries ago that mass production of munitions is impossible without standardization.

Mass production by machines is impossible without interchangeability of parts. And interchangeability is the offspring of military necessity. As far back as 1750 the French had made gun carriages, caissons, and wheels interchangeable. There they stopped. The English devised pulley blocks for the navy in the eighteenth century so that they were interchangeable from ship to ship. The principle was independently applied in the United States to musket-making by Eli Whitney, inventor of the cotton gin. In 1798 he received a government contract to make 10,000 muskets on the interchangeable principle, by which it became possible to assemble a complete weapon from a mixed mass of parts. This is the beginning of mass production. Whitney is the industrial ancestor of Henry Ford and all other mass producers of machines and goods.

The standardization of weapons was naturally accompanied by the standardization of army clothing into uniforms. When even small duchies framed specifications for cloth which was to be one quality and color, buttons of a given size and of a given metal, hats of one design and material, the old hit-and-miss system of clothing regiments had to give way. An order for 10,000 uniforms or shoes was gigantic. During the Seven Years' War the demand for military cloth was more than the weavers could meet. So it was with wagons, boots, harness, hats, belts. In the first quarter of the nineteenth century we first hear of the sewing machine. It was Thimmonier's — a Frenchman whose name is almost forgotten — and it was first used in making army uniforms (1829).

Cloth has to be washed and dyed. An enormous demand arose for soaps, colors, and bleaching agents. When prices soared in 1775 the French Academy of Science offered a price for a process whereby soda could be made cheaply. Nicolas Leblanc won it, and thus started the heavy chemical industry.

If France failed to reap full advantage of the soda process it was because of the French Revolution. The heavy chemical industry passed to England, which was supplying cloth for most of the armies of Europe.

Soldiers must have not only arms and uniforms but ammunition and food. A system of transport and supply is therefore necessary. Though Europe allowed the Roman military roads to collapse, it did make military use of the locomotive when it appeared. On the continent of Europe railways were laid out from the first with an eye to military necessity. Without the modern railway it would be impossible to shift whole armies from one front to another or to supply them with food and munitions. For this reason alone we must dismiss as pure myths the hordes with which Xerxes is said to have invaded Greece, the dense masses of Gauls with which Julius Caesar says he was confronted, and Attila's force of 700,000. Even if there had been good railroads, populations were not large enough to raise armies that ran into the hundreds of thousands. The largest army ever assembled before the railroad came was that with which Napoleon invaded Russia, a force of about 500,000 which came to grief because it floundered in mud and which starved and froze to death because it could not be supplied with necessities.

This brief historical sketch is necessary, because without it it is not easy to understand the enormous part that the scientist and the inventor have played in modern warfare. Wherever we turn we find these two behind the lines inventing new processes and new machines for the industrialist and the army.

The relation of even pure science to war goes very deep. Who would suspect that Newton's laws of gravitation owed much to the needs of artillery officers? Yet so it was. For artillery officers wanted to know how far projectiles could be fired and what paths the projectiles followed. Galileo and

Newton both applied themselves to this problem. And by studying it they arrived at the laws of gravitation. To be sure there were other considerations, but the influence of war in arriving at such laws as those of gravitation is undeniable.

SCIENCE MAKES WAR TOTALITARIAN

As science and invention advanced, both military and industrial needs increased. For Richard the Lion Heart coal was of little interest. Now nations are willing to fight for it, because the steam engine was invented. Rubber was only a curiosity to Napoleon. Today an army rolls into battle on rubber, and we need rubber for ten thousand different purposes. About 70,000 items are on the lists of requirements of the Army and the Navy. Who would suspect, for example, that blond hair from Sweden is a military necessity? Yet so it is. Swedish blond hair is particularly sensitive to humidity, hence it is used to measure the amount of moisture contained in the air. Without it the morrow's weather cannot be accurately foretold for the masters of ships, the heads of factories, or generals in the field. And so it is with lenses for cameras and range-finders; coal tar, from which explosives are made; paints; cameras used by pilots in the air to photograph positions below. This relation of science and technology is an old story, as we have seen. But it is also a story that is ever new, because war needs the scientist and counts upon him not only to make fighting more machinelike but also to improve industrial processes. Totalitarian war is so total that behind every soldier at the front some sixteen workers must stand to supply food, shells, all the many things that armies and navies need.

War began to be scientific with Napoleon, who was much of a scientist himself, coming as he did out of the artillery schools of France, where alone science was taught systematically in the eighteenth century. He concerned himself with production as much as he did with the organization and handling of arms. He infused new life into the chemical industry, and saw to it that sugar beets and potatoes were grown of a quality that was unprecedented.

The scientific preparations for the present war began many years ago — began, in fact, as far back as the middle of the last century. The first coal-tar dye, mauve, was discovered by an Englishman, William Perkin. But the coal-tar industry passed to Germany. Why? Because that nation was both scientific and militaristic. Many high explosives which we regard as modern were actually discovered back in the late eighteenth and early nineteenth centuries. Some of them, like picric acid and ammonium nitrate, were not even recognized as explosives, because they are so stable. They could not be made in large quantities for lack of a suitable raw material and knowledge. Coal tar is an abundant source of high explosives, and the particular source now exploited is known as toluene. TNT is trinitrotoluene. The Germans saw at once that not only could they make dyes and perfumes and drugs out of coal tar but also explosives. In fact a coal-tar dye plant can be turned almost overnight into an explosive factory. It was natural, then, that Germany, because of its chemical knowledge and its militaristic ambitions, should long have led the world in the production of explosives.

But explosives are not all. There must be food. So we find German chemists busying themselves long before 1914 with the conversion of sawdust into sugar. Rubber is needed in war. Accordingly early in the present century the Germans attempted to make in the factory a substitute for rubber; they finally succeeded about ten years ago. A synthetic ammonia process was developed because Germany knew that it would be cut off from the saltpeter beds of Chile by the British fleet and because it needed nitrogen, the principal constituent of all explosives. So with gasoline, which can now be obtained from coal. Processes for treating sewage to recover its fats were developed. The garbage pail became a source of values. Milk was converted into cloth. The tops of vegetables, ordinarily thrown away, were husbanded for conversion to fibers.

MOBILIZING AMERICAN SCIENTISTS

The democratic countries are just as scientific as Germany. But they do not prepare for war in this far-seeing way. When war comes they are usually cornered. In two, three, or four years they must catch up with a highly prepared enemy such as Germany or Japan. So they hurriedly mobilize science and industry when they are attacked. Even in our Civil War we find the beginnings of the process. We created the National Academy of Sciences then to give the Government scientific advice. The Academy is today one of our mainstays. But the industrial and military scale of modern warfare calls for organization of a type unknown when Gettysburg was fought.

Except perhaps for Russia, America spends more money on scientific research in peaceful times than any other country in the world. Our great philanthropic foundations have established astounding laboratories. Our universities have trained great mathematicians, great physicists, great engineers. Our industries conduct research at an enormous cost. According to a recently published report of the National Resources Planning Board we have been spending recently about $300,000,000 a year on research of all kinds, and we employ over 70,000 in our laboratories. If any nation has the scientific capacity to produce and to fight it is the United States.

The problem, then, is to mobilize science and engineering for the benefit of factories and the armed forces. When we decided to extend all possible aid to Great Britain in its struggle against Hitler and Mussolini, our first step was to create the Office of Scientific Research and Development. The experts that constitute it are not just military officers, but mostly civilian authorities on science. In other words, a civilian body is entrusted with the important business of solving the scientific problems of warfare. Its decisions cannot be vetoed by generals and admirals. What is more, it supervises even the laboratories of the Army and the Navy, which is something new in warfare.

Within this Office of Scientific Research and Development we find a National Defense Research Committee, with President James B. Conant of Harvard as its chairman, a committee which is more directly concerned with the mobilization of research scientists and resources; also a Committee on Medical Research, which indicates how medical science is to be mobilized and applied to improve the health of Army and Navy. Much is being done for the same purpose by specialists in nutrition.

The Office of Scientific Research and Development has a free hand. It spends its own money exactly as it pleases. It may or may not take the advice that it receives. The best brains in the country are consolidated into a collective master brain. It is a brain that concerns itself with almost everything under the sun — with armor, atom-smashing, searchlights, explosives, metals, signal lights, range-finders, and the industrial processes whereby munitions are made. About five hundred of the country's leading scientists are encompassed in the organization of the Office of Scientific Research and Industrial Development and the National Defense Research Committee. These men do not carry on research. They are advisers and consultants who pose problems which they believe to be important. The actual laboratory work is done by others. All told, about 3,000 scientists are at work as employees of contracting research organizations and another 3,000 as laboratory helpers and mechanics. And this does not include a host of engineers who are engaged in testing and similar work.

The scientists who conduct research are not housed in one huge building, but are scattered all over the country in university and research laboratories. All are under contract and an oath of secrecy and loyalty. All work behind locked doors.

Who are these top men? For the most part they are university professors and research engineers. Their names are as well known as are the names of prominent corporation presidents and bankers. The problem therefore reduces itself to finding assistants — men who can make instruments, men who know how to test, men who can perform difficult mathematical calculations. To find these we took a leaf out of the British book. That is, we compiled a great list or directory of engineers, artisans, mechanics, and specialists.

This directory is one of the marvels of our scientific organization. It was compiled by Dr. Leonard Carmichael, a distinguished psychologist who in happier times is the president of Tufts College. He combed the country for psychologists, biochemists, physicists, translators, librarians, historians, bacteriologists, mathematicians, experts on textiles and paints. He has a card index of about 200,000 of these technically trained persons. The facts regarding them are not written but punched in the cards. About everything is punched that can be thought of — age, sex, scientific affiliations, papers read, patents issued, academic honors, special abilities, experience. Pass the cards through a sorting machine and out come names classified mechanically in a score of different ways.

Suppose some chemist who is working on explosives wants half a dozen good assistants, three metallurgists, and six or seven handy men. He states his requirements. Dr. Carmichael's machine sorts out the names of men in the particular Army

Corps area where the chemist is working. It goes through the whole list of 200,000 and covers every expert from Alaska to Panama. If he is not satisfied with the selection a new and longer list is submitted. Ultimately the chemist gets the men he wants, unless they are already engaged in war work.

The directory was not compiled for the Office of Scientific Research and Development alone. Any government agency can draw upon it.

PROBLEMS TO BE SOLVED

What are the problems with which the Office of Scientific Research and Development concerns itself? They cannot be specifically described, because they are secrets. But we can state their general character.

The army uses a heat signal lamp. It weighs five or six pounds, and it comprises a flashlight, a red lens, a tripod, a pistol grip, and a coil of rubber-covered wire. The light can be flashed either by pulling the pistol trigger or by pressing a clicker on the end of the wire. Put the instrument next to the cheek and it can be " fired " like a rifle. Or set it up on a tripod and code signals can be flashed with the clicker from a trench or some hole in the ground. Use the red lens and the light is scarcely visible at over 400 yards without red goggles. But with the goggles — and the enemy is sure to have them — the flashes can be detected at three-quarters of a mile. Signaling with the lens is a dangerous task. Can the apparatus be lightened? Can it be made safer? Is there a better source of red rays? We have a problem to be assigned to some competent laboratory.

Consider the firing of a big gun on a battleship — no longer a matter of merely finding the range and pulling a lanyard. Wind direction, velocity of projectile, temperature and density of the air, state of the tide, rotation of the earth, must all

be allowed for.   More than twenty different operations must
be performed to train a 16-inch gun on its target.   Complex
machinery and range-finding equipment must be used.   Can it
be simplified, the twenty-four operations reduced in number,
and higher rapidity of fire achieved?   The problem is turned
over to a laboratory, which promptly engages a staff of
mathematicians, optical experts, and engineers, with the certainty that some improvement will be made.

There is the matter of armor plate for warships and tanks.
The elasticity of the metal and its ability to resist shells need
study.   The mathematician is called in.   He finds the needed
answers in his equations.

Or suppose the problem is one of searchlights.   The largest
of the army are of 800 million candle power.   They have their
own power plants to light the arcs and to train the beam on
the target.   But can the mechanism be improved and the
candle power be increased?   Another problem is presented to
the experts.

What is the penetration of a high-velocity bullet under given
conditions?   Would layers of airplane armor be better than
single sheets or plates?   Can shatterproof glass be used as
armor, as some experiments indicate?   For the answer, a contract is made with research metallurgists, experts on plastics,
authorities on ballistics.

Then there is the problem of increasing the firing speed and
the range of antiaircraft artillery.   This is again a matter of
range-finding, of making allowances for temperature, baro-
metric pressure, and wind velocity; of metals, of explosives.
Instruments are now available which make all the corrections
called for.   But are they the last word?

The number of such projects approved up to December 1,
1941, numbered about 550.   More than a hundred laboratories
are under contract to make investigations, at a cost of over

20 million dollars. Some problems can be solved for a few hundred dollars. Others call for the expenditure of $300,000 a month. In the first year of its existence (this was before the Office of Scientific Research and Development was created to supervise all research) the National Defense Research Committee spent about 10 millions.

How do the problems originate? Some are proposed by the Army and the Navy. Others emerge from group deliberations of the National Defense Research Committee. Still others are suggested by outsiders. Every question has to run the gauntlet of criticism. The nine men who comprise the National Defense Research Committee meet regularly once a month to consider proposals which have been called to the attention of subcommittees and discussed. With the opinion of the subcommittee before it the National Defense Research Committee decides what should be done and who shall do it.

CIVILIANS AND INVENTIONS

We have long prided ourselves on our inventive ability. What of the farm hands and the mechanics in the factories who take out patents by the tens of thousands every year? Surely they have something to contribute. Since the Government thinks so too, we have created a National Inventors' Council, with Charles F. Kettering at its head. It is the business of the Council to examine the proposals of unheralded McCormicks, Whitneys, Bells, and Morses in our midst. Though the Council has passed along a few suggestions for further consideration, it is not likely that epoch-making inventions will be discovered, and this for the simple reason that modern warfare is so intricate and complex that farm hands and mechanics can hardly be expected even to understand the problem to be solved. During the last war, for example, we had a Naval Consulting Board which received 110,000 suggestions. Of these only one was adopted — a device for jouncing and whirling a would-be pilot in a sort of cradle to discover how he would stand up in a " barrel roll," a " dead-leaf " turn, or some maneuver which would strain his nerves and physique to the breaking point. The Army had a similar experience. Out of the 25,000 suggestions with which it was swamped only 25 were retained for further study, and what became of these the official reports do not disclose. Despite this discouraging experience, the Office of Scientific Research and the National Inventors' Council proceed on the theory that though 99.9 per cent of the ideas submitted can be rejected at once, the remaining .1 per cent may be worth adopting.

The Patent Office is also a great repository of inventions that may have a wartime use. It has always been a clearinghouse of ideas — most of them of no great merit. The examiners of the Patent Office allow no patent to be issued which has even the germ of a good military or naval idea, but pass the idea along to the proper officials. It may be taken for granted that if any patent is granted for a new gun, torpedo, military metal, explosive, or searchlight, the reason is that it is either impractical or fundamentally old.

SLOWNESS IN ADOPTING INVENTIONS

Even though revolutionary inventions and discoveries may be made in the research laboratory, it is not easy to introduce them. An army is a highly standardized living machine. It may number millions. It is drilled in the use of standardized weapons for months and even years. Artillery, tanks, airplanes, rifles, machine guns — the whole equipment of an army is elaborately standardized, which means that it cannot be changed overnight. If, for example, it were possible to devise an explosive ten or twenty times more effective than trinitrotoluene — something very doubtful — it could not be fired with the utmost effectiveness in existing guns; new metals would have to be sought.

Standardization, tradition, inertia, account for the slowness with which revolutionary inventions are usually introduced and for the opposition with which inventors meet. After some experiments with 6-pounders had convinced him of the merit of his steel, Bessemer placed his results before the authorities of Woolwich arsenal, only to be rebuffed. It was not until many years later (1882) that the British discontinued the production of iron cannon. It was not until 1865, when the Civil War was about to end, that our Army decided to order 70,000 breech-loading infantry rifles, though breech-loaders had been experimented with in 1857. Maxim had to hawk his machine gun all over Europe before it was adopted, and then succeeded only with the assistance of Basil Zaharoff, a high-pressure salesman of munitions. Before 1904 the Krupps of Germany were the leaders in military and industrial metallurgy, yet so difficult did they find it to sell their wares that the military experts of the world were invited to see for themselves how the new steels were made and to witness tests of new guns at the proving grounds of Meppen. Though iron-clad ships had been suggested to Napoleon, and promising experiments had been made with them by the United States Government as early as 1846, and French armored ships had been successful against Russian forts during the Crimean War, Ericsson had to build his *Monitor* at his own expense. Despite all the bombing of the First World War, a pamphlet entitled *Aircraft Production Facts* published by the United States Army as late as 1919 reached the conclusion that " contrary to general belief outside military circles the principal function of the airplane is the securing of information with fatal accuracy." Gas might have been introduced in battle at any time after the French Revolution, but it remained for a

German scientist to suggest that chlorine be wafted at Ypres and Neuve-Chapelle during the last war, and it was only later that mustard gas, known for sixty years, was fired in shells.

GUARDING HEALTH

It has been dinned into us that the distinction between combatants and noncombatants has disappeared, that factories and armies constitute a unit. Hence the rising concern with the health of nations, which means not only the health of armed forces but the health of workers. Health has become of paramount importance. This means research in the detection and cure of disease. It means good nutrition. It means the rehabilitation of drafted men who have been rejected because of physical defects that can be corrected. It means the medical care of workers in war industries. So we find that we have an Office of Defense Health and Welfare Service with half a dozen medical committees. As a result we hear much more than we ever did before about the control of infectious diseases and about vitamins and mineral salts.

Just as we may expect to profit from the work done in purely military and industrial research, so we may expect to profit by all these medical studies. Even before the defense program was formulated there was a growing demand for a better distribution of medical services. About 50,000,000 in this country live in families with incomes of less than $1,000 a year — families that cannot pay for medical attention in severe illness. The doctor cannot be asked to care for these millions for nothing, even though he is sometimes willing to do so. The Government must step in and provide public clinics and hospitals. What type of organization shall be set up to achieve that end has not yet been decided, but we may be sure that the work done by the medical committees for the Army, the Navy, and industrial workers will indicate what policy will be adopted. It cannot be denied that though medical education ranks high in this country, medical care is not well distributed.

DEVELOPING SUBSTITUTES AND NEW MATERIALS

Only in Germany and Russia is industrial research more or less under government control. Neither Great Britain nor the United States has shown any inclination to interfere with its organization and methods. Possibly this is inevitable in a democratic country that believes in the preservation of free enterprise. Possibly industrial and military research may be more closely linked than we realize, for the simple reason that there is no longer much difference between the two. But it is certain that the Office of Scientific Research and Development and the National Defense Research Committee are strictly limited to the directing of military research; they branch out into industrial research only when military or naval problems must be solved. It follows that we must leave largely to industry the search for the substitutes that we so sorely need to take the place of natural rubber, tin, tungsten, and the three hundred materials which are so essential that they are catalogued in a Critical Priorities List.

Almost everything that we touch and wear is a war necessity, from the steel of which a pin is made to the wool on our backs, from the paint with which we coat a chair to the twine with which we tie a bundle. And many of these necessities come from abroad. Coconut oil from the Philippines and babassu oil from Brazil for soaps, asbestos from Canada, tung oil from China and citicica and castor oil from Brazil for paints, South American caroa for twine, tapioca from the Netherlands East Indies for box glue, cacao from Africa for carbon black — the supplies of all are curtailed today. Lipsticks may have to be husbanded because the bromine and chlorine required to produce them are the raw materials of some essential industries. The Government must even control the consumption of sodium and potassium which enter into permanent-wave solutions.

We have only to scan the list of what are now called essentials to realize the enormity of the task with which industrial science is confronted. War is the supreme opportunity of the substitute. Even the United States, one of the richest countries in the world in natural resources, must import essentials. It cannot produce everything that it needs; it cannot live off its own fat.

"Substitute" is a bad word for the new substances that science must find. What we call synthetic rubber — it is not rubber at all — is an example. For some purposes the half-dozen "synthetic" rubbers which are now being produced are better than the natural product. They are major necessities now. Besides, we are experimenting with some plants such as guayule, from which a milk is obtained that can be made into rubber. All told there are 1,200 such plants, among them varieties of dandelion, and some of them could be easily cultivated.

And then there are the plastics. We have been using them for fountain-pen cases, costume jewelry, bathroom fixtures and "glasses," spectacle frames, piano keys, buttons, cheap lenses for binoculars and cameras, wainscoting, and even furniture. Their possibilities are limitless. We shall hear more and more of them. Army experts have found that thirty-four of the parts in a bombing plane can be made of plastics.

THE WAR AS A STIMULUS TO SCIENCE

About everything which an army or a battleship needs thus becomes the subject of inquiry. As a result, not only the art of warfare but science itself receives an enormous impetus. We must not forget that as the result of the First World War scientific research was stimulated. And so it will be after this war is ended. When the treaties of peace are signed, we shall find ourselves using glass in new ways as a structural material. The dairies will no longer wonder what they will do with surplus milk. The farm is likely to become the purveyor of raw material for the factory. Synthetic rubber will be so cheap that it will probably compete with plantation rubber from the Far East. Tin will no longer be used as lining for cans of fruits and vegetables. We ought to dress better, live better, play better, as the result of this mobilization of science, even though the mobilization has primarily a military end in view. For this, it must never be forgotten, is totalitarian war, which means that every industrial process is under scientific scrutiny. Consider what happened in the last war. Our chemical and optical industries were nothing to boast of. Now we are the match of any country in both fields. We produced very little electric steel for special industrial purposes. Now we stand on our feet in that respect. Industrial research was conducted long before 1914; now we have many more and magnificent industrial laboratories. A few plastics were known in 1914; now we have about 2,000, with a new one appearing almost every month. Dyes, nitrates, substitutes for rubber, vitamins, hormones — we have laboratories for all of them now.

When the war is over, we shall find that we have entered a new, artificial world. It is not likely that we shall cease to weave cloth from the fibers of plants and animals for many a year, but we shall certainly be using more substitutes for leather and rubber and even clothing ourselves in cloth that came out of the vat and that is nothing but converted soybeans or milk. Our present search for substitutes is merely a more urgent search than that which has been conducted ever since synthetic chemistry was born. A hundred years ago, for example, Wöhler synthesized urea and threw a bombshell into science because he had produced something that only animals were supposed to make. Practical men asked: What good is it? Some of our plastics are now made of urea. No discovery is useless. The business of technology is to create an artificial environment for man, and the more we synthesize in our effort to discover substitutes, the more artificial that environment becomes.

The great lesson that science teaches is this: Change within science always means social change. Science touches us more and more. The area of its influence is widening because we invoke it both on the battle front and in the factories. If we can mobilize science in an emergency, why not permanently? The question is already in the minds of both social scientists and laboratory experimenters. The problems of peace press for solution as well as the problems of war. What are they? What is the order of their importance? For the first time we are giving such questions our systematic attention. The same type of scientific vigilance that we reveal in a crisis can be organized for peace. If the mobilization of physicists, engineers, chemists, and physicians proves anything, it proves what science can do to make the utmost use of our material and human resources.

XVI. How can the nation strengthen its health?

PAUL DE KRUIF

Before the First World War Paul de Kruif had studied and taught bacteriology at the University of Michigan. During the war he was a captain in the Medical Department of the United States Army. After the war he continued his researches at the Pasteur Institute in France, and the Rockefeller Institute in New York. More recently he has been writing about man's fight against disease. His 'Microbe Hunters,' 'Hunger Fighters,' and 'Men against Death' tell of gains already made. This chapter points to some remaining ills that weaken us in our fight for democracy and that must be overcome in our unending fight for life.

WHAT WE BELIEVE

In Germany, in Italy, and in Japan, boys are taught "You were born to die for the glory of your country." The Fascist leaders have no illusions; war is death, and they know it. Therefore they train their boys to die; they train them to believe in dying. Having been born Italians, the Italian boys are taught to die so that Italy may become an empire. The German boys are rigorously educated in death — to give it and to accept it — for the glory of Hitler and for the expansion of the Reich. When a German soldier is killed, his parents receive a card saying "You will see your son no more. Heil Hitler!" You shudder? You wouldn't if you had received a Nazi education. And the Japanese boys — well, they have been taught to look forward to their own explosion as human torpedoes carrying dynamite against their foes as a destiny almost divine.

American boys are taught to live. They are taught that if they live healthfully and honestly, they are making themselves and their country strong. They are taught to fight death, not to train for it.

To destroy this terrible cult of death, for good and all, we are going to have to be strong in more than battleships, tanks, and airplanes. For, in the long run, these weapons are no better than the spirit and the courage of the men who build them and man them. And that spirit and courage — to outlast that of our enemies — depend first and last on the strength of the bodies of our men and women, old and young.

We begin the long fight with a great advantage. It is really far more important than our admitted leadership of the world in medical and public-health science. That edge we have over our enemies — you never see it mentioned among our powerful resources — is something not made of steel, rubber, oil, or aluminum. It is the serene and simple faith of a handful of men who are not in general regarded as our leaders or our most important citizens.

Through all the last years of weather more and more stormy for the hopes and lives of mankind, these men of faith have gone on working as if there was no threat of mankind's or our own destruction. This is the faith of these men of medical science and public health:

That human life is good.

That, for medical science, there are no rich or poor, no high or low, no black or white, no Jews or Aryans — that there are only human beings all equal before science, all candidates for its power of salvation.

That the aim of medical science has been, remains, and will

always be the conservation of our human life, of all levels of humanity.

That it is not the duty of our men of medicine — as it now has become the duty of the Nazi scientists — to decide whether human life is worth perpetuating, or whether certain sections or levels of humanity are worth preserving.

Such are the articles of faith on which the stronghearts of our vanguard against death are fighting to make democracy come true. By what they are doing to raise the level of strength and life in our country, they show us that medical science in action is the highest in practical democracy yet achieved by mankind.

We must grant that there are still inequalities and abuses in the practice of medicine and public health, by gold-digger doctors, by incompetent physicians, by bungling bureaucrats. Yet even so, the life that our science already now offers to poor as well as to rich, to criminals as well as to saints — this is the best working blueprint of the Sermon on the Mount in action. This is a poignant prophecy that the legend of the Good Samaritan may yet come true for mankind. This is the extreme opposite of the baby-bombing, the torture of the innocent, the mass death of the defenseless, by which our enemies are trying to enslave us.

BUT WE HAVE OUR WEAKNESSES, TOO

Yet we as a nation are not by a long shot so strong, either in body or in spirit, as we might be or can be. Here is the dead hand on medical progress: the rich can buy medical treatment often impossible to obtain by those moderately well-off or by the poor. Lack of the wherewithal, both for sick individuals and in public funds, is still responsible for the weakness of millions who could be strong, for the myriads of the half-alive who might be living on the top step of energy. Even more of a deadweight on the drive for strengthening the nation's health than this outworn system that still puts money ahead of human life is our American weakness of not wanting to think of, to look at, to take action against, human suffering. So long as our noses are not rubbed in these infamies, then they are not there. Everything-gonna-be-all-right — such is the easy-going slogan of our great nation, so clownish and so powerful. And in the matter of our physical and mental strength, we croon to ourselves:

" You are an essentially healthful America."

During the last three years efforts were made to gain enactment of some start at a national health program. There was an effective opposition against the growing demand that the Government show more concern for the people's health — and a great complacency. Why should our Congress get excited about expanding our health services? And why be in a sweat about providing better and more widespread medical care? Aren't we really an essentially healthful America? Like all great democratic leaders, our President only urges congressional action when the demand of the people becomes widespread and stern enough, and insistent. It was easy for our legislators to postpone action in the complacent belief that . . . Oh, well . . . we are healthy enough.

Our easy-going good nature accepted many half-facts and confusing comparisons. The great Einstein explained his famous theory of relativity by saying " If you sit for an hour with a pretty girl, it seems less than a minute; if you sit for a minute on a red-hot stove, it seems more than an hour." The arguments against the health program were based on a similar theory; that is, that public health in a community could be estimated only in relation to public health in other communities. Unfortunately, however, there was one fundamental difference between Einstein's argument and those against the health law:

his made sound sense — and the others' didn't. The fact that there is an epidemic of typhus in Poland at this minute and no typhus whatever in New Orleans doesn't go to prove at all that New Orleans is a healthy city. Maybe it is, and maybe it isn't. Actually, the conditions in Poland have nothing whatever to do with the conditions in New Orleans.

Therefore, one can very comfortably admit that *relatively* we are healthy while still insisting that we should be much healthier than we are. India is swept periodically with epidemics of bubonic plague; and we are largely free from that disease. That fact doesn't make us healthy, though, does it? — even if we go further and admit that our diphtheria death rate is low. Children aren't starving to death here as they are in the occupied countries in Europe, but that fact doesn't mean that all our children are getting all the food they should. Relatively healthy. Yes. But we aren't talking about our health in comparison to the health of other peoples; we're talking about the *improvement* that ought to be, and could be, effected in our health.

When Surgeon General Thomas Parran of the United States Public Health Service stated in *Plain Words about Venereal Diseases* — a book that everyone should read — that the rate of rise of gonorrhea and syphilis in our new army was alarming, we told ourselves comfortingly that the venereal-disease rate was higher in the armed forces in the last war than it is in the forces we have at present. Anybody fool enough to find comfort in that kind of logic would be capable of saying "The arthritis that has made my right arm useless doesn't matter at all; my uncle had arthritis in his right arm *and* his left thumb."

Before the war perhaps we could afford to fool ourselves with half-truths and misleading parallel statements; they are even more dangerous than downright lies. Lies can be proved lies, but few of us think clearly enough or know enough to spot the half-lie that forms the other half of a half-truth. And in wartime we can afford neither half-truths nor lies.

The plain and undeniable fact is this: The erosion of our people by disease is formidable, shockingly so in the light of the already existing power of science to combat it. The gratifying low death rate from a given malady is a false index of the state of our general health. It is the terrible totality of all now preventable sickness and death, still existing, that we all must face. Only after we have faced it can we demand the national action that will make us a truly strong America.

SOME SIGHTS TO SEE

Of course we know that no one wants the people to be needlessly sick or to die when there's the power of science to prevent it. Maybe our complacent everything-gonna-be-all-right is thanks simply to our lack of information, to our not wearing out a little shoe leather, to our being too busy to bother to stir ourselves out of our own luxurious comfort to visit the underground inferno of sickness, pain, misery, and death that today helps to sabotage America's effort to go all-out against the world's would-be destroyers. How it would open our eyes, and maybe, too, our hearts if our President — he is a man of goodwill — would only appoint a commission of medical and public-health men and women who really know. With orders to lead the greatest doubters among us, gently but firmly —

Into our insane asylums, to live for a while among our hundreds of thousands of gibbering, stuporous, maniacal, vacant-eyed wretches. These today fill more than half the available hospital beds of America. . . .

Into tenements, trailer villages, and hovels, to spend a few weeks with thousands now rotting to death with tuberculosis. Sixty thousand of these are still dying yearly. One hundred and eighty thousand are yearly being newly smitten with this white death. And at least 90,000 are waiting, watching death approaching — because they have no beds for tuberculosis care. . . .

Into hospital wards, and homes, to spend days and nights sniffing the aroma of forlorn ones wanting only the mercy of death to end their torture from cancer. These number between 100,000 and 200,000. . . .

Into poor homes and shacks, reeking with poverty, to learn why it is that children born in the midst of new science to prevent it are wrecked by rheumatic heartbreak. Forty thousand at least of these are dying yearly. And many hundreds of thousands live half-lives, under the overhanging sword of death — in the years of what should be their prime — from rheumatic heart disease. . . .

Into families and institutions where the pale spirochete of syphilis is still a guest . . . where the little children are very gentle, not playful or mischievous, and have bulging foreheads . . . or where the older children started out healthy but are slowly going blind . . . or where a once happy family is now wrecked by the loss of a mother dead of syphilitic heartbreak, or a father taken away because of sudden deadly madness. Our yearly new cases of syphilis, from which disasters are recruited, number more than 500,000.

Then our allegers of an essentially healthful America should be made to live, too, for a while, in the industrial wasteland of tumble-down hutches that cluster round our starkly beautiful factories. Here they could discuss our country's vast productive power, with its victims, with fathers of families sitting looking at their now idle hands, their backs and their legs wrecked by not many years on the assembly line.

Then, for a change, our glad-eyed protesters that all is well might be led into the homes of the well-to-do as well as the homes of the poor. In both they would find children who have spasms, and jumping muscles, and they would find invalid mothers who couldn't care for their children because they are the victims of bungling obstetrics. No census has ever been taken of such women and children, but they number into the scores of thousands.

Our Pollyannas boast about America's bountiful food supply. It would be good for their education if they were conducted, by famine-fighting physicians like Dr. Tom Douglas Spies, through the agricultural desert in the midst of an industrial boom, through our sunny Southland, where millions of citizens are contemptuously called " poor white trash " — but who are really sick, with a now preventable hidden hunger.

Here, after seeing this, our sight-seers might attempt a feeble answer. They might say that this malnourishment has always been, after all, a peculiarly Southern problem. But how many of our hundreds of thousands of worried, jittery, gloomy, sleepless psychoneurotics — they are estimated to constitute at least half of the patients coming into doctors' offices — how many of these, *all over America*, are likewise really suffering from the newly discovered chemical starvation that comes from long-unsuspected malnutrition? Such a survey — there are now scientific tools to make it — has not yet even been begun.

By the time they have finished the excursion we have outlined, the doubters are likely to be doubters no longer. Truly horrified, they are more likely to say: " Something must be done. Something must be done at once! "

This half-life is shared by young and old. Its toll of the young is shown by the alarming proportion of nearly 50 out of every 100 of our men rejected in 1941 for military service. Of these 50, 10 are rejected for miserable teeth; 6 for dimly seeing eyes; 5 for heart disease; 1 for venereal disease; and 28 for miscellaneous kinds of human erosion, from feeble-mindedness to

THE HEALTH OF DRAFTEES

OUT OF EVERY 100

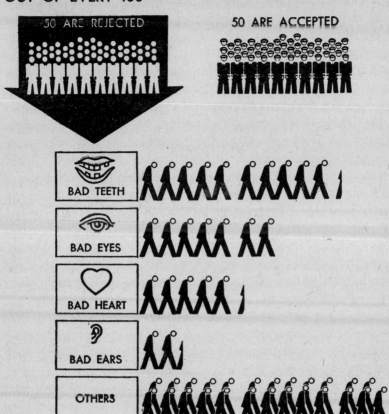

50 ARE REJECTED

50 ARE ACCEPTED

BAD TEETH

BAD EYES

BAD HEART

BAD EARS

OTHERS

Each symbol represents one man

PICTOGRAPH CORPORATION

Modern warfare puts a greatly increased strain on the individual soldier. Army standards therefore permit only those healthy of body and mind to get into active service. While many of those rejected are not seriously handicapped — many would have been acceptable after some treatment — the high rate of rejections indicates a serious situation.

fallen arches. There is a great deal of conversation about the need of the rehabilitation of these unfits and misfits, but no effective material program has been put into action.

Well, science stands ready to begin doing that something — ready and eager. The good and progressive physicians of our country — and they number scores of thousands — are not fooled by the protests that everything is fine, thank you, with the health of the nation. From their own experience they know better. The public-health men of our cities, counties, and states stand ready to organize with our doctors a great public-health arm.

Even the country's budget-balancers, its bankers, know that it is costing our taxpayers billions of dollars because millions of our citizens are needlessly sick or as needlessly dying. They would underwrite the bonds that will provide the money necessary for this fight for national health. The bankers, being no fools, know that the money saved by putting the sick back to work would pay off such bonds many times over in a generation. The present plan need frighten no one with the bogey of " socialized medicine " or " medical regimentation " that scared so many when an attempt was made three years ago to initiate a national health program. There is an army of health-fighters waiting for the call to action. The army has its leaders — the men of the United States Public Health Service, headed by Dr. Thomas Parran.

WHAT CAN BE DONE?

Even in peacetime 400,000,000 man days annually are lost to industry through illness. This is the equivalent of 1,000 factories with 1,500 men each — idle for a year! If our leaders, if our President and the Congress, wish really to strengthen the health of our nation so that we could cut down substantially the losses through illness, so that our forges and factories would really roar with all-out production, so that we could enormously cut down the shameful toll of the unfit young manhood now rejected by the fighting services — here are some of the weapons, here is the power of these tools that beg for all-out use by the fighters for our strength and life:

First, pneumonia. It is one of the chief causes of death, but in the past three years its toll has actually been cut in half, and that half can be cut again. Two of the sulfa drugs, sulfapyridine and sulfathiazole, when used in the treatment of this disease have shown their power — and also their menace. Now, fortunately, there is a new drug, sulfadiazine — " God's Powder," as it has been justly and beautifully called. It is far more safe than the other sulfa drugs, and if it is put into the hands of our physicians, it can make the possibility of death from pneumonia actually negligible.

Acute appendicitis still endangers the lives of 500,000 Americans yearly, most of them in the prime of life. The danger comes not from the operation itself but from the peritonitis that so often follows it. Peritonitis can be controlled by the sulfa drugs, and when it is, the mortality rate from appendicitis will sink toward the incredible figure of zero.

The new shock treatments for insanity, if they were now systematically and skillfully applied to those in the early stages of mental disease, would soon begin to empty the hospital beds of our asylums. And the permanent recovery of sanity of a high percentage of these now temporarily cured ones would be assured if they were then psychologically treated according to the principles of Dr. A. A. Low, as worked out at the University of Illinois Research Hospital in Chicago.

An enormous percentage — it approaches 80 out of every 100 — of our victims of syphilis do not now stick to the dangerous and arduous eighteen months of arsenic and bismuth treatment that will cure them, nor even to the eight months of the same treatment that will render them incapable of infecting others. But today there are two new and far more powerful weapons. The arsenical " drip " treatment bids fair to cure a high percentage of victims of early syphilis within a week. This drip treatment, highly technical, still has its dangers; but new methods of treatment are in the offing which bid fair to cure the majority of early cases of syphilis in from four to six weeks. And most astounding, the new combination of arsenicals and bismuth with artificial fever — still experimental but very hopeful — will rid early syphilitics of their disease in one day's time.

Syphilis has been a hideous curse for centuries upon centuries, but how long would it last if our doctors and nurses and hospitals had the equipment to fight it? And they could, and would, have the equipment under a national health program. Surely, the eradication of syphilis alone would justify the program a thousand times over.

Gonorrhea, though not fatal like syphilis, wastes more days of time than any other disease in our army. It saps the strength and cuts down the days of work of more than 1,000,000 of our young Americans, yearly. It makes hundreds of thousands of women unable to bear children. Systematically applied as it could be under a national health program, it would cure 90 out of every 100 cases of gonorrhea within one week's time. And with a mass onslaught on this sickness, sterilizing the disease in those now giving it to others, its blight could be reduced to negligibility in two years.

In 1940 tuberculosis, the white plague, began a sinister upsurge in nineteen of our leading industrial cities. It still kills 60,000 yearly, and attacks 180,000 others — most of them vigorous people sorely needed for our production. But it is the strain of industrial production that is making possible the deadly comeback that tuberculosis is now staging.

Industrial strain is making the comeback possible, but it need not. Detroit, where industrial strain is at its greatest, continues to drive the TB death rate down, so that it has already sunk in that city below that of the nation as a whole. Detroit's public-health men, TB-controllers, surgeons, physicians, and nurses actively fight tuberculosis by screening the community and industries for early symptoms, by X-ray, by an adequate supply of hospital beds for all tuberculosis cases, advanced as well as early. If the nation under a health program fought in the same fashion, the white plague would become hardly more than a memory within a generation.

Rheumatic heart disease kills more than 40,000 of our young Americans yearly, and it deprives another 500,000 of the strength necessary for productive work. The attacks of hemolytic streptococcus sore throat, which act like a trigger releasing the disease, can now be prevented by the systematic use of sulfa drugs — under our doctors' control! — during the months of the sore throat season. And better still, there is hope that means will be found actually to abolish the susceptibility of young Americans to rheumatic heart disease, by food that could be brought within the reach of everyone.

Even cancer, though it usually attacks those somewhat beyond the prime of life, must be considered a sapper of our nation's strength. Our older people are valuable; they have wisdom and experience to give to the effort toward production. The leaders are not youngsters; they are almost without exception people who have attained the age of those most likely to be attacked by cancer. Furthermore, cancer doesn't always wait for its victim to pass middle age before it strikes. Now and again it destroys even small children. If our physicians, the nation over, were trained to be constantly suspicious of the disease so that they would spot it in its first stages; if our X-ray men, our radiologists and surgeons, were given equipment and hospital facilities adequate for its proper treatment, formidable headway could be made in curing the disease. At present more than 150,000 people die each year of cancer. It is conservatively estimated that 30 per cent of those people could be saved.

And finally, there is a drain upon our nation's energy that does not yet go by the name of a definite sickness. Yet if its true extent were known, it would probably be found to be the master sapper of our people's strength and productive power. This is the widespread chronic chemical starvation for certain key chemicals, minerals, and vitamins, without which the cells of our bodies cannot truly function. In the midst of a possible plenty, our refiners of sugar and our millers and bakers, in response to the public's foolish demand, have taken these essential elements out of our daily bread and our sugar, and have actually turned them over to the feeding of cattle and swine.

The result is a vast feebleness, a half-life of mind and spirit, a draining away of energy and courage. Until recently there was no exact means of diagnosis for this immense hidden hunger. Its symptoms are so vague that it has been easy for old-fogey physicians, who have closed their eyes to the chemical magic of the new crystal pure B vitamins, to pooh-pooh even the possibility of this nation-wide chemical starvation.

But now there is a simple test for B-vitamin hunger. An inflammation in the cornea of the eyes gives evidence of starvation for the B vitamin — riboflavin — and where riboflavin is lacking, there is almost sure also to be a hidden hunger for B's vitamin brothers. This definite sign of B-vitamin starvation, which is revealed by inflammation of the cornea, first makes itself felt in eyestrain and sore eyes not correctable by glasses, and it can be detected by the use of the slit lamp. Practicing physicians could be trained by eye specialists in the use of the

BETTER DIETS FOR OUR SOLDIERS

16 OZ. BEEF

1 QUART SPRUCE BEER

1 OZ. RICE

16 OZ. FLOUR

16 OZ. MILK

7 OZ. PEAS

16 OZ. MEAT

ONE EGG

21 OZ. FRESH VEGETABLES

2.35 OZ. BEVERAGES

3.3 OZ. BUTTER & LARD

4.7 OZ. FRUIT

.25 OZ. CHEESE

.9 OZ. MILK

2 OZ. BACON

SPICES & SALT

5 OZ. SUGAR

2.5 OZ. DRY VEGETABLES & CEREALS

12 OZ. FLOUR, WHEAT

slit lamp in a couple of weeks, and once they were trained, a nation-wide survey of chemical starvation could be made. The results of such a survey can only be guessed at now, but once they were accurately known, the people could be told the foods they needed and taught by propaganda to eat them.

THE TIME IS NOW

This fight to strengthen our nation's health could begin now. Indeed, if we want to attain the fitness necessary for full war effort, it must begin now.

The fundamental principles of a noncontroversial health program have already been set down in writing. There are only seven of them, and they are the result of thought and experience, not by crackpots, but by leaders in medical and public-health work:

1. The basic purposes of a national health program are: (a) Federal aid to the states to strengthen the fight against those diseases and causes of death that we now know how to control or prevent, and (b) Federal aid to the states in establishing sound ways and means to provide medical care to those in the nation who cannot pay for needed medical, dental, nursing, and hospital care without depriving themselves of necessary food, clothing, and similar necessities of life. This establishes the fifth human right, the right of medical care, in addition to the rights to food, clothing, shelter, and fuel now recognized.

2. The law must state that the Federal Government's part in a national health program is only that of giving money and expert or technical aid — where needed and when requested — to help the states in developing and improving their own health programs.

3. The health law must safeguard the relationship of patient and doctor as now existing in private practice; it must not take paying patients away from doctors.

4. The law must be administered not by several agencies, but by a unified agency such as the United States Public Health Service.

5. The health program should be carried on by the states working with and through doctors of each state.

6. The Federal health program should provide facilities such as hospitals and clinics. The Federal health officials should not actually take care of sick people.

7. The Federal health program should encourage wherever possible voluntary rather than compulsory health insurance.

Upon the basis of these simple principles, a practical health law could be written inside of one week. There is every reason to believe that it would gain powerful, and possibly unanimous, support in both houses of the Congress, exactly as unanimous support was given when the Venereal Disease Control Act was passed three years ago.

Not even the most hard-boiled budget-balancers would oppose the law, for men of business stand ready to demonstrate to the budget-balancers that an adequate health program would be the greatest single act of economy ever carried out in our country's history.

The law would in all likelihood be opposed by quacks and health faddists and a few die-hards in organized medicine. But those die-hards oppose all health legislation on principle. Their principles are so well known, and so completely understood, that their opposition would hasten the passing of the legislation.

The barons of England forced King John to sign the Magna Carta that gave the English people the right to live as free men. The American people are their own barons, and it is up to them to demand a Magna Carta that will give them the right to *live*. They have the right to ask for the best and longest life medical science can give them; and if they demand the right, the Congress and the President will not withhold it from them.

AND WHY NOT?

The nation has now become united. No voices are heard protesting the necessity of the coming total expenditure of over 100 billion dollars for the production of the instruments of death to our enemies. But so far, for health there has been no significant increase in appropriations.

The effort of production (and mobilization of our armed forces) is going to dislocate profoundly our national life. It is going to affect — and not for the better, unless we are vigilant — our national health.

And as the strain of our all-out effort increases, as populations migrate to take their part in this production, as production comes to depend on older and less fit men and women, as more dollars go for guns and fewer for the strength of the men who forge them, more and more cracks are going to show in the pleasant façade of our " essentially healthful " America.

We know that this production for the nation's war effort is dependent on the enormous sums of money we have voted — and we have voted them gladly. We are proud to stand the tax burden and to make all the needed sacrifices.

We applaud the increase in expenditure of billions upon billions for death. Should we not, as citizens, demand appropriation of the comparatively paltry millions now desperately needed — for life?

XVII. How can young people help?

CHARLES H. JUDD

Charles H. Judd was for seven years a member of the faculty of Yale University. He resigned to become head of the Department of Education and director of the School of Education at the University of Chicago. While serving there he edited the 'School Review,' the leading journal in the United States dealing with high-school problems. He is author of numerous books and articles relating to high schools. He has served as government consultant on education and as a member of many national committees, and has written important reports on educational problems.

When the United States entered the First World War in 1917, many Europeans felt certain that it would be impossible for this country to train within any reasonable period of time soldiers who could compare with the trained veterans in the armies of Europe. It was true that American soldiers after they reached Europe found that they were deficient in some of the techniques of warfare. They showed, however, such dash and ability to meet emergencies, and such rapid improvement in the performance of all kinds of military duties, that when the war was over, commissions came from the leading countries of the Old World to study the educational system of the United States. Europeans were convinced from the way in which American soldiers successfully carried on that there must be something about the schools of a free, democratic nation that made young men competent and resourceful to an exceptional degree.

The evidence that comes from the First World War as to the kind of young man prepared for life in American schools suggests the direction in which young people today should turn their thinking and their activities in this much vaster war. The effort must be made now to prepare every young person for the future by multiplying manyfold all the virtues that were exhibited by the soldiers who fought in 1917 and 1918 on the oceans and on the battlefields of France.

There is another indication that comes out of the First World War of what ought to be done now by young people, including college and high-school students. The men who were in the American Expeditionary Force learned something about the importance of keeping fit and developing stamina. They also learned the advantages of living outdoors. When they came back home after the Armistice in 1918, they produced a veritable transformation in the ways of living of this nation. They knew the value of health for themselves and others. They went in for camping and outdoor activities. Swimming, skiing, and summer camps have gained popularity rapidly. Schools and colleges have provided games and sports for all students rather than for teams alone. To be sure, not all has been done that might have been done to cultivate robust physiques among the American people, but enormous advances have been made in the development of a program of personal and public health.

Initiative, resourcefulness, and health will be in great demand whatever comes. These virtues would be worth cultivating even if there were no war. They are now essential, first, to the survival of the nation, and second, to the reconstruction of a world shattered, as it will be, at the end of the war.

Many of the ways in which young people can help in the

war do not differ much from the ways in which older people can help. But young people, in school or out, should not feel that their part is unimportant. They are already citizens, with many of the responsibilities of citizenship. They will be called on sooner in wartime than in peacetime to assume the responsibilities of adults, some in our armed forces, others in civilian effort.

There are four kinds of need that they can help to meet: (1) conserving our natural resources, and protecting the health and strength of our people — our human resources; (2) keeping informed about the war and the problems and needs created by the war; (3) developing and practicing skills that become important in the war; and (4) supporting the war by helping to maintain good morale and by taking every opportunity to make their energy and their effort count.

CONSERVING NATURAL AND HUMAN RESOURCES

The word " conserve " is better than the word " economize," which is often used in telling people what they ought to do to help in the war. " Economize " as that word is commonly used implies saving or putting aside. This is no time for putting resources aside. For example, the Price Administration has said that everyone must conserve rubber, that people may not buy new automobile tires unless they are performing certain publicly necessary services. This ruling does not mean that rubber is to be laid aside. The reason that the ordinary citizen is asked to conserve rubber is that there is great need for it in Army equipment. There is also urgent need for all the metals, for petroleum, and for lumber. " Conservation " means putting all these materials and whatever else America has to the best possible use; it means *no waste*. The best possible use of the country's physical resources is public use for the good of us all as distinguished from use for satisfaction of merely one person or one family.

There are a great many things that it is entirely legitimate for people in school and college to use. One of these, for example, is paper. Since, however, the pulpwood out of which paper is made has to be cut down in the forest, transported to a mill, and manufactured into paper, which is in turn distributed to users, it is evident that the demand that paper be used properly is fully justified because of the effort involved in making and distributing it. Anyone who is careless about paper is subtracting from the sum total of the nation's energy. Conservation permits the use of paper in writing themes and in working out problems in mathematics. It is clearly desirable that paper be supplied for textbooks and for newspapers which distribute the news, but conservation dictates emphatically that only so much paper be used as is really needed for carefully considered purposes.

Furthermore, as the civilian-defense leaders have warned, all paper which has been used in school or anywhere else should be carefully saved so that it can be collected and reworked in the manufacture of bags, wrapping paper, and other necessary articles requiring only a low grade of material. The duty of young people with respect to paper is typical of their duty with respect to all other material resources, from school supplies to their own clothing.

Many of us have never had to consider that artificial light, heat, and water are made available only through the expenditure of valuable energy — energy that can well be used for war purposes. Americans have had in the past so much of everything that most of us have become careless and wasteful. It is easy to turn on an electric light and to forget entirely the long train of expenditures of power, material, and labor required for its production. These expenditures are completely hidden from view, and costs to us are small. But in wartime we cannot afford the carelessness or extravagance that leaves lights burning and heat and water turned on when they are not needed.

Food is another thing that a great many people consume without thinking of its value. The fact is that in many parts of the world there is not enough food to keep people physically fit. At the moment Americans still have plenty, but in Britain and in many other countries the need for food is great. Our Army and Navy will require much of what we produce. The civilian-defense agencies have asked everyone to conserve food. This request does not mean that anyone in this country ought to go without the food needed to keep his energy at the maximum. It does mean that there should be no waste.

Conservation is important not only in the use of material things but also in the use of human energy. Conservation of energy in the home is more possible than many young people realize. If the industries of the country are to be carried on with the highest efficiency, when the workers are in their own homes, their energy should be carefully conserved. Young people get so accustomed to being taken care of that they do not always think of the many ways in which they could easily contribute to the energy of their elders. Each member of a well-organized household ought to have stated duties which he or she is expected to perform. In city apartments opportunities are fewer than they are on farms, but they exist even in the smallest apartment. If everyone would take part in the performance of household duties, there would be energy for public services in greater measure than there is now.

It is also possible to reduce the amount of work, and perhaps the number of workers, needed for police and fire protection and for keeping streets and other public places clean.

Another type of conservation which can properly be urged

is conservation of money. Here again use and conservation have the same meaning. The government can use to advantage all the money that it can get. The purchase of Defense Stamps and Bonds means lending the Government for the time being financial resources that it needs for effective production of war materials and for payment for the services of those whom it employs.

Conservation means reducing expenditures of money, labor, and material for goods not really needed. Expenses of social parties, for example, can be reduced, and the savings applied to some worth-while war effort. The special advantage to the purchasers of Defense Stamps and Bonds is that in due time the investment will be returned with interest. Conservation in this case serves a double purpose.

All that has been said about conservation can be made somewhat more impressive by pointing out that, although the individual is a very small unit in a great population and each individual can accomplish only a little in the way of conservation, the aggregate nationally will be very large if each one of us does the best we can.

Hundreds of other examples of conservation could be cited. Perhaps it will reinforce what has been said if part of a release issued on December 26, 1941, by the Bureau of Industrial Conservation of the Federal Office of Production Management is quoted.

Wholesalers, retailers, farmers or any users of burlap bags were urged to return the bags to the source from which they had come, or to dispose of them with any other so-called waste materials, such as waste paper, scrap metals, old rags, and rubber. All of these items are currently being collected as part of the national "salvage for victory" program sponsored by the bureau. Waste dealers will now buy burlap, it was said, or collecting charities will accept the material.

In asking for a special effort on the part of the users of burlap toward conservation and salvage of the material, Lessing J. Rosenwald, chief of the bureau, pointed out that most of the nation's supply is imported from India. " All users of burlap should treat the material with care, and should see that it is returned rapidly and in good condition, or salvaged, for re-use," Mr. Rosenwald stated.

The Department of Agriculture has joined in the appeal, it was noted, in a nation-wide request to farmers to reduce their use of burlap as much as possible.

KEEPING INFORMED

Much has been written in the newspapers in recent months about the importance of a central war council to direct the activities of the United Nations. The earnest effort of each separate nation among them to attain victory is not enough to ensure success in this war. There must be unity of action. The lesson that unity of action contributes to success was learned by human beings long ago. It is easy to imagine how the earliest savage tribes discovered that joint action by a band of hunters or warriors was more likely to get decisive results than was the expenditure of energy by single individuals working for themselves. Indeed, many animals live in herds and flocks, in anthills and beehives, for the same reason that men hunt, fight, and work in organized bands.

While the necessities of protection and prosperity early compelled men to join in social groups, children are by no means intelligent enough at the beginning of their lives to recognize that each individual ought to assume his or her share in group activities. For long years after early childhood young people are slow in reaching an understanding of their social obligations. Only gradually do they learn the advantages of contributing to the lives of others in order that they may in turn have the help of others in achieving the purposes which will make their own lives successful. Group living is an art that has to be slowly and often painfully acquired. It can be learned by experience in the course of which the individual suffers whenever he refuses to play his part in the group, or it can be learned by deliberate study of the nature of social groups.

A war brings even one who is very shortsighted and dull of understanding to a new vision of the relations of human beings to one another. Americans did not realize a year or so ago how much this nation is concerned with the kind of government that exists in Indo-China or Borneo. Today one waits with anxiety for the day's news from these far-off lands.

During the decade from 1930 to 1940 the people of the United States had another demonstration of the closeness of the bonds that tie together the prosperous and the needy. The whole nation, like all the nations of the world, was engulfed in an economic depression which was as devastating as a war in which armies and navies clash. Men out of work could not buy goods which factories had to sell in order to keep running. Farmers who could not sell their products could not buy machines or paint, with the result that workers in more factories lost their jobs. Depression in Australia or Brazil affected automobile manufacturers and workers in Detroit. If convincing proof of the close relation between individuals and groups of individuals had to be supplied to make people socially conscious, the depression certainly furnished it.

All that has been said leads to the conclusion that young people ought to cultivate as broad a view of social relations as they can gain. There are some school and college subjects, such as history and literature, which make us aware of the problems of others. A student who studies these subjects should make certain that he gains from them an understanding of the realities of human life which they describe. Unfortunately, a great

deal of studying absorbs so much attention in mere mastery
of the details and facts of textbook statements that the student
does not gain an understanding of organized society and of
his relation to it.

Devices which are more direct than classroom exercises are
often helpful in starting one on the road of understanding. A
concrete suggestion for direct social training which has been
widely acted on in schools and colleges is that students organize clubs in which they practice social thinking and social
living. It is essential that the clubs organized be of the right
kind. The experience gained through participation in club
life is not always such that social consciousness results. In
general, it has been found that secret societies made up of exclusive memberships dull rather than sharpen the democratic
sense of those who belong. The purpose of a club in wartime
should be far broader than mere pleasure for individual members. Only when some large, comprehensive purpose is served
does a club develop attitudes which are truly sociable.

It is especially appropriate at this time to recommend that
clubs be organized which will afford forums for discussion of
the issues which will have to be faced when the war is over.
There is no way of gaining insight into the nature of society
and of one's place in society more effectively than a sober and
serious discussion of the problems of society.

Discussion of problems will often lead to the conclusion that
the group should unite in some kind of action. The creation
of a committee to be helpful to students new to the school and
to recent arrivals in the community is a demonstration of a social spirit that is educative to both those who help and those
who are helped. There are some communities in the United
States where the need for such a committee is at the present
time more urgent than ever before. The rapid development
of new industries and the shifting of families of workers to new

homes have resulted in grave social problems, both for the established communities and for those who move into new communities.

The value of social organizations for young people who live in sparsely settled areas has been recognized for many years. The United States Department of Agriculture sponsors the 4-H Club, and the Vocational Division of the United States Office of Education sponsors the Future Farmers of America. Other organizations operate in both rural and urban areas, such as the Boy Scouts, the Girl Scouts, the Campfire Girls, and the Girl Reserves. The Junior Red Cross contributes directly to the war activities of the nation.

On the social studies rests the special responsibility for making young people aware of local, national, and world problems, and of the part young people can take in all kinds of human activity. Until recently American schools have unfortunately been deficient in providing sufficient and well-balanced courses in these social studies — in world history as well as American history; in economics, or how people earn a living; in civics, or how people are governed. Students can do much to help improve such studies.

The people of the United States have only recently emerged from community life that was conducted on a small scale. Many a farm home was a short time ago, historically speaking, an independent and self-sufficient unit. Towns scattered across the continent were small. One could see the whole machinery of society, or at least a large part of that machinery, in operation. It is still within the memory of a great many of the older people in this country that the highways were built and taken care of by the people who lived near them. There were few public utilities; even the water supply and sanitary systems, such as they were, were under purely family control. The man who went to the legislature and often the man who went to the national House of Representatives were personally known to the men who elected them.

It is little wonder under such simple conditions that the idea was prevalent that the schools had no duty other than to teach the three R's and a few literary and scientific subjects. The older generation of the present time still holds to some extent this same attitude, which was more or less reasonable in the past. Some school boards have been reluctant to establish courses that deal with social problems, especially social problems about which there is sharp disagreement, such as the relation of labor to capital and some aspects of party politics.

The time will undoubtedly come when social studies will everywhere be part of the curriculum of the elementary school as well as of the high school and the college. But in any case, keeping informed about events and the world in which we live goes on outside as well as inside the classroom. Newspapers, magazines, and other reading, motion pictures, and the radio are all important. So are talking and working with others, and taking part in organizations to which we belong or which we can join. Keeping informed and building up experience that helps us understand the world about us is one of the most important responsibilities of citizenship, both in wartime and in peacetime.

DEVELOPING AND PRACTICING SKILLS

A plea which national leaders are addressing again and again to the people of this country is that they produce to the maximum of their ability — produce airplanes, tanks, shells, and guns, also agricultural crops, clothing for Britain and the other United Nations, ships to carry the world commerce, and coal and metals that will speed up industries. Essential to the production of all these things is human skill.

Human skill is not cultivated in many of the classrooms of

the nation. This statement is not intended to cast any reflection on the value of subjects of instruction which do not produce skill. Skill would be of little use in a world in which avenues of communication were closed because of lack of mastery of languages. Skill would never have been cultivated on a large scale in the modern mechanical world if there had been no mathematics to promote precise thinking. Skill would be without the materials with which to work and the guidance necessary for the best use of materials if there were no science. Nevertheless, after all has been said that can be said about the significance of subjects that do not produce skill, the fact remains that one of the greatest present needs of America is for constructive and technical skills.

Many thinkers and many educators have long believed that every young person should cultivate some kind of productive, constructive skill. The so-called white-collar jobs are overcrowded, primarily because of an utterly indefensible prejudice against hand labor. There can be no doubt that this prejudice has its historical roots in ancient life, in which all hand labor was performed by slaves while freemen devoted themselves to conquest and politics. Hand labor, now supplemented by machinery which has to be guided by skillful hands, is highly essential to national prosperity, and to winning the war. Every person should be sure that he or she has some kind of skill to contribute.

It hardly needs to be repeated, because it has been frequently pointed out, that the change in the character of American occupations has deprived a great many young people of the opportunities that used to be available to the majority of young people in earlier times to cultivate skills while they worked on farms. Those who could plow, sow, cultivate, and reap, those who could care for farm animals, repair farm machinery, cultivate gardens, grow fruit, build fences, and keep a farmhouse and farm building in repair, did not need to fear unemployment. In a city a young person often has to seek opportunities for work; such opportunities do not thrust themselves on him.

An interesting story is told by a high-school principal who had in his school a number of young people who were drawing wages from the National Youth Administration in return for work. A boy who was not working for wages to help pay his expenses while in school had observed the benefit which some of his schoolmates were deriving by adding manual labor to their studies. He went to the principal and asked whether he might have a nonpaid membership in the group working under the National Youth Administration so that he too might gain the advantages which he saw others gaining as they cultivated the ability to be productive members of society.

The CCC camps gave many boys a chance to develop skills, and the Army and the Navy are now training many more to be skilled workers. Recently the possibility of work camps for all youth has been suggested.

A nation at war needs all the personal initiative its people can muster. It needs young people who will take the initiative in finding ways of being constructively skillful. In some schools and colleges opportunities for work are provided. There are shop courses and courses in home economics and nursing, in first aid, and in civilian protection. There are courses in agriculture and gardening.

Where such courses do not exist or where the opportunities that they afford are limited, out-of-school work has to be devised. Boys have built camps in the woods. They have cleaned up city parks and have built apparatus for recreation. They have stayed after school and built school furniture and ping-pong tables. Girls have made garments for orphan homes and have volunteered as helpers to nurses. Both boys and girls have beautified school yards and classrooms. College students have planted trees and gardens, painted murals, and even done much more routine tasks of repairing buildings.

It is safe to say that in every community in the land there are quite within the capacity of young people endless opportunities for work which can be made useful to the workers themselves in cultivating skills and can be made highly productive for the public good. These opportunities need to be discovered by ingenious youth. Two pamphlets published by the National Association of Secondary-School Principals under the titles *Youth and Work Opportunities* and *Youth at Work* give numerous examples of projects which have been worked on in public schools.

MAINTAINING MORALE AND EFFICIENCY

One key question will probably have arisen in the minds of readers of this chapter: How is anyone who has all the engagements that a college or high-school student has going to be able to do the extras demanded in helping the nation win the war? The question is merely putting in a personal way what the nation as a whole has had to ask itself. When a nation is at war, it has to use all its resources of materials, energy, and intelligence. When a nation is at war, everyone ought to contribute to national efficiency by conserving materials and energy, working as hard as possible, and cultivating and exhibiting intelligence.

Two suggestions can be made as to steps that everyone should take. First, plan a reasonable program for the day's work and recreation and do not let any minor distractions disturb the plan. A writer who prepared a widely used manual on how to study began his advice by saying " Have a regular place and time for study." If he had gone on advising in the same vein about other activities, he would have said " Have a time to get up in the morning, a time to leave for school, a time for recreation, and a time each day for the cultivation and employment of constructive skill." This will be especially important if the school year is shortened, and if high-school and college programs are speeded up.

Second, include in the day's plan a specific allotment of time to be taken from that which would under ordinary circumstances be devoted to recreation, and dedicate this time to some kind of socially useful service. There are schools in the United States in which girls have voluntarily stayed after school every day and spent an hour knitting and sewing clothes for the needy and for people in war-ridden countries, or in studying first aid or civilian defense. Boys have done work on buildings. Rural boys have planted crops and raised animals. Many young people have been willing to devote not merely a fraction of their recreation time but the whole of it to such useful work. Girls and boys alike have offered their services to school libraries and public libraries. Relief organizations need workers. Part-time and summer jobs can help in increasing national production or in releasing workers for more important activities.

The authors of a recent book on education, commenting on activities of enrollees in the National Youth Administration, gave the following examples of social services of a research type performed by high-school and college students.

In Dodge City, Kansas, NYA-aided youth received experience with research on school records. In Hurley, Wisconsin, a study of the success of athletes after graduation was conducted under the supervision of the superintendent and the coach. One of the novel research projects reported was the experimental attempt to perfect a peach tree which will withstand any kind of weather. This project, undertaken by six youths in the Chaffey Junior College, Ontario, California, was very beneficial to the boys who participated, because they were all majoring in agriculture and were all very much interested in the assignment.

Perhaps the best way to summarize all that has been said in this chapter is to point out that conservation, study of social problems, labor, and contribution to the public good are to be recommended as ensuring that balanced and calm view of the war which is described by the phrase " high morale." People who are constructively occupied do not worry. They do not listen to pessimistic reports. They do not gossip and criticize others. They are hopeful and earnest in all that they do. They make a courageous, co-operative attack on present and future problems in the spirit which has always been characteristic of aggressive, hard-working, intelligent Americans. In short, they show initiative in making themselves into good, enthusiastic citizens of the United States and of the world.

XVIII. How can artists and writers help the war effort?

DOROTHY CANFIELD FISHER

Dorothy Canfield Fisher, one of our leading novelists, belongs to a Vermont family who, since 1764, made their home in the village of Arlington. Her father was an educator, and in her childhood and youth she was taken to the several state universities where he was professor or president. During the First World War, she lived in France for nearly four years, as she has recorded in 'Home Fires in France,' 'The Day of Glory,' and 'The Deepening Stream.' She is a member of the Editorial Board of the Book of the Month Club.

Americans are great people for "forming a committee" to get something done. Wherever there is a group of Americans, young or older, they are sure to be organized into active committees. We all belong to committees. Or if we don't, we should. For this way of getting things done is one of the finest elements in our democracy, one of our finest American habits. People from other countries have, for more than a century, admired this acting together of our own accord as much as any other of our institutions. In fact they realize, as we do not, that many of our institutions depend on this habit. Such observers say, wonderingly: "Those Americans! When they want something done in their communities, they don't wait for the government to do it. They form a committee and make plans for getting it done themselves. And who is on that committee? Not officials. Not specialists. Just citizens. They get astonishingly skilled in practical affairs that way, in getting on with other people, in getting things accomplished. It is a skill they practice from their youth on."

Those observers of our ways are right. The national habit of spontaneously acting in common with other people is one of the finest parts of the grand American tradition we are so fortunate as to inherit.

WORKING BY OURSELVES

But there are some things — and they are among the most valuable in human life — which can't be done, not at all, not a single bit, by acting in common with other people. It's just a waste of time to try. If you want to get a new piano for your club or church, you can't do better than to form a committee and collectively make plans to raise the money to buy a piano. But when the piano is bought, a committee can't, by acting together, find out how to use it for making music. If you want to improve your own piano-playing, belonging to a committee wouldn't do you a bit of good. No matter how many meetings you attend, your playing will not get better until you yourself sit down at the piano and practice with your own ten fingers. Nobody else can do that for you. And the only way to improve your tennis game is to get out on the court, you yourself, and practice to learn how to play better. Nobody else can learn for you. Somebody who knows much more about playing the piano or about playing tennis than you do can be of use to you, can steer you, can inspire you to keep on, can encourage you when you are doing better, can tell you where your mistakes are, but nobody can learn anything for you, or enjoy anything for you, or understand more for you — any more than anybody else can nourish you by eating beef-steaks for you, or than somebody else can give you the joy of seeing the sunrise by getting up early and looking at it while you are still in bed. There are many things, and some of them the very best things in life, which you must do for yourself.

WHAT THE ARTIST MAKES YOU SEE

And yet, not always entirely by yourself. What you often need is an individual relationship with one other person who is specially gifted, specially trained, specially experienced. You need contact, occasional or frequent, with one or another personality of heightened value and skill along certain lines, somebody who — perhaps because he has given more thought to a subject than you, perhaps because he was born with a special understanding of it, with specially warm appreciation of it — can help you see more in it, feel a keener interest in it, understand its value, more than you would otherwise.

That specialized personality, that individual with heightened value and skill along certain lines, is the writer, the painter, the sculptor, the musician, the architect, the fine dancer — in short, the artist. The part such people play in our human life is to help make each one of us more interested in what goes on around him, to stir us up to try to understand more fully the real meaning of what we do, what other people do, to open our eyes more widely to see what there really is all around us to look at, to make us have some definite sound ideas about why some ways of acting or feeling are better than other ways, to make our hearts respond more sensitively, more warmly, more intelligently, more ardently, more vitally, to human existence.

This greater responsiveness and deeper understanding and appreciation do not by any means always make us jollier or happier at the moment. But they make us amount to much more all the time; and in the long run they make us value human life more, enjoy it more, find it more steadily worth living, worth fighting for in its best phases. Nobody in his senses would, if the choice were given him, prefer to remain ignorant and shallow and childish — even if by doing so he could be amused by foolish trifles, no matter what was happening around him. A baby in a high chair, playing with a feather, goes right on being interested and cheerful, even if at the other end of the street a beautiful cathedral, fruit of centuries of artistic effort, is being bombed to pieces. He doesn't feel any of the pain and sorrow and wrath which shake a person capable of appreciating the golden value of the sculpture, the architecture, the incalculable skill, and the noble religious fervor which have created the cathedral. Yes, the baby with the feather, *at that moment*, is enjoying life more than the grown person weeping helplessly over the senseless destruction of exquisite beauty. But would you, if you had the choice, prefer to live like the baby? You know you would not.

For when the baby loses his plaything — when the feather is blown away, perhaps into a fire on the hearth where it is crisped into nothing, he weeps as heartily as the person shocked by the destruction of a noble building. *And he has nothing left.* Whereas after the destruction of the stones and mortar of which the cathedral is made, the man or woman who loved it has the most noble memories; and better than these, he has the proof of the skill, devotion, and endless perseverance of which human beings are capable in the service of a great ideal. He also has the hope that human endeavor will sometime once more glorify the life of the spirit. And he can't but be fired by an intense determination to do his level best to protect and

cherish future efforts to build up a world in which such beauty
will be valued. Since he, being human, is one of the great clan
— the fact that the cathedral existed proved this — which *can*
create beauty, *can* worship an ideal, he feels human life to be
infinitely more worth while, no matter what happens. His
whole personality is deepened and enriched by this complex
of strong emotions, coming from his appreciation of the in-
estimable value to mankind of a great work of art. The baby,
frantic over a lost toy, has none of all this rich faith and ener-
getic determination, and beautiful memories, and forward-
looking faith. When his feather is burned up he can feel nothing but despair.

This kind of service, then, is what an artist, a writer, a
musician, an architect, does for the country in peacetime. Nobody can claim that he can give much help in getting material,
useful things constructed, or workable organizations set up.
But he is of the greatest possible help in making good use of
such things once they are constructed, in stirring others up to
appreciate them, in showing how to get the greatest amount
of enjoyment from them. As in getting good tennis or good
music in your club or community, there are two parts to
every effort. The first is to get the court constructed, to raise
the money to buy a piano. But there's no enjoyment in having a fine tennis court or a piano if there's nobody who knows
how to get the good out of them. The artists — that is, the
writer, sculptor, poet, painter, and all the rest — are the people
who continually reinspire human beings to get the good out of
being alive. Even if the finely trained, specially skilled tennis-
player doesn't actually give you lessons, it is through him that
you see what well-played tennis can be. It is from watching
him that you get the idea (one of the most valuable anybody
can have) that it is really much more enjoyable to practice
hard, to struggle with all your might, day after day, to be ac-

curate and controlled and swift with your racket than just to take it easy and knock the balls around aimlessly. You would soon be bored with that. You wouldn't be any less bored because the court was in good shape. Nor would you enjoy your hour on the court more just because you had spent a great deal of money on your racket and balls. The only way to get the good out of equipment for tennis is to learn how to play tennis well. And — again — nobody can learn this for you. Nor can anybody learn for you how to get the good out of living — the real good, which is not to own a lot of expensive possessions, but to know how to enjoy doing something with them.

The fine piano-player makes us aware of what can be done with those black and white keys and taut strings. The Sioux Indian, just off the reservation, wrapped in his blanket, can't see anything in a grand piano but a funny-looking black box on legs, with a hinged lid. When he lifts the lid, there's nothing inside but a lot of wires fastened down so tightly nobody can get any use of them. By pounding on the keys with his fists he can make a noise. But you have to be a very young child to get much fun out of just making a noise. A person untrained, uncultivated, uninspired by contact with the creative mind and skill of the writer, poet, musician, saint, sculptor — all the artists — stands gaping at human life just as helplessly as the Sioux Indian in front of the piano. What can you do with living to get real enjoyment out of it? Very few people can, without specially creative minds, see the wonderful possibilities in human existence. They can make a noise. But that's a bore, after a little of it.

It takes the fine musician to reveal to us what beauty, what joy, what comfort, what fun, what deepening of the heart, can flow from good music. It takes the painter and the sculptor to make us aware of what beauty and joy and deepening of the heart can flow from what we have to look at — no matter where we live. For no matter where we live, we have the magnificence and infinite variety of light and shade. A great French artist once fancifully wrote that there is nothing more beautiful than a mud puddle, mirroring as it does all the million shades of color in the sky and clouds. Our own literal, unimaginative, unawakened eyes might see in a mud puddle only danger to our clean shoes. But you can't go on seeing only dirt in it, after someone has succeeded in calling your attention to its mother-of-pearl iridescence and the way in which its tiny pool reflects the greatness of the sky. When you have seen a fine painting of a summer field, green and rich, or one of a blue-and-silver country landscape in winter, or of a city street at night, melodramatic with yellow lights against the blackness — from that time on you can't help having more interest in whatever you look at out of your own window.

The worth-while writer of fiction does this same kind of service for you in helping you see more interest, meaning, depth, joy, sorrow, complexity, in human life than you would without his specialized skill in understanding why human beings act as they do, and portraying them so that his readers too understand more of what goes on around them. The more you understand anything, of course, the more interesting it is to you. Placed in the room with an egg-beater, a small child who has had the normal chance to exercise his curiosity about the workings of things, has a bright-eyed, fascinating time learning what the queer wire contraption is for, and how to make it whir around and around. A child of the same native ability and same age who has always been repressed and told "Keep still!" and "Don't touch!" may spend the same time idly sucking his thumb and gazing at a blank wall, the egg-beater lying untouched beside him.

HOW POETS AND NOVEL–WRITERS HELP US

In telling us stories (which are true to human nature whether they ever literally happened just that way in actual fact), what the sound, honest, really good fiction-writer does for us is to make us stop passing the time away in gazing at a blank wall and sucking our thumbs (so to speak). He shows us how to look at the people we know and at ourselves, trying to understand what makes human beings act the way they do, appreciating the beauty, or the weakness, the strength, or the evil — the drama of human life. Could any woman or girl read, really read, *Tom Sawyer* and *Huckleberry Finn* and not understand boys much better, appreciate them more, find more fun in watching them, have more sympathy for them, get on better with them? What Mark Twain does for the readers of those stories of boy life is just what the fine tennis star does for beginning players; he gives them, at the same time that he fascinates and delights them, a wholly new idea of what there is to a good tennis game, of what goes on in a boy's heart and mind as he grows toward being a man.

The person who has been absorbed in a masterpiece of fiction emerges from reading it changed from what he was before. He is wiser, he is stronger, he is encouraged to keep on trying to understand life and to manage his own life with sympathy and compassion and resourcefulness, rather than just bullheadedly to muddle his way through it, by main strength. After reading a noble novel of Tolstoy's, the reader may (although there has not been in the story a single word about how to get on with an exasperatingly cross old great-aunt) see what it is in her life which has made his old kinswoman so disagreeable. Once he sees that, he can try to rearrange her background and his attitude toward her to avoid what is specially distressing to her. And he may feel a healing pity for her, which will do him as much good as it does her. After having had his emotions deeply stirred by a fine poem, such as Benét's *John Brown's Body,* a reader may (although of course Benét says nothing about jobs in that epic poem) see to his great relief that his having lost his job is not an irrevocable catastrophe for the world or for him, that the important thing is to keep on trying.

What fine poets do for us can only be compared to what is done for us by a trip in an airplane over a region we have known very well from walking and driving around in it. Looking down from a plane, we suddenly see as a whole what we have, before, only seen parts of. We see that what has looked like a valley is really only a little dip in a much bigger one. We see that what we have taken for a mountain is only a foothill to a much greater range behind it. We see why the river takes that sudden turn with which fishing trips have made us so familiar. And when we are landed again, down on the earth, we can never look at the country around us with the same narrowed, limited notions about its various parts. We have seen how they fit into the great whole. Our very minds seem to have grown larger to take in the wider meaning of what is before our eyes as we trudge along over path and road and street. Looking up at the foothill, we see in our imagination the greater bulk of the real mountain behind it. It is such a far, true glimpse of the real proportion of things in our life, or of the beauty or meaning beyond our ordinary sight, which fine poetry brings to us.

SOMETHING ELSE WRITERS CAN DO FOR US

And finally there is something else which artists and writers often do for us, very different from giving us a new revelation of meaning and interest and beauty in human life. It is very valuable too, and only people with a specialized skill can do it for us, and each one by himself, each one differently from every other one. It is again something which can't be accomplished for us by the most efficient committee. This service can perhaps be best described by comparing it to tap dancing.

If somebody should ask you to explain just why you enjoy watching a skilled tap dancer click out complicated rhythms with his feet, you'd hardly know what to say. But we all do. There is not a single bit of wisdom to be learned from the crisp, rapid clatter of skilled heels and toes. We don't understand human life any more for having watched those strong, finely muscled legs so perfectly under the control of the dancer. But as we watch, we are stirred out of dullness and boredom. The faces of people looking at a lively tap dance done by a skillful professional are always interested, alive, and often smiling. For the moment they have forgotten the examinations they didn't pass, the bills they can't pay, the sour, cross-grained fellow worker who darkens the job. Whatever troubles them is, for the time their eyes are fixed on those sparkling, dynamic feet, pushed away from the center of their attention. Their pulse quickens cheerfully in harmony with the heels and toes tapping rhythmically at machine-gun-fire speed. As they watch the supple elastic body, spinning, twisting, flaming in what looks like an ecstasy of enjoyment, the spectators forget for a moment that they themselves are clumsy, sad, unsuccessful, or anxious. Such a moment of forgetfulness refreshes as a drink of cold water refreshes a hot, thirsty man. It does not, like a meal of good food, make him stronger and more enduring. It is like sitting down for a while when your legs are tired — very agreeable. It is not like sitting down at a well-spread dinner table.

Now there is a kind of writing which also gives a momentary refreshment by making us forget what is really going on around us. Like the lively clickety-clack of the expert tap dancer's feet, it distracts the attention of the reader for a while. People who read " to pass the time away," or " for entertainment," get out of their reading neither more nor less than people get who sit passive, watching an expert tear through an excitingly rapid and complicated dance program. What it does for them is that for the time being they can't think of anything else. It is true that when it is over they don't understand any more than before how to deal with their own lives, except that, having had a little rest, they can often see their problems in a new perspective. But sometimes people are so tired and bothered by their difficulties that a temporary breathing-spell is what they need more than anything else.

The effect of contact with a living work of art lasts on and on in the lives of those who have come under its influence, strengthening and nourishing. The effect of the tap dancer and the kind of writing — we might say detective stories and tales of pure adventure — which entertains as tap dancing does ends the moment the dancer stops or the reader closes the book. *We need both kinds of art.*

THE ARTS IN WARTIME

And we need them *both* infinitely more in wartime than in peace. For our questions and problems and emotions are terrifically heightened and intensified in wartime. Because life presses upon us so hard, we desperately need the occasional half-hour of vacation which is brought to us by the writer who writes as the tap dancer dances, only to make us forget what is going on around us. There never was a time when he who can make us laugh is more pricelessly valuable than when life makes us feel like screaming in pain, weeping in sorrow and anxiety, gnashing our teeth in rage. But just laughing, delicious as mirth is, just the momentary refreshment which comes with forgetting a problem, doesn't get us on at all toward solving it.

To understand problems, and hence to deal competently with them, we need the vivid light of the imagination. That shows us their true meaning. And only the creative-minded writer primarily concerned with understanding complex human life can turn the switch so that the light of our imagination is on.

Somebody has said that the long, scientifically accurate research on the town of Muncie, Indiana, which was reported in *Middletown* does not make us understand what life in a small Middle Western town can feel like nearly as much as the novel *Main Street.* Shakespeare was no classical scholar. From his century down to ours any professor of Latin has known more facts about Rome than he did. Ben Jonson knew more. But neither Ben Jonson nor any Latin scholar made his readers feel and hence understand the real Roman spirit as Shakespeare did in *Julius Caesar.* Keats was not a well-educated man, as the English think of education. Yet Matthew Arnold (who himself had " education " as England thinks of it, with every trimming) said that Keats has made his readers feel and understand the Greek spirit far more than anyone else writing in English. Learned people had written about China for centuries, had heaped up mountains of facts about it. But not until Pearl Buck's *The Good Earth* did we really understand the primer-simple fact that the Chinese people are human beings like ourselves. Our whole attitude toward China has been transformed by having our imaginations aroused to new life by a fine novel.

TELLING THE TRUTH VERSUS PROPAGANDA

There is one kind of presentation of facts which is sometimes called propaganda. In its bad meaning, propaganda is the presentation of facts so arranged as to make us believe that the whole of which each fact is a part is quite different from what it really is. In everyday, plain language, propaganda, as it is often practiced, is just lying. And like any other kind of lying, it is dangerous to the very cause it is trying to help, because it does not take long for people to lose faith in a voice which tells lies. Here the " real " writer, responsible, experienced, can help a good cause as nobody else can, because when he speaks it is from a lifelong professional effort to try to tell the truth about human life.

If there were in our town an epidemic of sickness, we wouldn't pay much attention to politicians telling us excitedly that it was typhoid fever, and that we must give our last cent in taxes to pay for a new water-supply system. In the back of our minds would be the notion " *Maybe* they just want a big piece of public work done so their friends can make money out of the contracts." And " *Maybe* it's typhoid fever, and maybe it isn't." But if a group of M.D.'s announced that we needed an expensive new water system because people were getting sick with typhoid fever, there would not be, not in the farthest corner of our minds, the notion that maybe the sickness was really pellagra, and that they were telling us something else to make us willing to pay more taxes. In just the same way there is a sort of not-to-be-imitated conviction of truth which comes with a statement of human reality made by a real writer or poet or artist who is using his highly trained capacity to grasp the true meaning of human events.

For this reason, it is the real writer who can be counted on to throw his weight as needed on this side or the other of the great scales where " morale " hangs in the balance. Suppose that we, the general public, are getting mortally weary of the small monotonous tasks we are set to do as our part of the war effort. Along comes Carl Sandburg with a ringing poem which stirs our hearts like a bugle shout. He awakens our imaginations, drowsy with monotony, and makes us see that we too, in our small corner, are truly fighting to keep the doors of opportunity open, for all men and women everywhere, against the insane notion of a so-called master race that that door must be shut to most of the human race, and open only to them.

Or, take an opposite example — suppose that we have become so enraged and excited by the murderous orgy of destructiveness going on all over the globe that our own destructive instincts (for of course we have our fair share of them, like everybody else) are aroused to fever, till we can't think of anything else. Statisticians can't help us get back a normally sound conception of what we are doing, no matter how many facts they tell us over the radio. Propagandists soon lose their influence because we learn to distrust every word they say. Only the person who is a writer in the best sense of the word can stir our imagination with some living, vividly true presentation of the complex truth which makes us remember that (a) what we are out to do is in the last analysis creatively to construct and that (b) all we have to construct with is the human race, so that (c) if all the race becomes absorbed and obsessed with destruction — why, then indeed we are all lost.

HOW A STORY CAN TELL THE REAL TRUTH

A fine example of this unique usefulness of the creative writer is in John Steinbeck's last novel (it is presented as a play too), *The Moon Is Down*. It is a story of what happens in one of the free European countries, now invaded, conquered, and run by the Nazis. It might be Norway, Belgium, Holland, Czechoslovakia — any country where men and women are civilized and free. Imagine what the propagandist, trying to stir us up to hate the Nazis, would make out of such a story. He would present the German conquerors as all black, each one of them a maniac, a neurotic, a monster; and the Norwegians all white, each one of them saintly, blameless victims.

But he wouldn't make much real impression on us because, not having a creative imagination, he wouldn't be able to make his story sound real. We wouldn't believe what he told us.

What Steinbeck does for us is to make us see what our lives would be like if we were conquered by a nation which feels contempt for all other peoples. Because he has a creative imagination, trained to divine what really happens in human lives, he shows us the German invaders not as rotten degenerates by nature, but as ordinary human beings who have been brought up all wrong, who have been carefully trained in the thoroughly bad principles of self-seeking ruthlessness, moral insensibility, admiration for treachery, ignorance of freedom, hatred for justice, indifference to the rights of others. The horrifying picture of what ordinary people do who have been brought up all wrong makes us feel with our hearts as well as understand with our minds that our real purpose in this terrible struggle we are making is to get people brought up more nearly right, not only to punish those who have been brought up wrong. To have lived for a while with those simple, small-town Norwegians who take it for granted that brave men and women must resist tyranny — it makes us passionately admire the beauty and dignity which freedom gives to human beings, as well as passionately hate and detest the dreadful idea that ruthless contempt for the rights of others is the only solid basis for human existence.

We are wiser, after reading such a creatively true presentation of the clash between the lovers and haters of human dignity. After a factual presentation of the situation in Norway under the Germans, we are only more informed. Steinbeck doesn't say a single word about the right way to train human beings. What he shows us is that the wretched position of those Nazi officers in the small Norwegian village is not because each one of them was born bad, but because the will to

dominate and destroy can be taught to human beings.   He
makes us realize that our real goal is not, ourselves, to dominate
or destroy, but so to organize the world's life that everywhere,
in everybody's heart, there will be less desire to destroy and
dominate.

ESPECIAL NEED IN WARTIME TO UNDERSTAND

War changes the whole of human life — hence it creates an
immensely greater need to understand it than ever before, because the old solutions don't solve, the old keys don't unlock
the new door.   What we are trying to accomplish by going
to war seems to us, at first sight, entirely different from what
has been the purpose of our lives before.   It takes the long-
range view of the creative brooding mind of the true writer to
see that it is not different, that it is only more intense.   The
myriad details in our everyday life seem to be in a pattern entirely other than the old one we know so well.   Unless we
understand that the new pattern is only the fine old one,
served by Washington and Jefferson and Lincoln, and revered
by all Americans, we can't do our share in ordering our lives
to fit into it.   We are apt to take a part of the great effort before us as too large a part of the whole.   For instance, if we
think that just to " beat Hitler " is our aim, we will be as far
away from understanding what we are really up to as a student
is who thinks that what he is doing is just trying to pass examinations.   Beating Hitler is only a part of what we have been
aroused to do with all our might; namely, to try, as never before, to construct a decent way of life open to all the people of
the globe, which will allow everyone, everywhere, to develop
his finest qualities.   Our American Revolution would have
been a failure if we had thought that we were out just to " beat
the British."   If we had not gone from destruction to construc-

tion, our great Federation would never have come into existence.

How are we going to make living sense out of the strange wild struggle before us, if not with the help of the same people who, in ordinary life, have best helped us make real sense out of human life — the writers, the spiritual leaders, the artists, the poets? It is significant that one of the first preparations made for the war has been a quick instinctive rush to gather together in anthologies the *writings* of the spiritual ancestors of our country — of the world. In *The Democratic Spirit*, Bernard Smith has collected statements from American writings from our earliest days down to the present which are full of the contagious, burning fire and enthusiasm which Americans have felt for the idea of human freedom. And in two other collections, this spiritual ancestry of devotion to freedom is traced far back before the beginning of our nation, before the discovery of America, to the dawn of human history — in Irwin Edman's *Fountainheads of Freedom* and in Norman Cousin's *A Treasury of Democracy*. As much as tanks and ammunition do we need the backing of farseeing, gifted, sincere writers and poets and artists, whose occupation is always to try to see through the surface confusion of mixed-up details to the clear, enduring, immortal pattern of which each detail is a part. Without such divining spirits, gifted in expressing what they divine, we get lost in isolated facts.

Our government, and the learned and scholarly, have it as their duty to keep us, the general public, informed of as many of the new facts bursting upon human life as they can be sure of. And we have it as our duty to inform ourselves about those new facts. But just facts are more like the queer-shaped pieces of a jigsaw puzzle than anything else. They make no sense, no picture, unless they are put together. It takes imagination to put them together.

And who is it who arouses, stimulates, and warms our imaginations and cheers us on by showing us what depth of understanding can come through a combination of intelligence and creative imagination? Not the statistician who lays the facts before us.

And who is it who uses his own imagination to put the facts together right? Not the propagandist who forces them into the pattern which suits his own purposes.

It is to the creative writer and artist that we must look for true understanding of complex human life. The function of the " real " writer (that is, the author who does not write just to help the reader forget for a minute what things are like, but to help him permanently understand why things are as they are, and hence by implication how to handle them better) is to keep us from just pawing facts over and over aimlessly, like a discouraged person pawing over the pieces of a jigsaw puzzle. It is the creative writer who makes us feel the eager certainty that those facts can make sense. It is the creative writer who tries, from his long experience in interpreting the facts of human life, to make us see what honestly seems to him to be the truth.

Can you think of anything — anything at all — which is more needed in wartime than this kind of stimulation? I can't. Without it, we can't " win " a war, no matter how many cannon and submarines and tanks our splendid industrial system manufactures, because we will not have a clear idea of what it is we want to win.

Our nation has now joined with others in what, quite literally, is a life-and-death struggle on a world-wide scale such as the people on our globe never before imagined could be possible. In the current phrase, we will " need all that we have " to survive it, to emerge with our ideals alive.

Yes, " all that we have " will be none too much to see us through the ordeal before us. And in this tragic and heroic crisis, which so heightens all our needs, an irreplaceable part of that " all " is what the artist and the writer can do for us.

XIX. What are we fighting for?

WINSTON CHURCHILL
FRANKLIN D. ROOSEVELT

This is a war for freedom and democracy. For the two great countries, Britain and the United States, it is a life-and-death struggle against the Axis Powers, led by Nazi Germany, who seek to loot, to dominate, and to enslave the rest of the planet. It is a war that must be won, whatever the cost in blood and toil; and when it is won, it will be the task of the United Nations to organize a peace so solid, so implemented with justice and power, that never again may outlaw nations imperil the foundations of civilization.

These are the beliefs passionately held and powerfully expressed by the two most distinguished leaders of democracy — Winston Churchill, Prime Minister of Britain, and Franklin D. Roosevelt, President of the United States.

I. WINSTON CHURCHILL

ON DEMOCRATIC CIVILIZATION

(This is the full text of a brief speech on "Civilization" delivered by Prime Minister Churchill to the University of Bristol, July 2, 1938.)

There are few words which are used more loosely than the word "Civilization." What does it mean? It means a society based upon the opinion of civilians. It means that violence, the rule of warriors and despotic chiefs, the conditions of camps and warfare, of riot and tyranny, give place to parliaments where laws are made, and independent courts of justice in which over long periods those laws are maintained. That is Civilization — and in its soil grow continually freedom, comfort, and culture. When Civilization reigns in any country, a wider and less harassed life is afforded to the masses of the people. The traditions of the past are cherished, and the inheritance bequeathed to us by former wise or valiant men becomes a rich estate to be enjoyed and used by all.

The central principle of Civilization is the subordination of the ruling authority to the settled customs of the people and to their will as expressed through the Constitution. In this Island we have today achieved in a high degree the blessings of Civilization. There is freedom; there is law; there is love of country; there is a great measure of good will between classes; there is a widening prosperity. There are unmeasured opportunities of correcting abuses and making further progress.

In this very week we have seen a Prime Minister at the head of a large and loyal majority bow with good grace to the customs of Parliament, and we have heard Socialist Members speaking with pride of the precedents of the early seventeenth century, and the principle of the Petition of Right. In this respect for law and sense of continuity lies one of the glories of England. And more than that, there also lies in it an important part of her strength and safety. Such episodes are astonishing, but also educative, to countries where dictatorships prevail, and where no one dares to raise his hand against arbitrary power. They stir and cheer the minds of men in many lands.

We have, however, to face the problem of the turbulent, formidable world outside our shores. Why should not the same principles which have shaped the free, ordered, tolerant civilization of the British Isles and British Empire be found serviceable in the organization of this anxious world? Why should not nations link themselves together in a larger system and establish a rule of law for the benefit of all?   That surely is the supreme hope by which we should be inspired and the goal towards which we should march with resolute step.

But it is vain to imagine that the mere perception or declaration of right principles, whether in one country or in many countries, will be of any value unless they are supported by those qualities of civic virtue and manly courage — aye, and by those instruments and agencies of force and science which in the last resort must be the defense of right and reason.

Civilization will not last, freedom will not survive, peace will not be kept, unless a very large majority of mankind unite together to defend them and show themselves possessed of a constabulary power before which barbaric and atavistic forces will stand in awe.

Here, then, we see the task which should command the exertions of the rising generation which fills this spacious hall, and which may bring to the life of Britain the surge of a new impulse towards the organization of world peace, and across the gulf of these eventful years prepare and bring nearer the Brotherhood of Man.

CHURCHILL ON GERMANY AND HITLER

(From a speech delivered in the House of Commons on October 24, 1935.)

I have no prejudice against the German people.   I have many German friends, and I have a lively admiration for their splendid qualities of intellect and valour and for their achievements in science and art.   The re-entry into the European circle of a Germany at peace within itself, with a heart devoid of hate, would be the most precious benefit for which we could strive, and a supreme advantage which alone would liberate Europe from its peril and its fear, and I believe that the British and French democracies would go a long way in extending the hand of friendship to realize such a hope.

But that is not the position which exists today. We cannot afford to see Nazidom in its present phase of cruelty and intolerance, with all its hatreds and all its gleaming weapons, paramount in Europe.

(From a speech delivered in the House of Commons on April 13, 1933.)

New discord has arisen in Europe of late years from the fact that Germany is not satisfied with the result of the late war. I have indicated several times that Germany got off lightly after the Great War. I know that that is not always a fashionable opinion, but the facts repudiate the idea that a Carthaginian peace was in fact imposed upon the German people. No portion of Germany inhabited by Germans was detached, except where there was the difficulty of disentangling the population of the Silesian border. No attempt was made to divide Germany as between the northern and southern portions, which might well have tempted the conquerors at that time. No state was carved out of Germany. She underwent no serious territorial loss, except the loss of Alsace and Lorraine, which she herself had seized only fifty years before. The great mass of the Germans remained united after all that Europe had passed through, and they are more vehemently united today than ever before. We know what has happened to the war indemnity. They have lost their colonies, it is true; but these were not of great value to them, and it is not at all true for them to say that these colonies could ever have afforded any appreciable outlet for their working-class population. They are not suited for white colonization.

On the other hand, when we think of what would have happened to us, to France, or to Belgium if the Germans had won; when we think of terms which they exacted from Rumania, or of the terms of the Treaty of Brest-Litovsk; when we remember that up to a few months from the end of the war German authorities refused to consider that Belgium could ever be liberated, but said that she should be kept in thrall for military purposes for ever, I do not think we need break our hearts in deploring the treatment that Germany is receiving now. Germany is not satisfied; but no concession which has been made has produced any very marked appearance of gratitude. Once it has been conceded it has seemed less valuable than when it was demanded.

" THIS IS NO CLASS WAR "

(From the speech broadcast on June 22, 1941, shortly after the Nazi invasion of Russia.)

Hitler is a monster of wickedness, insatiable in his lust for blood and plunder. Not content with having all Europe under his heel or else terrorized into various forms of abject submission, he must now carry his work of butchery and desolation among the vast multitudes of Russia and of Asia. The terrible military machine which we and the rest of the civilized world so foolishly, so supinely, so insensately allowed the Nazi gangsters to build up year by year from almost nothing; this machine cannot stand idle, lest it rust or fall to pieces. It must be in continual motion, grinding up human lives and trampling down the homes and the rights of hundreds of millions of men.

Moreover, it must be fed not only with flesh but with oil. So now this bloodthirsty guttersnipe must launch his mechanized armies upon new fields of slaughter, pillage, and devastation. Poor as are the Russian peasants, workmen, and soldiers, he must steal from them their daily bread. He must devour their harvests. He must rob them of the oil which drives their ploughs and thus produce a famine without example in human history.

And even the carnage and ruin which his victory, should he gain it — though he's not gained it yet — will bring upon the Russian people, will itself be only a stepping-stone to the attempt to plunge the four or five hundred millions who live in China and the 350,000,000 who live in India into that bottomless pit of human degradation over which the diabolic emblem of the swastika flaunts itself.

It is not too much to say here this pleasant summer evening that the lives and happiness of a thousand million additional human beings are now menaced with brutal Nazi violence. That is enough to make us hold our breath.

But presently I shall show you something else that lies behind and something that touches very nearly the life of Britain and of the United States.

The Nazi regime is indistinguishable from the worst features of Communism. It is devoid of all theme and principle except appetite and racial domination. It excels in all forms of human wickedness in the efficiency of its cruelty and ferocious aggression. No one has been a more consistent opponent of Communism than I have for the last twenty-five years. I will unsay no words that I've spoken about it. But all this fades away before the spectacle which is now unfolding.

The past, with its crimes, its follies, and its tragedies, flashes away. I see the Russian soldiers standing on the threshold of their native land, guarding the fields which their fathers have tilled from time immemorial. I see them guarding their homes; their mothers and wives pray, ah, yes, for there are times when all pray for the safety of their loved ones, for the return of the breadwinner, of the champion, of their protectors.

I see the 10,000 villages of Russia, where the means of existence was wrung so hardly from the soil, but where there are still primordial human joys, where maidens laugh and children play. I see advancing upon all this, in hideous onslaught, the Nazi war machine, with its clanking, heel-clicking, dandified Prussian officers, its crafty expert agents, fresh from the cowing and tying down of a dozen countries. I see also the dull, drilled, docile, brutish masses of the Hun soldiery, plodding on like a swarm of crawling locusts. I see the German bombers and fighters in the sky, still smarting from many a British whipping, so delighted to find what they believe is an easier and a safer prey. And behind all this glare, behind all this storm, I see that small group of villainous men who planned, organized and launched this cataract of horrors upon mankind. . . .

We have but one aim and one single irrevocable purpose. We are resolved to destroy Hitler and every vestige of the Nazi regime. From this nothing will turn us. Nothing. We will never parley; we will never negotiate with Hitler or any of his gang. We shall fight him by land; we shall fight him by sea; we shall fight him in the air, until, with God's help, we have rid the earth of his shadow and liberated its people from his yoke. . . .

This is no class war; this is a war in which the whole British Empire and Commonwealth of Nations is engaged without distinction of race, creed or party. It is not for me to speak of the action of the United States, but this I will say: If Hitler imagines that his attack on Soviet Russia will cause the slightest division of aims or slackening of effort in the great democracies who are resolved upon his doom, he is woefully mistaken. On the contrary, we shall be fortified and encouraged in our efforts to rescue mankind from this tyranny. We shall be strengthened and not weakened in our determination and in our resources.

This is no time to moralize upon the follies of countries and governments which have allowed themselves to be struck down one by one, when by united action they could so easily have saved themselves and saved the world from this catastrophe; but when I spoke a few minutes ago of Hitler's blood lust and the hateful appetites which have impelled or lured him on his Russian adventure, I said there was one deeper motive behind his outrage. He wishes to destroy the Russian power because he hopes that if he succeeds in this he will be able to bring back the main strength of his army and air force from the east and hurl it upon this island, which he knows he must conquer or suffer the penalty of his crimes.

His invasion of Russia is no more than a prelude to an attempted invasion of the British Isles. He hopes no doubt that all this may be accomplished before the winter comes, and that he can overwhelm Great Britain before the fleets and air power of the United States will intervene; he hopes that he may once again repeat upon a greater scale than ever before that process of destroying his enemies one by one, by which he has so long thrived and prospered, and that then the scene will be clear for the final act without which all his conquests would be in vain: namely, the subjugation of the Western Hemisphere to his will and to his system.

The Russian danger is, therefore, our danger and the danger of the United States, just as the cause of any Russian fighting for his hearth and home is the cause of free men and free people in every quarter of the globe. Let us learn the lessons already taught by such cruel experience. Let us redouble our exertions and strike with united strength while life and power remain.

CHURCHILL ON THE COST OF VICTORY

(Unlike the bragging Hitler or the vainglorious Mussolini, he is not afraid to let his people see for themselves the desperate plight they are in. These were his words on March 3, 1940, when the Battle of the Atlantic was going none too well for the British.)

We must not boast or speak in terms of vain conceit and overconfidence. We have never underrated the terrible nature of what we undertook when, after striving so long for peace, we set ourselves to the task of dealing with the Nazi and German menace, and of dealing with it in such a fashion as would clear a path of progress and enable all countries, the great and small, the old and new, to breathe freely for a long time to come.

We do not minimize our job, but we can now measure it in its enormous magnitude more exactly than we could before we came into contact with our adversary on the sea and in the air. We do not conceal from ourselves that trials and tribulations lie before us far beyond anything we have so far undergone, and we know that supreme exertion will be required.

(At the same time, Churchill's confidence and courage shone in these words, right after Dunkirk, June 4, 1940.)

We shall not flag nor fail. We shall go on to the end. We shall fight in France and on the seas and oceans; we shall fight with growing confidence and growing strength in the air. We shall defend our island whatever the cost may be; we shall fight on beaches, landing grounds, in fields, in streets and on the hills. We shall never surrender and even if, which I do not for the moment believe, this island or a large part of it were subjugated and starving, then our empire beyond the seas, armed and guarded by the British Fleet, will carry on the struggle until in God's good time the New World, with all its power and might, sets forth to the liberation and rescue of the Old.

(Earlier in the conflict, when Churchill was still First Lord of the Admiralty, he made this ringing declaration, January 20, 1940.)

Certainly it is true that we are facing numerical odds, but that is no new thing in our history. Very few wars have been won by mere numbers alone. Quality, will power, geographical advantages, natural and financial resources, the command of the sea, and, above all, a cause which rouses the spontaneous surging of human spirit in millions of hearts, these have proved to be the decisive factors in the human story.

If it were otherwise, how would the race of men have risen above the ape? How otherwise would they have conquered and extirpated the dragons and monsters of the brine? How would they have evolved the moral theme? How would they have marched forward across the centuries to broad conceptions of compassion, of freedom, and of right? How would they ever have discerned those beacon lights which summon and guide us across rough dark waters and presently will guide us across the flaming lines of battle toward better days which lie beyond?

In the bitter and increasingly exacting conflict which lies before us we are resolved to keep nothing back and not to be outstripped by any in service to the common cause. Let the great cities of Warsaw, of Prague, of Vienna banish despair, even in the midst of their agony. Their liberation is sure. The day will come when the joy bells will ring again throughout Europe and when victorious nations, masters not only of their foes but of themselves, will plan and build in justice, in tradition, and in freedom a house of many mansions where there will be room for all.

CHURCHILL ON THE PURPOSE OF THE WAR

(As to the character of final victory, Churchill has expressed himself, as might be expected, in vigorous and unmistakable terms. The following is an excerpt from a speech delivered in London at the Lord Mayor's luncheon on November 10, 1941.)

We are told from many quarters that we must soon expect what is called a peace offensive from Berlin.

All the usual signs and symptoms are already manifested (as the Foreign Secretary will confirm) in neutral countries. All those signs point in one direction: They all show that the guilty men who have let hell loose upon the world are hoping to escape with their fleeting triumphs and ill-gotten plunder from the closing net of doom.

We owe it to ourselves, we owe it to our Russian allies, and to the Government and people of the United States to make it absolutely clear that whether we are supported or alone, however long and hard the toil may be, the British nation and His Majesty's Government at the head of that nation, in intimate concert with the governments of the great Dominions, will never enter into any negotiation with Hitler or with any party in Germany which represents the Nazi regime.

(And when victory comes, Churchill foresees a close and continuing co-operation between Great Britain and the United States. These words are taken from a speech in the House of Commons, August 20, 1940, shortly after arrangements had been made to lease to the United States certain bases owned by the British.)

These two great organizations of the English-speaking democracies, the British Empire and the United States, will have to be somewhat mixed up together in some of their affairs for mutual and general advantage.

For my own part, looking out upon the future, I do not view

the process with any misgivings. No one can stop it. Like the Mississippi, it just keeps rolling along. Let it roll. Let it roll on in full flood, inexorable, irresistible, to broader lands and better days.

(From Churchill's address to the United States Congress on December 26, 1941.)

Here we are together, facing a group of mighty foes who seek our ruin. Here we are together, defending all that to free men is dear. Twice in a single generation the catastrophe of world war has fallen upon us.

Twice in our lifetime has the long arm of fate reached out across the ocean to bring the United States into the forefront of the battle. If we had kept together after the last war, if we had taken common measures for our safety, this renewal of the curse need never have fallen upon us.

Do we not owe it to ourselves, to our children, to tormented mankind, to make sure that these catastrophes do not engulf us for the third time? It has been proved that pestilences may break out in the Old World which carry their destructive ravages into the New World, from which, once they are afoot, the New World cannot escape. Duty and prudence alike command, first, that the germ centers of hatred and revenge should be constantly and vigilantly served and treated in good time and that an adequate organization should be set up to make sure that the pestilence can be controlled at its earliest beginnings, before it spreads and rages throughout the entire earth.

Five or six years ago, it would have been easy, without shedding a drop of blood, for the United States and Great Britain to have insisted on the fulfilment of the disarmament clauses of the treaties which Germany signed after the Great War, and that also would have been the opportunity for assuring to the Germans those materials, those raw materials, which we declared in the Atlantic Charter should not be denied to any nation, victor or vanquished. The chance has passed; it is gone. Prodigious hammer strokes have been needed to bring us together today.

If you will allow me to use other language, I will say that he must indeed have a blind soul who cannot see that some great purpose and design is being worked out here below, for which we have the honour to be the faithful servants. It is not given to us to peer into the mysteries of the future; yet I avow my hope and faith that in the days to come, the British and American peoples will, for their own safety and for the good of all, walk together in majesty, in justice, and in peace.

II. FRANKLIN D. ROOSEVELT

ON FREEDOM AND DEMOCRACY

(From the speech delivered to the Pan-American Union on April 15, 1940.)

In my conception, the whole world now is struggling to find the basis of its life in coming centuries.

I affirm that that life must be based on positive values.

The value of love will always be stronger than the value of hate, since any nation or group of nations which employs hatred eventually is torn to pieces by hatred within itself.

The value of a belief in humanity and justice is always stronger than the value of belief in force, because force at last turns inward, and if that occurs each man or group of men is finally compelled to measure his strength against his own brother.

The value of truth and sincerity is always stronger than the value of lies and cynicism. No process has yet been invented which can permanently separate men from their hearts and consciences, or can prevent them from seeing the results of their ideas as time rolls by. You cannot make men believe that a way of life is good when it spreads poverty, misery, disease, and death. Men cannot be everlastingly loyal unless they are free.

We acclaim today the symbol of fifty years of the American way. We are determined to continue on that way in friendship. We are determined that our mutual relations be built upon honor and good faith. We are determined to live in peace and to make that peace secure. We are determined to follow the path of free peoples to a civilization worthy of free men.

(Mr. Roosevelt has vigorously expressed his convictions on the deep and unresolved conflict between the democratic Powers and the Axis Powers. This excerpt is from a broadcast from the White House on May 27, 1941.)

Today the whole world is divided, divided between human slavery and human freedom, divided between pagan brutality and the Christian ideal.

We choose human freedom — which is the Christian ideal.

No one of us can waver for a moment in his courage or his faith.

We will not accept a Hitler-dominated world. And we will not accept a world like the postwar world of the nineteen-twenties, in which the seeds of Hitlerism can again be planted and allowed to grow.

We will accept only a world consecrated to freedom of speech and expression — freedom of every person to worship God in his own way — freedom from want — and freedom from terror.

Is such a world impossible of attainment?

Magna Carta, the Declaration of Independence, the Constitution of the United States, the Emancipation Proclamation, and every other milestone in human progress — all were ideals which seemed impossible of attainment — yet they were attained.

As a military force, we were weak when we established our independence, but we successfully stood off tyrants powerful in their day, tyrants who are now lost in the dust of history.

Odds meant nothing to us then. Shall we now, with all our potential strength, hesitate to take every single measure necessary to maintain our American liberties?

Our people and our government will not hesitate to meet that challenge.

As the President of a united and determined people, I say solemnly:

We reassert the ancient American doctrine of freedom of the seas.

We reassert the solidarity of the twenty-one American republics and the Dominion of Canada in the preservation of the independence of the hemisphere.

We have pledged material support to the other democracies of the world — and we will fulfill that pledge.

We in the Americas will decide for ourselves whether and when and where our American interests are attacked or our security threatened.

We are placing our armed forces in strategic military position.

We will not hesitate to use our armed forces to repel attack.

We reassert our abiding faith in the vitality of our constitutional republic as a perpetual home of freedom, of tolerance, and of devotion to the word of God.

(The shortsightedness of the isolationist view is pointed out in the following excerpt from a speech the President delivered at the University of Virginia, June 10, 1940.)

Some indeed still hold to the now somewhat obvious delusion that we of the United States can safely permit the United States to become a lone island, a lone island in a world dominated by the philosophy of force.

Such an island may be the dream of those who still talk and vote as isolationists. Such an island represents to me and to the overwhelming majority of Americans today a helpless nightmare, the helpless nightmare of a people without freedom. Yes, the nightmare of a people lodged in prison, handcuffed, hungry and fed through the bars from day to day by the contemptuous, unpitying masters of other continents.

It is natural also that we should ask ourselves how now we can prevent the building of that prison and the placing of ourselves in the midst of it.

Let us not hesitate — all of us — to proclaim certain truths. Overwhelmingly we, as a nation — and this applies to all the other American nations — we are convinced that military and naval victory for the gods of force and hate would endanger the institutions of democracy in the Western World — and that equally, therefore, the whole of our sympathies lie with those nations that are giving their lifeblood in combat against those forces.

ROOSEVELT ON HITLER

(The President pays his respects to the Führer and to the principles underlying the Nazi assault on civilization in no uncertain terms in the following passage from a speech broadcast on December 15, 1941.)

But, in the year 1933, there came to power in Germany a political clique which did not accept the declarations of the

American bill of human rights as valid; a small clique of ambitious and unscrupulous politicians whose announced and admitted platform was precisely the destruction of the rights that instrument declared. Indeed the entire program and goal of these political and moral tigers was nothing more than the overthrow, throughout the earth, of the great revolution of human liberty of which our American Bill of Rights is the mother charter.

The truths which were self-evident to Thomas Jefferson — which have been self-evident to the six generations of Americans who followed him — were to these men hateful. The rights to life, liberty, and the pursuit of happiness which seemed to the founders of the Republic, and which seem to us, inalienable, were, to Hitler and his fellows, empty words which they proposed to cancel forever.

The propositions they advanced to take the place of Jefferson's inalienable rights were these:

That the individual human being has no rights whatever in himself and by virtue of his humanity.

That the individual human being has no right to a soul of his own, or a mind of his own, or a tongue of his own, or a trade of his own; or even to live where he pleases or to marry the woman he loves.

That his only duty is the duty of obedience, not to his God, and not to his conscience, but to Adolf Hitler; and that his only value is his value, not as a man, but as a unit of the Nazi state.

To Hitler the ideal of the people, as we conceive it — the free, self-governing, and responsible people — is incomprehensible. The people, to Hitler, are " the masses " and the highest human idealism is, in his own words, that a man should wish to become " a dust particle " of the order " of force " which is to shape his universe.

To Hitler, the government, as we conceive it, is an impossible conception. The government to him is not the servant and the instrument of the people, but their absolute master and the dictator of their every act.

To Hitler the church, as we conceive it, is a monstrosity to be destroyed by every means at his command. The Nazi church is to be the " national church," a pagan church, " absolutely and exclusively in the service of but one doctrine, one race, one nation."

To Hitler, the freedom of men to think as they please and speak as they please and worship as they please is, of all things imaginable, most hateful and most desperately to be feared.

The issue of our time, the issue of the war in which we are engaged, is the issue forced upon the decent, self-respecting peoples of the earth by the aggressive dogmas of this attempted revival of barbarism; this proposed return to tyranny; this effort to impose again upon the peoples of the world doctrines of absolute obedience, and of dictatorial rule, and of the suppression of truth, and of the oppression of conscience, which the free nations of the earth have long ago rejected.

What we face is nothing more nor less than an attempt to overthrow and to cancel out the great upsurge of human liberty of which the American Bill of Rights is the fundamental document; to force the peoples of the earth, and among them the peoples of this continent, and this nation, to accept again the absolute authority and despotic rule from which the courage and the resolution and the sacrifices of their ancestors liberated them many, many years ago.

It is an attempt, an attempt which could succeed only if those who have inherited the gift of liberty had lost the manhood to preserve it. But we Americans know that the determination of this generation of our people, our generation, to preserve liberty is as fixed and certain as the determination of that earlier generation of Americans was to win it.

We will not, under any threat, or in the face of any danger, surrender the guarantees of liberty our forefathers framed for us in our Bill of Rights.

We hold with all the passion of our hearts and minds to those commitments of the human spirit.

We are solemnly determined that no power or combination of powers of this earth shall shake our hold upon them.

We covenant with each other before all the world that, having taken up arms in the defense of liberty, we will not lay them down before liberty is once again secure in the world we live in. For that security we pray; for that security we act — now and evermore.

ROOSEVELT ON AMERICA'S TASK

(In another portion of the same speech Mr. Roosevelt indicates his belief that the Japanese attack at Pearl Harbor, following as it does the Nazi pattern, is an integral part of the same conspiracy against the forces which stand in the way of Axis domination.)

The course that Japan has followed for the past ten years in Asia has paralleled the course of Hitler and Mussolini in Europe and in Africa. Today it has become far more than a parallel. It is collaboration — actual collaboration — so well calculated that all the continents of the world, and all the oceans, are now considered by the Axis strategists as one gigantic battlefield.

In 1931, ten years ago, Japan invaded Manchukuo — without warning.

In 1935, Italy invaded Ethiopia — without warning.

In 1938, Hitler occupied Austria — without warning.

In 1939, Hitler invaded Czechoslovakia — without warning.

Later in 1939, Hitler invaded Poland — without warning.

In 1940 Hitler invaded Norway, Denmark, the Netherlands, Belgium, and Luxemburg — without warning.

In 1940, Italy attacked France and later Greece — without warning.

And this year, in 1941, the Axis Powers attacked Yugoslavia and Greece and they dominated the Balkans — without warning.

In 1941 also, Hitler invaded Russia — without warning.

And now Japan has attacked Malaya and Thailand — and the United States — without warning.

It is all of one pattern.

(The following is taken from the President's speech broadcast on October 27, 1941.)

It has not been easy for us Americans to adjust ourselves to the shocking realities of a world in which the principles of common humanity and common decency are being mowed down by the firing squads of the Gestapo. We have enjoyed many of God's blessings. We have lived in a broad and abundant land and by our industry and productivity we have made it flourish.

There are those who say that our great good fortune has betrayed us, that we are now no match for the regimented masses who have been trained in the Spartan ways of ruthless brutality. They say that we have grown fat and flabby and lazy — and that we are doomed.

But those who say that know nothing of America or of American life.

They do not know that this land is great because it is a land of endless challenge. Our country was first populated, and it has been steadily developed, by men and women in whom there has burned the spirit of adventure and restlessness and individual independence which will not tolerate oppression.

Ours has been a story, a story of vigorous challenge which has been accepted and overcome — challenges of uncharted seas, of wild forests and desert plains, of raging floods and withering droughts, of foreign tyrants and domestic strife, of staggering problems, social and economic and physical. And we have come out of them the most powerful nation — and the freest — in all of history.

Today, in the face of this newest and greatest challenge of them all, we Americans have cleared our decks and taken our battle stations. We stand ready in the defense of our nation and in the faith of our fathers to do what God has given us the power to see as our full duty.

(From his Labor Day broadcast, September 1, 1941.)

The task of defeating Hitler may be long and arduous. There are a few appeasers and Nazi sympathizers who say it cannot be done. They even ask me to negotiate with Hitler — to pray for crumbs from his victorious table. They do, in fact, ask me to become the modern Benedict Arnold and betray all that I hold dear — my devotion to our freedom — to our churches — to our country. This course I have rejected — I reject it again.

Instead, I know that I speak the conscience and determination of the American people when I say that we shall do everything in our power to crush Hitler and his Nazi forces.

American workers, American farmers, American businessmen, American church people, all of us together, have the great responsibility and the great privilege of laboring to build a democratic world on enduring foundations.

(President Roosevelt, it is clear, will be content with no vague or indecisive outcome to the struggle for world freedom. These uncompromising words were delivered in a radio speech two days after the Pearl Harbor attack.)

I repeat that the United States can accept no result save victory, final and complete. Not only must the shame of Japanese treachery be wiped out, but the sources of international brutality, wherever they exist, must be absolutely and finally broken.

(And the President concludes this notable speech in a strain of resolute and solemn confidence.)

The true goal we seek is far above and beyond the ugly field of battle. When we resort to force, as now we must, we are determined that this force shall be directed toward ultimate good as well as against immediate evil. We Americans are not destroyers — we are builders.

We are now in the midst of a war, not for conquest, not for vengeance, but for a world in which this nation, and all that this nation represents, will be safe for our children. We expect to eliminate the danger from Japan, but it would serve us ill if we accomplished that and found that the rest of the world was dominated by Hitler and Mussolini.

We are going to win the war and we are going to win the peace that follows.

And in the dark hours of this day — and through dark days that may be yet to come — we will know that the vast majority of the members of the human race are on our side. Many of them are fighting with us. All of them are praying for us. For, in representing our cause, we represent theirs as well — our hope and their hope for liberty under God.

(Looking beyond the war to victory and the establishment of enduring peace, the President, in an address delivered on March 15, 1941, sees a future in which the American people will intelligently and manfully shoulder their responsibility for making that peace endure.)

And, when dictatorships — no, I didn't say if, I said when — dictatorships disintegrate — and pray God that will be sooner than any of us now dare to hope — then our country must continue to play its great part in the period of world reconstruction for the good of humanity.

We believe that the rallying cry of the dictators, their boasting about a master race, will prove to be pure stuff and nonsense. There never has been, there isn't now, and there never will be any race of people on the earth fit to serve as masters over their fellow men.

The world has no use for any nation which, because of size or because of military might, asserts the right to goosestep to world power over the bodies of other nations and other races. We believe that any nationality, no matter how small, has the inherent right to its own nationhood.

We believe that the men and women of such nations, no matter what size, can, through the processes of peace, serve themselves and serve the world by protecting the common man's security: improve the standards of healthful living; provide markets for manufacture and for agriculture. Through that kind of peaceful service every nation can increase its happiness, banish the terrors of war, and abandon man's inhumanity to man.

Never in all our history have Americans faced a job so well worth while. May it be said of us in the days to come that our children and our children's children rise up and call us blessed.

ROOSEVELT AND CHURCHILL ON THE TERMS OF THE PEACE

(Behind the brief and simple words of the following declaration, now called the Atlantic Charter, looms the most dramatic and stirring movement of all time. Twenty-six nations, most of them democracies, some strong, some weak, some the victims of conquest and defeat, rise against the " savage and brutal forces " that threaten liberty and human rights, and pledge themselves to fight together until freedom and justice are finally secure. Later, in January, 1942, most of the Latin-American countries also broke with the Axis and pledged their adherence to the Atlantic Charter.)

THE JOINT DECLARATION
(Issued by the White House, August 14, 1941)

The President of the United States of America and the Prime Minister, Mr. Churchill, representing His Majesty's Government in the United Kingdom, being met together, deem it right to make known certain common principles in the national policies of their respective countries on which they base their hopes for a better future for the world.

First: Their countries seek no aggrandizement, territorial or other;

Second: They desire to see no territorial changes that do not accord with the freely expressed wishes of the peoples concerned;

Third: They respect the right of all peoples to choose the form of government under which they will live; and they wish to see sovereign rights and self-government restored to those who have been deprived of them;

Fourth: They will endeavor, with due respect for their existing obligations, to further the enjoyment by all states, great or small, victor or vanquished, of access, on equal terms, to the trade and to the raw materials of the world which are needed for their economic prosperity;

Fifth: They desire to bring about the fullest collaboration between all nations in the economic field, with the object of securing for all improved labor standards, economic adjustment and social security;

Sixth: After the final destruction of the Nazi tyranny, they hope to see established a peace which will afford to all nations the means of dwelling in safety within their own boundaries, and which will afford assurance that all the men in all the lands may live in freedom from fear and want;

Seventh: Such a peace should enable all men to traverse the high seas and oceans without hindrance;

Eighth: They believe that all of the nations of the world, for realistic as well as spiritual reasons, must come to the abandonment of the use of force. Since no future peace can be maintained if land, sea or air armaments continue to be employed by nations which threaten, or may threaten, aggression outside of their frontiers, they believe, pending the establishment of a wider and permanent system of general security, that the disarmament of such nations is essential. They will likewise aid and encourage all other practicable measures which will lighten for peace-loving peoples the crushing burden of armaments.

Franklin D. Roosevelt
Winston S. Churchill

DECLARATION OF THE UNITED NATIONS

Behind the brief and simple words of the Declaration by the United Nations looms the most dramatic and stirring movement of all time. Twenty-six nations, most of them democracies, some strong, some weak, some the victims of conquest and defeat, rise against the " savage and brutal forces " that threaten human rights, and pledge themselves to fight together until freedom and justice are finally secure. Later, in January, 1942, most of the Latin-American countries pledged their adherence to the Atlantic Charter.

A joint declaration by the United States of America, the United Kingdom of Great Britain and Northern Ireland, and the Union of Soviet Socialist Republics, China, Australia, Belgium, Canada, Costa Rica, Cuba, Czechoslovakia, Dominican Republic, El Salvador, Greece, Guatemala, Haiti, Honduras, India, Luxembourg, Netherlands, New Zealand, Nicaragua, Norway, Panama, Poland, South Africa, Yugoslavia.

The governments signatory hereto,

Having subscribed to a common program of purposes and principles embodied in the joint declaration of the President of the United States of America and the Prime Minister of the United Kingdom of Great Britain and Northern Ireland dated Aug. 14, 1941, known as the Atlantic Charter, being convinced that complete victory over their enemies is essential to defend life, liberty, independence and religious freedom, and to preserve human rights and justice in their own lands as well as in other lands, and that they are now engaged in a common struggle against savage and brutal forces seeking to subjugate the world, declare:

(1) Each government pledges itself to employ its full resources, military or economic, against those members of the Tripartite Pact and its adherents with which such government is at war.

(2) Each government pledges itself to co-operate with the governments signatory hereto and not to make a separate armistice or peace with the enemies.

The foregoing declaration may be adhered to by other nations which are, or which may be, rendering material assistance and contributions in the struggle for victory over Hitlerism.

Done at Washington, January First, 1942

The United States of America
The United Kingdom of Great Britain and Northern Ireland
The Union of Soviet Socialist Republics
The Republic of China
The Commonwealth of Australia
The Kingdom of Belgium
Canada
The Grand Duchy of Luxembourg
The Kingdom of the Netherlands
The Dominion of New Zealand
The Republic of Nicaragua
The Kingdom of Norway
The Republic of Panama
The Republic of Poland
The Republic of Costa Rica
The Republic of Cuba
The Czechoslovak Republic
The Dominican Republic
The Republic of El Salvador
The Kingdom of Greece
The Republic of Guatemala
La République d'Haiti
The Republic of Honduras
India
The Union of South Africa
The Kingdom of Yugoslavia

xx. Foundations of the peace

HENRY A. WALLACE

Henry A. Wallace, who became Vice-President of the United States in January, 1941, has long been known as a leading agriculturist, following in the footsteps of his grandfather and father. After being associate editor and editor of the family paper, 'Wallace's Farmer,' for thirteen years, he became Secretary of Agriculture — as his father had been before him — in 1933. Among his books are 'America Must Choose,' 'Statesmanship and Religion,' and 'Paths to Plenty.' This chapter is reprinted from the January, 1942, 'Atlantic Monthly,' by permission of the publishers.

In these days of world crisis, there are many who say, " Let us have no talk of peace until the war is won." There are others who have said, " Let us not think of helping to win the war until the details of the peace are completely settled." I believe the sensible and constructive course to take is this: Do everything we can to speed our drive for victory, because unless Hitler and his Italian and Japanese partners are defeated there will be only the cold, bleak hopelessness of a new Dark Age. At the same time, think hard and often about the future peace, because unless we and the other democracies have confidence in that peace our resistance to our enemies may not be strong enough to beat them.

Thinking of the future peace, in other words, is not searching for an escape from the stern realities of the present, not taking refuge in airy castles of our minds. From the practical standpoint of putting first things first, at a time when there are not enough hours in a day and every minute counts, planning for the future peace must of necessity be a part of our all-out war program. More than that, the daily actions being taken now by both Britain and ourselves are determining to a large extent the kind of postwar world we can have later on.

It seems almost certain that sometime within the next few years another peace will be written. If it should be a Hitler peace, no one but Hitler and his henchmen would be allowed any part in writing it. But if, with this country's determined participation and support, the Allies are successful, the world will have a second chance to organize its affairs on a basis of human decency and mutual welfare.

Again, as in 1919, there will be the question of what to do about the world's armies, the question of machinery to prevent new aggression, the question of what to do about national boundaries. And again, as in 1919, at the roots of all these knotty questions will be the fundamental problem of restoring the world's trade and of expanding economic activity so as to improve living-standards everywhere.

We are now aware, after our experience of the last twenty-five years, that the most careful delineation of national boundaries is not in itself enough to prevent the world from suffering a repetition of the catastrophe of general war. Nor can this be prevented simply by the establishment of an international league. We know now that the modern world must be recognized for what it is — an economic unit — and that wise arrangements must be made so that trade will be encouraged. The foundations of democracy can be rendered safe only when people everywhere have an opportunity to work and buy and sell with a reasonable assurance that they will be able to enjoy the fruits of their work.

Actually, the seeds of the present world upheaval were sown in the faulty economic decisions that followed the war of a generation ago. The vast sums of reparations imposed on Germany, however justified they may have been on moral grounds, were an indigestible lump in Europe's financial stomach. The war debts owed to the United States by the Allies were equally a handicap to trade. All over the world, the old international gold standard had broken down, and nothing effective was done to replace or restore it. Europe was left cut up into many small national units, and each of these units was left free to erect tariff and trade barriers as it pleased. Many nations, including our own, tried to buy as little as possible from the rest of the world and sell as much as possible. European countries that normally bought wheat and meat from overseas shifted their production policies with a view to becoming self-sufficient in food. This not only lowered their own standard of living, but upset the economies of the exporting countries. The United States, newly become a creditor nation, adopted tariff policies which only a debtor nation could hope to live with, and in so doing helped make it certain that the world would go through hell.

The dislocations brought by that First World War and by the unwise management of the peace were especially hard on the raw-material producers of the world. Prices of raw materials are extremely sensitive to changes in demand or supply. Therefore, various groups of raw-material producers, including the farmers, found themselves in serious trouble when their supplies were greater than demand. Wheat, cotton, sugar, coffee, rubber, copper — all these commodities were in chronic world-wide surplus during the postwar period. Producers of these commodities, wherever they were — in this country, in South America, in the Netherlands East Indies, in the British colonies, in other widely scattered areas — were faced again and again with overproduction, underconsumption, and appalling losses. The fall in raw-material prices and the resulting lack of purchasing power of the raw-material producers became a serious threat to the well-being of countries everywhere.

For ten years after the First World War, the deadly economic malady afflicting the world was covered up by the billions in private loans floated by foreign borrowers in the United States. These loans were usually floated at high rates of interest and used for purposes which, for the most part, did not increase the borrowing countries' ability to pay either the interest or the principal. Thus they produced a temporary, though basically unsound, prosperity. When the stream of loans suddenly dried up, the flimsiness of this prosperity of gaudy tinsel was revealed, and the whole thing came crashing down.

We all are familiar with the sequence of events after 1929 — the Hawley-Smoot Tariff Act in this country, the immediate retaliations in Canada and other countries, the failure of the Credit-Anstalt in Austria, the German financial collapse, the moratorium on war debts, the departure of England from the gold standard, the British Empire conference at Ottawa and the adoption of Empire preference tariff policies, the world-wide depression, the bank panic in this country, the rise of Hitler in Germany, the gradual loss of prestige by the League of Nations in one crisis after another, and, finally, the outbreak of the present war.

In very truth this nation, during those early postwar years, was sowing the wind by its policies of isolation, high tariffs, unwise foreign loans, and high-pressure sales abroad. It could not avoid reaping the whirlwind. Hindsight is always easier than foresight, and millions of Americans now look back upon those earlier policies as tragically mistaken. It would be a prolongation of the present world agony if, after this war is over, any of us again put blinders on our hindsight.

Spokesmen for the isolationist point of view did not support President Roosevelt in his stand for a peace built around freedom of speech and expression, freedom of worship, freedom from want, and freedom from fear. They were quick to condemn the President for having joined with Winston Churchill in subscribing to the Atlantic Charter. They saw dangerous foreign entanglements in such simple words of the President as these: " The co-operation which we seek is the co-operation of free countries, working together in a friendly civilized society."

We may wonder whether the long and bitter fight put up by the isolationists in the decade of the twenties to keep the United States from behaving as if it were part of the world is to be renewed when the time comes for building a new peace. What they do will have an important bearing on political alignments in the United States. The injection of such an issue into politics would ordinarily be nothing of which to complain, for surely the people have a right to choose the policies they want the nation to pursue. But the really serious aspect of the matter is that the whole future not only of this country but of human civilization itself may depend on the ability and willingness of the American people to take the broad view.

For my part, I believe that the American people have profited from their experiences of the last twenty-five years. I believe that they will perceive, with increasingly clear vision, the place of leadership in the world which the United States can scarcely avoid occupying; and that they will support policies and arrangements for sensible co-operation with other countries.

One evidence of the more enlightened point of view is found in the wide understanding of the great practical difficulties in the way of this country's trying to receive billions of dollars in goods and services when the war ends, in exchange for the weapons and food now being shipped abroad under the Lend-Lease Act. There seems some merit in the often-heard suggestion that the United States will be well repaid if Britain and the other recipients of lend-lease materials enter genuinely, intelligently and wholeheartedly into co-operative relationships to ensure the world's economic and social stability after the war.

II

The peace aims which Roosevelt and Churchill have enumerated are splendid statements of principle. They open up big fields for exploration. The job now is to work out, as definitely as we can while the war is still in progress, practical ways and means for realizing them.

Preliminary studies of some of the expected postwar problems already are being made by the Economic Defense Board and the Cabinet departments whose chiefs are members of that board. This is being done in accordance with the Executive Order of July 30, 1941, which directed the Board to " make investigation and advise the President on the relationship of economic defense . . . measures to postwar economic reconstruction and on the steps to be taken to protect the trade position of the United States and to expedite the establishment of sound, peacetime international economic relationships."

Now, what must be considered in establishing such " sound relationships " in peacetime? There are certain basic facts which cannot be ignored. One of these is the universal necessity of access to raw materials and the need for an economic arrangement to protect the raw-material producers of the world from such violent fluctuation in income as took place after the First World War. Another is the indispensability of markets for goods produced. A third is the present existence in all countries of tariffs and other barriers to imports. A fourth is the use of gold as a base for national currencies and as a means of settling international trade balances. A fifth is the place of credit in stimulating international trade. A sixth is the close relationship between stable national currencies and the exchange of goods and services. A seventh, and most important of all, is the essential role of adequate purchasing power within the various countries that are trading with each other — for full employment within nations makes broad trade possible with other nations. All these facts and factors are of prime importance in determining the state of the world's health, and they will naturally form some of the main ingredients of postwar economic planning, if it is to be done on a comprehensive scale.

Each of these aspects of world trade is a vast subject in itself, and I do not have space here to discuss them all. However, I do wish to point out that basic to any sensible ordering of the world's economic life is the stabilizing of the production and prices of raw materials.

During the '20's and '30's, when the raw-material producers were in such frequent trouble, various methods were developed to help them adjust themselves to the painful realities of diminishing demand. There were the Stevenson rubber plan, the Chadbourne sugar arrangement, the beginning of an international wheat agreement, and in the United States an Ever Normal Granary program. The plight of the producers was so difficult that in most of these remedies very little effort was made to think about the consumer. More than any of the other plans, the Ever Normal Granary in this country recognized consumer needs by setting up huge stock piles of wheat, cotton, and corn. The stated objective was to carry over the surplus from the fat years to the lean years, thus benefiting the producer in the years of overproduction and very low prices and helping the consumer in years when the supplies otherwise would be short and the prices high. As things turned out, our Ever Normal Granary stocks of corn made possible our quick and heavy shipments of pork and dairy products to Great Britain during this last year. Those of us who formulated the Ever Normal Granary program had in mind that supplies might eventually be very helpful in case of war. But none of us at that time visualized also how important these supplies might be to the war-stricken territories during the years immediately following the declaration of peace.

As part of the effort to win the peace, I am hoping that what might be called the " ever normal granary principle " can be established for a number of commodities on a world-wide scale. It will be remembered that the fourth point of the eight points agreed upon by Roosevelt and Churchill in the Atlantic Charter mentioned the enjoying by all the states, great or small, victor or vanquished, of access on equal terms to the raw materials of the world. To give this lofty ideal a more definite substance should be one of our chief objectives in the months that lie immediately ahead. The people of all Europe should feel that there are available, in the United States, in Latin America, and in the British Dominions, tremendous quantities of raw materials which can be used for food, clothing, and shelter within a short time after the war comes to an end.

Thus far, there have been no definite arrangements between the United States and the British Empire or between the United States and Latin America with regard to handling the raw-material problems of the world in such a way as to make for a just peace. A beginning has been made along this line with the international wheat agreement meeting which was held in Washington last July. Nothing has yet been signed, but it is apparent that the United States, Argentina, Canada, and Australia, as well as Great Britain, are moving in the direction of a World Ever Normal Granary, with export quotas and with prices stabilized at a point to be fair to producers and consumers.

The world cotton problem is similar in some ways to the world wheat problem, but less progress has been made toward orderly marketing arrangements for cotton than for wheat.

Huge surpluses of both cotton and wheat are piled up in the exporting countries, waiting to be used whenever the stricken countries are able once more to handle them. Of cotton, there is stored in the United States a supply sufficient to take care of the normal needs of all Europe for at least a year. Of wheat, the United States last July 1 had a carry-over about four times the normal of the '20's, and it is evident that next July 1 the carry-over will be nearly seven times the normal of the '20's. In Canada the situation is somewhat similar, while in Argentina and Australia large surpluses loom for the near future. Four great wheat-exporting nations of the world now have a billion more bushels on hand than they did during the first half of the '20's. This is approximately twice as much wheat as moved in world trade in the years preceding the outbreak of the war. It is enough wheat to feed the entire population of continental Europe for a large part of a year, or to cover the Continent's import requirements for nearly three years.

When the curse of the Nazi mailed fist is at last removed from the stricken countries overseas, the first and most pressing need will be action to bring food to the starving and the undernourished. For this purpose the accumulated surplus stocks of wheat and the increased production of other foods for which farmers are now pushing will be enormously helpful. The pity is that there is no practical way to get this food to these people now without helping the Nazis and thus postponing the day of real liberation of these people from the Nazi yoke.

Besides food, the devastated regions will have urgent need of other materials and equipment to assist in their reconstruction. Homes, factories, office buildings, schools, churches, highways, railroads, bridges, have been destroyed in large numbers. In the tremendous job of rebuilding which must be undertaken, the United States and the other countries of the Western Hemisphere can play a vital part. Meanwhile, both strategy and humanity will be served if we take every opportunity to let the people of the occupied countries know that we intend to stand behind them in their efforts to get back on their feet. That will give them something to which to cling during their months or years of misery and will speed the day of a Nazi collapse and the emancipation of the world.

The democratic countries are in splendid position to organize themselves for rapid relief work as soon as peace comes. I am confident that we can do this job and do it well. But we must be looking ahead to the longer future and laying plans on more than just a temporary basis.

III

It is now clear that by the end of the war the non-Axis nations will have a greater production of raw materials, a greater output of manufactured products, and a greater number of skilled workers than ever before in their history. Nearly half of their production may be going to the British and American governments by the time Hitler is overthrown. If two such customers were to drop out of the market abruptly, it would break everyone. Businessmen know this.

We in the democracies must begin to realize, therefore, that if we can afford tremendous sums of money to win the war, we can afford to invest whatever amount it takes to win the peace. If that necessity were accepted today, both here and in England, we could be writing a very important part of the peace now. Both nations could be making contracts with pro-

ducers of raw materials throughout the world for delivery of
their goods during the war and for several years beyond the
armistice at reasonable prices and not at inflated prices. That
would sharply reduce the cost of winning the war and give
more assurance than any other single action that business is
not going to be allowed to collapse after the fighting is over.
There would be no better use to which this country's gold
could be put than in making such purchases. Many of the
goods bought in this manner for postwar delivery would have
to be sold on credit by the British and ourselves for reconstruction within the devastated nations.

Just as individuals here and in England are being encouraged
to build up future purchasing power for themselves through
Defense Bonds and other devices, so raw-material-producing
countries would by means of such a plan as this be accumulat-
ing purchasing power in the form of gold. This gold could be
used in the future for buying the finished goods of Europe and
America.

Not only would the gold which these countries would
thereby obtain make it possible for them to buy finished goods
of Europe and America, but it could also be used in part to
provide much needed strength for their currency and banking systems, and make it possible for them progressively to
relax the stringent exchange controls, import quotas, and clear-
ing arrangements which serve so effectively to restrict the flow
of goods from country to country. Without adequate gold
reserve and without the ability to obtain the kind of credit
which can be utilized to pay for imports, a country is greatly
handicapped in its conduct of foreign trade, and, in order to
prevent its currency from depreciating in the foreign exchange
market and its credit from deteriorating, finds itself forced to
adopt illiberal trade policies and severe restrictions on its imports. With increased gold holdings countries will be able to

pursue more effectively a policy of stable foreign exchange and liberal trade practices.

If we get the right kind of peace, we are sure to see the whole world within a few years operating on a much higher level of production than ever before and this would of course mean a greater world market for raw materials.

Given the right kind of peace, this prospect of greater world trade is certain to materialize, for it rests on the sure prospect of continued industrialization everywhere. The process of industrialization is the way to attain higher standards of living. Everywhere there are communities that must increase their proportion of people engaged in industry and reduce the number of people engaged in the production of farm products. Even in the United States there are many areas where we want to see as soon as possible a shift in the degree of industrialization. Communities that are now only 40 per cent industrial could, in the course of the next ten years, become perhaps 50 per cent industrial. Similarly, there are many communities in southern Europe, Latin America, and the Pacific countries where that kind of shift would be of tremendous value from the standpoint of raising living-standards. For every unit of gain in per capita living-standards that a shift to a higher proportion of industrialization would mean in the United States, it would mean proportionately a much greater gain in the countries where industrialization is just begun. One of the difficult problems which we have to face is the need for helping numerous countries shift to increased industrialization without encouraging them to resort to high tariff schedules to accomplish that end.

Fortunately, in many cases the low level of industrialization is not a result of circumstances for which there is no remedy, but a consequence of the scarcity of capital and lack of proper technicians. It should be possible with intelligent effort to help those countries get both. Such growth in industrialization will assure the raw-material countries, which will be exchanging present production for gold, a continued market for their raw materials far into the future.

Some such program as here suggested might be worked out in collaboration with the British, and the democracies of Europe and Latin America, and put into effect boldly long before we come to an armistice. Probably the English-speaking peoples of the world will have to take the lead in underwriting world prosperity for a generation to come. They must begin now to prove by their actions that they are as interested in winning the peace as they are in winning the war. If this long-term, businesslike purchase of raw materials were working within six months, it would be worth a thousand blueprints at the peace conference. It is one of the ways in which we can build up morale for the struggle ahead. It is one of the ways in which we can build an economic future solid enough to be worth fighting for.

IV

The overthrow of Hitler is only half the battle; we must build a world in which our human and material resources are used to the utmost if we are to win a complete victory. This principle should be fundamental as the world moves to reorganize its affairs. Ways must be found by which the potential abundance of the world can be translated into real wealth and a higher standard of living. Certain minimum standards of food, clothing, and shelter ought to be established, and arrangements ought to be made to guarantee that no one should fall below those standards.

In this country we have already made a start in this direction. Through the food-stamp plan, the cotton-stamp plan, the school-lunch program, the low-cost milk program, and the homemade mattress program, the abundance of the farms is being put to use instead of being allowed to go to waste. Similar programs are in effect in greater or less degree in a number of South American countries, notably Argentina, Uruguay, Brazil, and Chile. In England, the Government is subsidizing consumption of certain foods so as to make sure that the population is as well nourished as possible during the time of stress, and to keep the prices as near as possible to the prewar level. Among the kinds of food subsidized are flour, bread, meat, tea, oatmeal, milk, and orange juice.

Is it not time to recognize that minimum standards of nutrition are as important for growing children as minimum standards of education? Is it not just as important that children should have sound and healthy bodies as that they should have trained minds? If we can afford $100 a year to educate a child, can't we afford $15 or $20 a year to keep that child physically fit for study?

If there is general recognition of this principle, then vast new markets for the world's production can be opened up. Perhaps the various countries can do still more than they have already done with relief distribution programs based primarily on their own domestic products. In certain instances these could be supplemented with foreign-grown products. For example, we could exchange our pork and lard and flour for South America's tropical fruits and cocoa. In terms of the residual balance, the cost of such a program may be less than the financial loss coming from demoralized raw material markets, needy producers, and hungry consumers.

In the field of food, minimum standards would mean that vastly increased quantities of dairy products, poultry products, meat, fruits, and vegetables would have to be produced. This would mean a shift from the production of staples such as wheat.

Perhaps the heavily populated countries of Europe can reorganize their own agriculture along those lines. This would mean a higher standard of living for their own people, and would restore to producing countries elsewhere the job of producing the wheat that is needed.

I do not mean to imply that I consider such mechanisms as the food and cotton stamp plans the final answer to the problem of assuring an economy of abundance. In that part of the world where democracy and capitalism prevail, the permanent answer lies in finding ways to make our system of production and exchange work more effectively and more consistently. That can be done by removing trade barriers and enlarging markets; by stimulating and guiding investments where they can be productive; by reducing — through appropriate fiscal policy and social-security program — the inequalities in incomes, so that a higher and more stable demand for consumers' goods will be attained; by applying advanced techniques and skills to the development of undeveloped areas; by re-equipping our own industrial and transportation system; and by providing to those people in greatest need better housing, schooling, and recreation.

Most people do not want charity. They want paying jobs. They will be able to have paying jobs, with few interruptions, if prices, production, and purchasing power can be held in balance with one another, and the economic machine can be kept running steadily and smoothly. This is the challenge to the leaders of industry, agriculture, labor, and government. It is a challenge to the highest statesmanship of our own and other nations. Of course there are difficulties and obstacles. Only by recognizing and studying obstacles can they be surmounted. A " new order " is truly waiting to be created — not the " new order " which the Nazis talk about and which would cloak the new form of slavery they would impose, but a new order of democracy where security, stability, efficiency, and widely distributed abundance would prevail.

Many persons in the United States are deeply disturbed over the heavy government borrowing and the drastic shifts in our economy made necessary by the defense program. They fear an end of the war almost as much as the war itself, because they believe the return of peace would bring another bad depression. But one of the hopeful signs for the future is the very fact that the possibility of depression is so widely recognized. This increases the chance that action will be taken in time to prevent it or at least cushion the shock. The basis for such action can best be laid now, while the war is still in progress. It must be laid, at least in part, in the plans for expanding and regularizing world trade, world production, world consumption. This is the new frontier, which Americans in the middle of the twentieth century find beckoning them on.

Index

Date Due

MILITARY AND
CIVILIAN INSIGNIA

ARMY

GENERAL

LIEUTENANT GENERAL

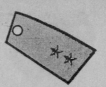

MAJOR GENERAL

BRIGADIER GENERAL

COLONEL

LIEUT. COLONEL: SILVER
MAJOR: GOLD

CAPTAIN

1ST LIEUTENANT: SILVER
2ND LIEUTENANT: GOLD

MASTER SERGEANT

FIRST SERGEANT

TECHNICAL SERGEANT

STAFF SERGEANT

SERGEANT

CORPORAL

PRIVATE FIRST CLASS

CIVILIAN DEFENSE

AUXILIARY
POLICE

BOMB SQUADS

AIR RAID WARDENS

MEDICAL FORCES

MESSENGERS